LEWIS A. COSER

GENERAL EDITOR

ÉMILE DURKHEIM, by Robert A. Nisbet, *with selected essays,* S-118
GEORG SIMMEL, edited by Lewis A. Coser, S-119
PARETO & MOSCA, edited by James H. Meisel, S-122

FORTHCOMING VOLUMES

KARL MANNHEIM, edited by Paul Kecskemeti
MAX WEBER, edited by Dennis Wrong
SIGMUND FREUD, edited by Harold Lasswell
KARL MARX, edited by Thomas Bottomore
GEORGE HERBERT MEAD, edited by Herbert Blumer

MAKERS OF MODERN SOCIAL SCIENCE
PARETO & MOSCA

EDITED BY
JAMES H. MEISEL

A SPECTRUM BOOK
Prentice-Hall, Inc.
Englewood Cliffs, New Jersey

CONTENTS

PARETO & MOSCA

PARETO & MOSCA

JAMES H. MEISEL

OF COUNTER-REVOLUTION

THIS VOLUME DEALS with two authors; both were Italians, both of the period reaching from the halcyon days of Victorian liberalism into the twentieth century of Fascism and Bolshevism. The older of the two, Vilfredo Pareto (1848-1923), lived to see the beginnings of Benito Mussolini's regime; Gaetano Mosca (1858-1941) almost survived it, living his last years in silent opposition to the dictator.

Mosca had emigrated from his native Sicily to Rome, where he became editor of the Italian equivalent of the *Congressional Record* and began his academic career as a specialist in constitutional law. A public servant in the best sense of the word, Mosca served his country—both in his scholarly pursuits and in his journalistic work—as a severe critic of a regime which had failed to fulfill the heady promises of the *Risorgimento*. His gadfly role did not exactly help him along the trail to academic eminence, but he finally achieved the rank of full professor at the University of Turin, and his negative view of the liberal establishment did not deprive him of the highest reward the government had to dispense: he was made a royal senator. He was, and remained, in all the vicissitudes of his life, an Italian first and last.

In contrast, Pareto, of a well-to-do upper-class family, was almost as much of a Frenchman as he was an Italian. Born in Paris, Pareto left an engineering career in Italy and went into a Swiss exile from which he was never to return. As the eminent mathematical economist of the University of Lausanne, he was removed from the political quarrels of the Italian regime. Bilingual, and writing some of his works first in French, Pareto was in a good position to reach a wider, more international audience than the more parochial Mosca. But these were not the only differences between the two.

When two authors are discussed in one book, they either share a common intellectual property or serve as a study in contrasts. Mosca and Pareto meet both requirements. They had much in common, but they differed on essential points. That may well be the reason that they disliked each other so intensely: their dispute has all the characteristics of a family quarrel.[1]

What is it that they share?

Both authors pioneered a new approach to social science. Mosca developed a model of historical power structures which transcended and denied the traditional, Aristotelian classification of governments. No matter what the constitution says, Mosca maintains, the few will always rule the many. Democracy and popular sovereignty are unmasked as mere myths. But Mosca's concept of the political class also supersedes the Marxian notion of the economic class, and politics no longer are mere "concentrated economics"[2] but the very fulcrum of control. It is in Mosca's ruling class that the salient social forces of the period find their optimal expression. To the extent that no important parts of the community are repressed or excluded from articulation, the ruling class—the elite—will last or be replaced by one more responsive to communal needs. This is not quite so antidemocratic as it sounds; still, Mosca insists that the contest for control is not between the many and the few but between one elite and another.

What determines the success or failure of a ruling class? This question generates a great deal of moral heat in Mosca's mind. Much as he wishes to remain the scientifically detached historian, he cannot but search for the solution which would make it possible for domination to endure while at the same time meeting the demands of changing times. Empirical and normative concerns are not easily separable in Mosca's work.

Pareto, too, aims at a system through which to predict the laws of change as well as of stability. But unlike Mosca, who cannot dissimulate his preference for an "ideal" balance, Pareto—the mathematician turned sociologist—remains undisturbed by the grim findings of his own investigation. At least, he claims noncommitment. Paradoxically, Mosca, with his normative nostalgia, strikes one as the more detached observer; his very reluctance—or inability—to mold his thoughts and observations into a coherent system reinforces the sense of detachment. Pareto's "scientific" construct, his professed empiricism, never quite allays one's fear that the repression of his privately held values was somewhat less than

[1] For more biographical detail, see pp. 47-49. See also n. 57, below.
[2] Lenin's phrase.

complete and, in fact, more self-defeating than Mosca's open avowal of his very similar values.

What were these values? It is easier to say what dislikes the two had in common. Both reacted to the general consequences of the Industrial Revolution, but they comprehended it in their own, specifically Italian context. Their country was a backward province of world capitalism. This fact may well explain the tendency of both writers to recoil from the political and social consequences of the general trend while advancing beyond the current leading ideologies. On that the two Italians are agreed; both are fighting on two fronts: against democracy and (Marxist) socialism—which, to them, are one and the same thing. They were, essentially, old-fashioned laissez-faire liberals—at least, their starting point is a firm belief in the "free" interplay of economic forces and, concomitantly, a distrust of extraeconomic intervention, whether it originates with the government or with strong "intermediary associations" (business and labor pressure groups or parties).

Such a negative reaction to modernity might easily end in a conservative posture, a mere hankering for *tempi passati*. That, however, was not the case with Mosca and Pareto. Their negation led them forward: they turned, not conservative, but counterrevolutionary, if counterrevolution be viewed as another form of revolution—one leading in a direction opposite to that of the temporarily successful current. Its revolutionary character is obscured by the fact that a counterrevolution is the result of conflicting pulls. The radical reversal of the main trend, the unqualified return to "normalcy" may be the initial aim. But when that aim is frustrated, the radical intention is deflected into a direction counter to that of the ruling passions of the day, making use of existing but frustrated revolutionary energies.

That conversion will derive its own strength not from the provocative successes of the "competition," but from its defeats. The counterrevolutionary learns from the very blunders of the revolutionary, by unmasking his illusions and replacing them with the pragmatic wisdom of the realist. The professed aim is still a better world—but to be implemented at a price which only the Unhappy Few are able—and only they elect—to pay. It is the burden which the Grand Inquisitors of this world must assume: the knowledge that the total liberation of mankind is fated to remain a myth. At best, the advances of freedom will be a mere by-product of the recurring quarrels between dominant minorities.

It is this outlook of the counterrevolutionary which gives his teachings the dark hues of ambiguity. If he is driven on by disappointment over the achievements of the socialist or the democrat, he is also envious of their revolutionary roles. He desperately wants to prove them wrong and himself right—the better, the real, revolutionary. He will borrow Lenin's method, and if the result is travesty, it may work *precisely* because imitation often drives out the original . . . The counterrevolutionary radical will often be a revolutionist *manqué*, and his success is predicated on the failure of the revolution—failure because it is of today, while counterrevolution knows the sadness of the morning after.

Mosca's and Pareto's Italy, with its arrested democratic and proletarian revolutions, could avail itself of the excuse of backwardness; but it could also claim that "privilege of backwardness" [3] which permits a leap across stages traveled by the more advanced societies. It has been intimated that both Mosca and Pareto favor the rule of elites because they were conditioned by a milieu which was still semifeudal (in the south) and generally not yet permeated by bourgeois democracy.[4] But it is equally permissible to say that Mosca and Pareto benefited from the "privilege" of Italian backwardness to transcend both socialism and democracy— that they were forced to transcend both ideologies because they had failed to transform the country, forced to grope for intimations of a social structure for which there were, in their lifetime, only misleading labels— first *fascism,* later *totalitarianism.* These labels were misleading as far as our authors were concerned, but at the time they were just as plausible as that other label by which they themselves were known: *Machiavellian.*[5]

Mosca's lack of methodology and his naïve faith in recorded "facts," Pareto's "biological materialism" and aberrant psychology—all this might have been forgiven them, but not the ambivalence that is the hallmark of the counterrevolutionary mind, a mind that is at once retrograde and futuristic. It made Mosca and Pareto instantly and forever "controversial" figures: to have strayed from the broad path was the unpardonable offense.

Yet it might be pleaded on their behalf that, if they erred, theirs was the error of great minds, from which one may learn more than from the correct findings of lesser lights.

The critical essays which follow this introduction focus on the two authors' master works: Mosca's *Elementi di scienza politica* (1896 and 1923), translated as *The Ruling Class* (1939), and Pareto's *Trattato di*

---

[3] Trotsky's phrase. See ed. by Marshall D. Sahlins and Elman R. Service (eds.), *Evolution and Culture* (Ann Arbor, Mich.: 1960), p. 99.

[4] See Carl J. Friedrich, *The New Image of the Common Man* (Boston: 1950), p. 265; Georg Lukacs, *Die Zerstörung der Vernunft* (Berlin: 1955), p. 496.

[5] See n. 87, below.

sociologia generale (1916), translated as *The Mind and Society* (1935). The publications that preceded or followed these two works are not well-known outside the circle of specialists. That is, in a way, a pity, because the so-called minor works of an important author (particularly his early works) may frequently reveal the springs of inspiration covered up by the completed structure. It is more than idle curiosity to seek to detect the genesis of an idea, to find out when it occurred and how it grew and changed—or failed to change. The origins of his ideas reveal more about a man's mind than his ultimate, "definitive" conclusions.

Gaetano Mosca hit on his *idée maîtresse* at the age of twenty-five, and to the end of his days he went on elaborating his original discovery, which like most seminal discoveries was simple to the point of triteness. Mosca candidly acknowledged his indebtedness to earlier thinkers, just as Karl Marx never claimed to have discovered the idea of the class struggle.[6] The genius of innovation is not necessarily tied to the—in our days overrated—notion of originality: the important point is what the discoverer makes of his find.

In this sense, Mosca's doctrine may be understood as his own variations on a theme anticipated by Machiavelli, Guicciardini, Rousseau, Saint-Simon, Taine, Gumplowicz, Novikov, and Ammon.[7] His main inspiration came from Saint-Simon, who held that

> . . . power in all organized societies is split between two orders—one controls the intellectual and moral; the other, the material forces. These two powers are exercised by two organized minorities which together form the ruling class.[8]

This sharp dichotomy is Mosca's starting point in the first work devoted to the problem of the ruling class:

> In all regularly constituted societies in which something called a government exists, we find that all authority is being exercised in the name of the entire people, or of an aristocracy, or of a single sovereign. . . .

Having thus restated the Aristotelian categories, Mosca instantly declares that he has little use for them:

> But besides that fact we find unfailingly another: the ruling class, or those who hold and exercise the public power, will be always a minority, and below them we find a numerous class of persons who do never, in any real

---

[6] See Marx and Engels, *Selected Works*, Vol. II, p. 410.

[7] See Gaetano Mosca, *The Ruling Class*, pp. 329-31; James H. Meisel, *The Myth of the Ruling Class* (Ann Arbor, Mich.: 1958), pp. 29, 170-71, 173, 192-93, 383-84.

[8] Gaetano Mosca, *Histoire des doctrines politiques* (Paris: 1936), p. 239.

sense, participate in government but merely submit to it: they may be called the ruled class.[9]

Two points must be noted here. The ruling class is narrowly identified by Mosca as *the public power* and equated with governmental personnel. Only in his later works does Mosca abandon the sharp dichotomy between the two groups and distinguish, in the ruling group itself, two strata: one comprising the official rulers; the other, much larger, composed of the executive class which transmits, communicates, and *mediates* the orders of the high command to the ruled masses. It is this second stratum which alone is capable of bridging the gap between the few and the many. Without the labors of these mediators, no minority rule could endure. In the last analysis, this stratum is the more important of the two groups making up the ruling class:

> . . . The stability of any political organism depends on the level of morality, intelligence, and activity that this second stratum has attained. . . .[10]

The concept will be further broadened to include other leading groups not necessarily part of the official governmental apparatus. But even in the early stages of his investigation, Mosca insists that his concept of the ruling class applies to all regimes—to those based on the doctrine of popular sovereignty as well as aristocracies or monarchies. In democratic states, too, "a governmental machine is bound to be in existence" which will "naturally" be composed of a minority in control. Therefore, "that special class of persons forms the government, and it is in that class entirely." The masses merely furnish that class "with the means by which it sustains and justifies its action, and they do so either voluntarily," because they find it advantageous, "or else they do it under duress." [11]

Sometimes the dominant minority rules by virtue of "superior moral fiber." Later on, Mosca discards this notion and maintains that the rulers are those endowed with the aptitudes and skills of rulership, not necessarily those of moral sensitivity. But the decisive reason why the Many will submit, more or less readily, is that

> . . . an organized minority, acting in concert, will forever triumph over a disorganized majority of people without common will or impulse.[12]

The idea that organization prevails over the unorganized (by definition) or disunited multitude is as old as Machiavelli and as recent as

---

[9] Gaetano Mosca, *Teorica dei governi e sul governo parlimentare* (Turin: 1884), p. 16.
[10] Mosca, *The Ruling Class, op. cit.,* p. 404.   [11] Mosca, *Teorica . . . , op. cit.,* p. 18.
[12] *Ibid.,* p. 19.

Robert Michels' "iron law of oligarchy." [13] Mosca would readily grant the fact that the masses, too, may—and indeed do—organize, but he would insist that the organized mass will, in turn, be led by an elite.

This new concept of a counterelite, and of a plurality of elites functioning outside the governmental class, each representing an important social force, makes its appearance in *The Ruling Class*. Now Mosca recognizes that, whenever the communication gap between rulers and ruled becomes too wide,

> . . . within the lower classes another ruling class, or directing minority, necessarily forms, and often this new class is antagonistic to the class that holds possession of the legal government. When this class of plebeian leaders is well organized, it may seriously embarrass an official government.[14]

With this charming understatement, Mosca introduces Marx's concept of the class struggle under another name; but in his own scheme the plebeian masses merely act as a discordant background chorus: the decisive battles are still fought between the minorities who hold power and those who aspire to it. Sometimes, the ruling class splits up into factions, each of which will, in a democratic setting, bid for popular support at the polls. But that does not mean that the people really decide the outcome:

> When we say the voters "choose" their representatives, we are using a language that is very inexact. The truth is that the representative has *himself elected* by the voters, [or] that his friends have him elected.[15]

His friends are the kingmakers in the party, the manipulators of the electoral machines—in short, the various sectors of the ruling class, now understood as the sum total of all organized minorities.

But the notion of the social process as a contest between heterogeneous groups is really more typical of Pareto's thought than of Mosca's *Weltanschauung*. Mosca's universe is pluralistic only on the surface; it rests on the *terra firma* of communal unity. The ruling class controls but it does not create the intellectual and the moral codes. What Mosca calls *the political formula*—the ideology by which the rulers justify their governance—not only "must respond to a true need of human nature," it is the joint product of the whole society.[16] In its institutionalized form it becomes "juridical defense" (or government of law), the guarantee of

---

[13] Mosca, *The Ruling Class, op. cit.*, p. 329, cites Machiavelli, *The Discourses* XVI; Robert Michels, *Political Parties* (New York: The Free Press of Glencoe, Inc., 1949), pp. 377 ff.

[14] Mosca, *The Ruling Class, op. cit.*, p. 116. [15] *Ibid.*, p. 154. [16] *Ibid.*, pp. 70 f.

civil liberties. These liberties are safe when the ruling class incorporates and represents the most important social forces, slighting and repressing none. That government will not simply mediate clashing interests; rather, it will put each in its place. The state must be strong enough to control the neofeudal baronies of large-scale business and labor organizations. But, at the same time, the state ought not to be too strong: the best system is that which gives rise to a class of public-minded citizens who stand above the battle because they are economically independent. Alas, that class, the glory of the nineteenth century, was disappearing rapidly in Mosca's day—turning into a dependent class of salaried employees, or committing Benda's "treason of the intellectuals" by deserting to the proletarian Left.[17]

Mosca was aware of the incipient bureaucratization of society. He was not opposed to change as such, provided it did not occur too fast (he knew how many aristocracies had sealed their own doom by refusing to absorb new forces), but he was opposed to wholesale change because it destroyed continuity. The price of revolution was too high. The most desirable arrangement, in his view, was one in which the forces of renewal and stability complement one another in a state of flexible equilibration.[18]

These are the lessons Mosca learned from history, and often the historian seems to be forgetful of the other Mosca, the theoretician of the ruling class. The doctrine loses its rigidity and becomes, in its final version,[19] almost democratic, an ingenious scheme of balanced moderation in the liberal tradition. Mosca knew this tradition could not be restored; what was left for him was not to build but to destroy, to help remove the intellectual obstacles of democratic "metaphysics" and plebeian millenarianism. He was fated to do yeoman service for the forces generated by the failing revolutions of his time. When the *terrible simplificateur,* Benito Mussolini, staged the real counterrevolution—fusing nationalist, proletarian, and mass-democratic elements into his ruling class—the theorist was horrified and hid his face.

Pareto came to sociology after a long and illustrious career as a mathematical economist. The theory of economic equilibrium became vital to his model of society, which he viewed as a congeries of human atoms. The Paretian system, unlike Mosca's, achieves unity, not by consensus,

---

[17] *Ibid.,* pp. 100, 120, 126 ff. (juridicial defense), 268-70 (independent middle class).
[18] See Meisel, "Power Source and Power Flow," reprinted here.
[19] The last chapter of Mosca, *Histoire* . . . , *op. cit.,* translated as the Supplement to Meisel, *op. cit.*

but by force. As force is diluted, the social equilibrium has to be restored by elements to which the use of force comes naturally. This is Pareto's famous *circulation des élites* (anticipated sketchily by Mosca[20]). But Pareto predicates his law on biological constancies of behavior which defy analysis. How do we know that they exist?

> [Through the] manifestations, verbal or through conduct, of [these] instincts, sentiments, inclinations, appetites, interests, *etc.*, and the logical or pseudological inferences that are drawn from such manifestations.[21]

As Mosca's aim is to unmask all metaphysical pretensions, so Pareto states in his great *Trattato:*

> One of the purposes of this work is to strip realities of such veilings of sentiments.[22]

Underneath the logical or pseudological manifestations (*derivation* is Pareto's term for rationalizations and myth-making) lie the *residues*—unchanging or, at best, slow-changing attitudes. Pareto has a list of six residues, but only the first two are really important to his purpose. The first, called *the residue of combination,* corresponds to the progressive and inventive type—in business it is the speculator; in politics, the Machiavellian fox, who prefers cunning and appeasement to brute violence—whose methods are "humanitarian," democratic, corrupt, and corrupting. The second, *the residue of persistent aggregates,* is Pareto's term for the mentality of the herd, worshipping tradition, and fond of forceful action.[23]

The terms of the *Trattato* are already clearly understood in Pareto's first sociological works. The elite makes its debut in the *Cours d'économie politique* (1896-97), although that felicitous phrase had not yet been coined:

> The differentiation of human societies generally begins with the formation of an aristocratic class. But it constitutes only one phase of the evolution. When the differentiation continues, the aristocratic class loses power. . . .[24]

The circulation of elites is defined in these words:

> The aristocracies maintain themselves only by constant renewal and absorption of the most distinguished individuals from the lower classes. As a

---

[20] But fully elaborated only in the second volume of *The Ruling Class, op. cit.,* Chap. 15, published seven years after Pareto's *Trattato.*
[21] Vilfredo Pareto, *The Mind and Society,* Vol. IV, p. 1915, I-b.
[22] *Ibid.,* p. 10. [23] *Ibid.,* Vol. II, Sec. 887 ff.
[24] Vilfredo Pareto, *Cours d'économie politique,* Vol. II, p. 56.

rule, all closed aristocracies deteriorate sharply after a certain number of generations. That fact is of the greatest importance for the entire social evolution.[25]

That fact is all the more important to Pareto, for he views the social structure as a hierarchy of aptitudes. In an ideally competitive society, the best in any given field are bound to achieve eminence. What is considered to be "best," however, depends on the values dominant in the particular society. If it is one of thieves, the nimblest thief will become chief.[26]

The selective process operates, ideally, in favor of the democratic principle: the lower classes are "the crucibles of the new aristocracies which replace the old, degenerated ones." This all the more so as selection is slowed down in the top stratum (the aristocracies take care of their less gifted members), "while in the lower classes Malthus' 'positive checks' are most rigorous." [27]

Democracy, however, does not automatically work for progress, nor does the great cause of freedom necessarily benefit from the equalitarian tendency:

> Despotism may be tantamount to progress if it results in differentiating an anarchically homogeneous society. The aristocracy [replacing it] is an advance and . . . one might say that, in a certain sense, the nations owe their freedom to their aristocracies. . . . The character of the Greek *tyrannis* was essentially democratic; it was a case of decadence, a return to less heterogeneous forms of life.[28]

For both Mosca and Pareto, the criterion of a "higher stage" of civilization was social differentiation, and both authors praise aristocracy in this sense as a liberating and progressive force, whereas democracy, according to Pareto, may have a retarding effect on society.

But here the similarities end. "Societies," declares Pareto, "are not homogeneous [unless they are 'anarchically homogeneous']. . . . Nor does any one society present a homogeneous whole; it is composed of heterogeneous individuals and classes. . . ." [29] Mosca approached the notion of class conflict gingerly. He abhorred Marx, while Pareto, much more the Manchester *laissez-faire* liberal, could never hide his admiration for Marx and his followers. "The socialists," he wrote, "are entirely right to attribute great importance to the 'class struggle' and to call it the great factor dominating history." [30]

---

[25] *Ibid.*, p. 29. [26] Pareto, *The Mind and Society, op. cit.*, Vol. III, Secs. 2027-28.
[27] Pareto, *Cours* . . . , *op. cit.*, p. 372. [28] *Ibid.*, p. 57. [29] *Ibid.*, p. 347.
[30] *Ibid.*, p. 385. See also J. H. Meisel, "A Question of Affinities: Pareto and Marx," *Cahiers Vilfredo Pareto*, V (1964), pp. 154-63.

Pareto's emphatic attitude toward the proletarian movement is still very much in evidence in *The Socialist Systems,* published five years later[31]—which is all the more remarkable as the main purpose of that work is to demolish the scientific claims of Marxist theory. The introduction to the study clearly states the methodological principles fully developed in the *Trattato:*

> In this work all questions will be successively considered, as much as this is possible, under their double aspect: . . . one we shall call objective; the other, subjective. *On the one hand we are going to enquire into the real facts which either favored the establishment of certain social systems or else were unfavorable to their realization. . . . On the other hand, we are going to examine the reasonings used to justify these systems or the failure of these systems. Finally, our aim is to determine the extent to which the premises used were derived from experience and the deductions based on logic.*[32]

The reasonings men use to justify their actions and inactions are not yet called *derivations,* but the meaning is clear. Pareto proclaims his intention to examine his data in an "exclusively scientific manner"— in other words, with objectivity. He has often been accused of violating his own principle. He was aware of it:

> Each of us has a secret enemy within who tries to make it difficult for us to follow the road [of reason] and avoid injecting our own sentiments into our logical deductions from the facts. Pointing out this general human failing, I well know that I am not exempt from it. My sentiments draw me toward liberty, so I took care not to be swayed by them. But in so doing, I may have gone too far and, afraid of being too partial to the arguments for liberty, it is possible I did not give them quite their due. Equally, in order not to be grossly unfair to sentiments of which I disapprove, I may have valued them too highly. . . .[33]

His sense of fairness is in evidence when he discusses derivations:

> It is a mistake to assume that men who deceive another [about their real motivations] must invariably act in bad faith; on the contrary, that is very rarely the case, and most of the time the deceiver had first to deceive himself. . . .[34]

It is a real need of humans to endow these credences with all the dignity of logical causation: "they believe . . . that their convictions have been

---

[31] Vilfredo Pareto, *Les Systèmes socialistes* (Paris: 1902), followed by the *Manuale di economia politica* (1906), which, in its first two chapters, represents a further stage in the development of the Paretian system.

[32] Pareto, *Les Systèmes* . . . , *op. cit.,* p. 16. Pareto's italics.   [33] *Ibid.,* p. 6.

[34] *Ibid.,* p. 9.

formed by a series of rigorous syllogisms starting from facts true and incontestable." [35]

No uniformity can be discovered in the major ethical or intellectual currents of a given epoch. All we can say is that "for reasons in part known and in part unknown, which must, to some extent, stem from the psychological structure of man, the moral and religious movements, like the economic movement, proceed rhythmically." [36] Sociology must, therefore, turn for help to the psychologist. But Pareto's psychology is his own almost entirely: a psychology based, in part, on his assumption of biological constants; in part, on the study of the historic rhythm which governs particular religious attitudes.[37]

Prediction in these matters is difficult because the social movement proceeds in an "undulating curve." [38] The fact that certain tendencies in the development of literature, law, or ethics appear to accelerate and to intensify is no reason to expect that such tendencies will win out in the end: a reaction may well be imminent.

> . . . when a movement is about to change direction, the reversal will not usually start with a decrease in intensity, which would facilitate prediction; on the contrary, the movement will attain its maximum intensity precisely at the moment prior to the change of general direction.[39]

In this emergent structure, the elite—the term makes its official debut now—falls into place, becoming a mere part of the whole project— an illustration rather than the starting point it is in Mosca's scheme. Again, Pareto's social pyramid—which, as he hastens to remark, is shaped rather like a "spinning top" [40]—still constitutes a hierarchy of social apti- tudes: "The so-called superior classes are also generally the richest." [41] But they cannot endure without renewing themselves from the lower classes, particularly from rural elements. Pareto says what he has said before, but says it beautifully. The lower classes he now calls

> . . . the dark crucible in which the new elites are being formed. They are the roots which feed the flower blossoming into elites. The blossoms fold and wilt, but they are soon replaced by others, if the roots remain inviolate.[42]

The circulation of elites is now described with almost mathematical precision:

> Let us assume an elite A, which is in control; another elite, B, which tries to replace it; then C represents the rest of the population, comprising the inept, the people lacking energy, character, intelligence . . . an army with-

[35] *Ibid.*, p. 17.   [36] *Ibid.*, p. 21.   [37] *Ibid.*, pp. 21-22.   [38] *Ibid.*, p. 22.   [39] *Ibid.*
[40] *Ibid.*, p. 26.   [41] *Ibid.*, p. 28.   [42] *Ibid.*, pp. 31-32.

out leaders which acquires importance only if led by either A or B. As a rule, the B's will lead them, while the A's are lulled by a false sense of security or underestimation of the C's. . . . However, sometimes the A's will try to outbid the B's by offering the C's concessions more apparent than real. . . .[43]

The situation is different if the B's take the place of the A's by a process of gradual infiltration. In that case, "the C's are deprived of leaders to prod them into revolt. . . ." However, if a showdown between the "in" elite and an "out" elite is unavoidable, the B's will need all the assistance of the C's. "If they succeed and assume power, a new elite, D, will come into existence and play the same role vis-à-vis the A's. And so on and so forth." [44]

The subject of these contests does not concern Pareto:

Often these events appear to historians only through the veil of their own passions and prejudices, and we will be told about a glorious war for liberty when what took place was a mere struggle between two elites competing for supremacy.[45]

In the Paretian universe, ideas and human aims become mere levers in the power struggle; history is an interminable struggle for control.[46]

This truth is documented by a close analysis of Roman history, to be repeated and expanded in the *Trattato*. But the truth of any matter is one thing; the utility of the truth is another. Socialism, for instance, did not make much of a direct impact on society, but "indirectly, it was an essential element of progress in our time, and this quite independently of its intrinsic value and logical content. Little does it matter if a theory is, from a certain viewpoint, false, provided the emotions it inspires are useful. . . ." In this case, they were useful to the proletarians.[47]

Given the relevance of the distinction between a truth and its usefulness, one must ask: What is the utility of the Paretian system? To be sure, Pareto has no "message" other than the exhortation to distrust all messages. Still, does his work perhaps contain some cryptic program that might be translated into action?

Ever since Marx had declared war on the European bourgeoisie, its intellectual defenders had been looking for an equally militant counter-ideology. But the only club with which to beat the Marxists proved to be —not the democratic creed, congenitally unfit for the purpose—but its stepchild Fascism. For a moment it appeared as if Pareto served the purpose. Had he not approved of Mussolini?[48] Not quite without reason,

[43] *Ibid.*, pp. 35-36. [44] *Ibid.*, p. 36. [45] *Ibid.*, p. 59. [46] See pp. 32-33 of this introduction.
[47] Pareto, *Les Systèmes* . . . , *op. cit.*, pp. 62, 64. On utility and truth, see also *The Mind and Society, op. cit.*, Vol. I, Secs. 72-74.
[48] See pp. 34-35 of this introduction.

he was variously known as "the bourgeois Karl Marx," [49] "the Karl Marx of Fascism," [50] or even "an old man who aspired to be the Machiavelli of the middle classes." [51]

It was a strange revival and reversal of the Marxist theory of class conflict, with Pareto as the Marx of counterrevolution. But that counter-revolution was directed both against the proletariat and against the bourgeoisie.[52]

THE RELUCTANT PARTNERS

When one says *Mosca,* one usually adds: *and Pareto.* The reverse, how-ever, is not always true; there can be no question that Pareto is by far the better known of the two men. The irony is that, whenever he is paired with Mosca, it usually concerns a subject which, if not exactly minor in Pareto's work, is definitely not his main or sole concern but only one of his four variables, and treated only at the very end: when there is talk of the elite, then Mosca and Pareto usually appear together, just as in the early period of the Russian revolution, people would not speak of Lenin without, in the same breath, also saying Trotzky. (The comparison must not be taken literally.)

Frequently, such a combination adds strength to each member. Not so in the case of Mosca and Pareto: both lost by it. Pareto's fame today does not rest on his methodology; it is not based on his conceptual groundwork, which fills almost three of the four volumes of the English version of the *Trattato.* No, "the lasting interest of Pareto, as of Mosca, . . . is their contribution to our understanding of what, since Pareto, we refer to as *the study of elites.* . . ." [53] Especially in the United States, Pareto "began to be known among social scientists as the originator of the theory of the elites. . . ." *Nomen est omen:* Mosca's label for the

[49] Joseph A. Schumpeter, "Vilfredo Pareto" in *Ten Great Economists: From Marx to Keynes* (New York: 1951), p. 110, citing G. H. Bousquet, *Vilfredo Pareto, sa vie et son oeuvre* (Paris: 1928), p. 237, who in turn cites the Italian socialist daily, *Avanti.*
[50] William McDougall, "Pareto as Psychologist," *Journal of Social Philosophy,* I: 1 (October 1935), 36, n. 1, citing R. V. Worthington, "Pareto: The Karl Marx of Fascism," *Economic Forum* (Summer and Fall 1933).
[51] Ellsworth Faris, "An Estimate of Pareto," *The American Journal of Sociology,* XLI: 5 (March 1936), 668.
[52] For Raymond Aron's interpretation of Pareto as a proto-totalitarian, see pp. 35-36 of this introduction and the excerpts from his 1937 essay reprinted here. H. Stuart Hughes, in his *Consciousness and Society* (New York: 1958), takes a more lenient view: "One of the great virtues of Pareto's schema is that it cuts across the conventional Left-Right cleavage" (p. 269). This splendidly defines the counterrevolutionary attitude.
[53] W. G. Runciman, *Social Science and Political Theory* (Cambridge: Cambridge University Press, 1963), p. 64.

dominant minority was less apt or felicitous: "The success of Pareto is, we think, the success of his skillfully or luckily chosen word *elite*. Mosca . . . used the expression *classe politica*. . . . Pareto's conventional term . . . has met with better fortune and has carried with it the reputation of the author." [54]

Perhaps, but not necessarily so. There is good reason for believing that, on the contrary, Pareto's greater reputation gave his term, *elite*, the wider currency.

Today, Pareto would be mortified to find his *Summa Antitheologica* known for what was a mere detail and illustration of his theory. But Mosca had two complaints: an unjust fate had robbed him of his claim to have originated the contemporary theory of the elite. "That Mosca, instead of having precedence, did make his appearance in Pareto's footsteps, is a historical joke." [55] If it had been merely a misfortune, owing to Pareto's already established international prestige as an economist, it would have been bad enough:

> The theory which is known today as the theory of the elite is nothing more than the theory of Mosca with some of its elements emphasized, some of its points amplified, and with its fundamental name changed. Its author is not Mosca. He is Vilfredo Pareto.[56]

But it was still worse.[57] Mosca's grudge against Pareto was nursed by his strong and never weakening suspicion that Pareto had knowingly appropriated his *idée maîtresse:* that at all times and under any form of government the organized few will rule over the unorganized majority. Suspicion became fury when Pareto haughtily dismissed the charge and even deleted references to the younger author from a new edition of an older work.[58]

Thus the intellectual association hurt both authors: Mosca lost the copyright to his idea, while Pareto found his moral reputation damaged and himself demoted to the theorist of the elite. The unknown jester who writes intellectual history decreed that the two enemies were to re-

---

[54] Renzo Sereno, "The Anti-Aristotelianism of Gaetano Mosca and Its Fate," *Ethics,* XLVIII: 4 (July 1938), 514, 515. In almost identical terms: Hughes, *op. cit.,* p. 254.

[55] Fritz Morstein Marx, "The Bureaucratic State—Some Remarks on Mosca's *Ruling Class,*" *Review of Politics,* I: 4 (October 1939), 459.

[56] *Ibid.*

[57] Readers interested in the old feud (irrelevant to the purpose of this study) are referred to Hughes, *op. cit.,* p. 255, and to his essay reprinted here. See also Meisel, *op. cit.,* pp. 170-76.

[58] What follows is an extended version of the present editor's study, "Mosca 'Transatlantico'" in *Cahiers Vilfredo Pareto* IV (1964), 15-23. Reproduced by permission of the publisher.

main forever Dioscuri, the inseparable twins of the school launched by
Gaetano Mosca when he published his first major work in 1884.[59]

It is not hard to prove that the two authors are as different in their
approach as in their ultimate conclusions:

> The main outlines of Mosca's and Pareto's thought may be similar: in both
> cases it suggests aristocratic fastidiousness and a distrust of mass democracy.
> . . . Yet the form of Pareto's and Mosca's works and the methodological pre-
> suppositions behind them differed sharply, and these differences, despite the
> most curious overlappings and internal contradictions, help explain the ulti-
> mate divergence that brought Pareto down on one side of a major political
> divide and Mosca on the other.[60]

Nevertheless, generation after generation chose to fasten on the superficial similarities; the myth that had conjoined the two survived all
learned refutations. If one adds that Mosca and Pareto treated socialism
and democracy as one and the same aberration, the confusion of their
images is complete. The twin attack on Marx and on democracy caused
still a different confusion: Western democrats would love the anti-Marxist
strictures but resent the anti-democratic bias, while the socialists would
have rejoiced in the rejection of bourgeois democracy, if only it had not
included socialism too.

The scholarly observer was not slow to see that Mosca and Pareto, in
rejecting Marx, remained obliged to him. H. Stuart Hughes remarks that
their critique of political ideologies, organized around the notion of the
elite, "completed the work of Marx by subjecting to his own sort of
treatment the socialist aspirations and the socialist view of history that
the founder of dialectical materialism had respected as the sole ideology
worthy to survive." [61] And Carl J. Friedrich finds Pareto's "contention
that a 'governing elite' is the projection of a class which happens to be
dominant in society . . . in close parallel to Marxist views. . . ." [62]
Ralf Dahrendorf observes that Mosca "has fallen victim to a Marxian
overestimation of class analysis." And he cited from *The Ruling Class:*
"One could explain the whole history of civilized mankind in terms of
the conflict between the attempt of the rulers to monopolize and be-
queath political power and the attempt of new forces to change the relations of power." [63] Mosca's "social forces easily remind" another writer

---

[59] Mosca, *Teorica* . . . , *op. cit.*   [60] Hughes, *op. cit.*, p. 253.   [61] *Ibid.*, p. 254.
[62] Carl J. Friedrich, *Man and His Government* (New York: 1963), p. 320.
[63] Ralf Dahrendorf, *Class and Class Conflict in an Industrial Society* (London: 1959),
p. 198, citing from the German edition of Mosca's *Elementi* (*Die Herrschende Klasse*
[Bern: 1950], p. 64; *The Ruling Class*, p. 65) differs slightly.

. . . of Marx's classes, as their "ideologies" recall our author's "formulas." And like the Marxian classes, Mosca's social forces closely reflect all the changes—economic, social, cultural—of an evolving civilization. . . . If that is so . . . then the distinction between the class struggle and the struggles of [Mosca's "political class"] becomes rather labored. Did Mosca draw the line so sharply because he was so uncomfortably close to Marx?[64]

One would expect the general reaction to such authors in the democratic West, particularly in America, to be one of uneasiness, if not outright hostility—the more so because their main works became available in English in the 1930's, at the very moment of truth for democracy. It was the Fascist decade, and both Mosca and Pareto were believed to be at least the intellectual parents if not the open partisans of Fascism. But it also was, in the United States, a time of questioning and self-reproach. The Wall Street gods had failed, and the planting of new seeds, even imported ones, seemed favorable. Mosca and Pareto found a small but eager audience, of which Pareto took the lion's share. The intellectual temper of the Great Depression found his cynical detachment more congenial than the liberal nostalgia of a Mosca. By the same token, the Paretian system of fixed archetypes, with its decree of cyclical recurrence made some sense in a society which was just shedding its naïve belief in a constant linear progress. The America of pragmatism and technocracy found Mosca's diffident analysis of "social forces" not so reassuring as Pareto's massive scientism. Mosca's legalistic labels (like *juridical defense* for government of law, and *formula* for myth) were less impressive than Pareto's novel *residues* and *derivations,* and not as dramatic as his Machiavellian *lions* and *foxes.*

Mosca suffered from a further disadvantage: he came to the New World four years after Pareto. Once again the privilege of intellectual priority had been denied him. There was worse to come: fate had decreed that Mosca and Pareto share the same American editors.[65]

Arthur Livingston, the scholar who presided over the translations of both the *Trattato* and the *Elementi,* was a man divided in his loyalties. His introduction to *The Ruling Class*—a title, incidentally, too narrow to do justice to the scope of Mosca's work—could not be bettered as an exercise in equitable and astute comparison:

> Pareto's research, based on an analysis of the social equilibrium, leads out to a comprehensive view of all society and results in a monument of gigantic

---

[64] Meisel, *op. cit.,* p. 303.
[65] *The Mind and Society* was published first (1935); *The Ruling Class* followed four years later (1939).

architectural proportions. . . . In such a research the problems of political organization that Mosca sets out to solve are mere details, yet in solving them Mosca has to take account of many of the facts that are basic in Pareto's larger structure, and he does take account of them in the form of observations, asides, intuitions, remarks that delight and astound for their shrewdness and profoundness. . . .

But with Mosca this "remains a literary finesse. . . . In Pareto the same perception . . . becomes scientific hypothesis. . . ." [66]

Scientific reassurance for Americans that the disrupted equilibrium of their society was bound to be restored—could that have been the great attraction prompting editor and publisher to launch Pareto first?[67]

Publication of *The Ruling Class* (1939) started Mosca on his transatlantic pilgrimage. A few attentive readers of the learned journals had already spotted him the year before, when an American from Italy, Renzo Sereno, introduced his compatriot in a memorable essay which became a "must" for all would-be *cognoscenti*. He was followed by Fritz Morstein Marx, who dealt with Mosca's contribution to the theory of bureaucratic government.[68] Otherwise, American response remained perfunctory or negative. When Sidney Hook, the eminent New York philosopher, dissected Mosca, the Italian's rather uninformed critique of dialectical materialism must have been painful to the man who had done more than any other writer in the 1930's to inform America about Karl Marx.[69] He could agree with Mosca's strictures on political democracy, but otherwise made short shrift of his scientific and methodological deficiencies— just as Hook's Italian colleague, Benedetto Croce, had done sixteen years earlier.[70]

World War II, with its mobilization of prodemocratic sentiment, was not conducive to the spread, in America, of the idea of a ruling class. Hegel, Nietzsche, and a host of minor figures were blamed for the rise of the fascist ideologies. Mosca and Pareto were, of course, among the culprits, chained in unholy brotherhood once more.

[66] Mosca, *The Ruling Class, op. cit.,* pp. xxxvii-viii, ix.

[67] Livingston says that the translation of the *Elementi* "was planned in 1923 as part of an enterprise for making the monuments of Italian Machiavellian thought available to English-speaking scholars. Normally it should have appeared, and but for difficulties associated with the crisis of [19]29 [the beginning of the Great Depression] would have appeared, in advance of my American edition of Pareto's *Trattato.* . . ." *Ibid.*, p. xxxvi.

[68] See n. 55, 56 above. In his most recent work, *The Rulers* (New York: 1962), Sereno took a dimmer view of Mosca (and Pareto).

[69] See n. 34

[70] See Sidney Hook, "The Fetishism of Power," reprinted here. About Croce, see pp. 34, 43. Croce's essay in *La Critica,* XXI (November 20, 1923), on the whole benevolent, became the Preface to the Fourth edition of the *Elementi* (Bari: 1939), not of the Fifth, as Professor Ferrarotti has it (see p. 133, n. 11).

Thus Carl J. Friedrich, Harvard University's political philosopher, declared war against the two and left them on the battlefield for dead. (More recently, he reconsidered the whole question in a calmer mood, but 1942 was not a year to favor scholarly detachment.[71])

At this juncture, the Furies who were dogging Gaetano Mosca's every step determined that he should have a defender. He reminds one of the man who said that he could take care of his enemies, but who was going to protect him from his friends?

James Burnham, after he had broken with Leon Trotzky (then an exile in Mexico), did not take long to identify the revolutionary class that would supplant the disappointing proletariat: the new class of managers. Because this class was short on theory, Burnham furnished it in *The Machiavellians: Defenders of Freedom* (1943). They were the four tough-minded realists: Sorel, Pareto, Mosca, and Michels. It is through this work that the majority of American students first encountered Gaetano Mosca.[72] It was probably inevitable that the Mosca of James Burnham was the one who held that "only power can control power." [73] Yet there is another side to Mosca that Burnham could not—or would not see. But Burnham must not be censured too severely: Mosca was himself ambiguous. Sometimes, he honestly believed that freedom could exist only where it was buttressed by sufficient social power; but he also considered power as collective energy, as source—and product—of cooperation. That force —though not always manifest—is spelled out by the "formula" used by the ruling class to justify its dominance. When Mosca deplores the weakening of those "forces of moral cohesion which alone are capable of uniting in a consensus of sentiments and ideas all the atoms that make up a people," [74] one is instantly reminded of an author very much disliked by Mosca: Rousseau, and his General Will.

Most of the time, the pragmatist of power and of conflict seems to hold the upper hand. But he has moments of despondency in which he will call for a disinterested class of economically independent citizens, who are to be the guardians of the social value system which is being structured as "the balance of the social forces." With that concept Mosca paces Talcott Parsons, who developed it, however, not from Mosca but from Pareto.

---

[71] Friedrich, *The New Image of the Common Man, op. cit.*, pp. 238-70.
[72] Such standard texts as George H. Sabine's *History of Political Theory* (1937 and 1950), Francis W. Coker's *Recent Political Thought* (1934), and John H. Hallowell's *Main Currents in Modern Political Thought* (1950), have nothing to say about Mosca.
[73] *The Machiavellians*, p. 110. [74] Mosca, *The Ruling Class*, p. 481.

Mosca's power balance resembles, but is not necessarily identical with, David Riesman's congery of independent "veto groups": each poised to frustrate—singly or in combination—any drive for absolute control.[75] For there was nothing Mosca feared more than the emerging feudal baronies of large-scale corporate or syndicalist character. Again and again, Mosca stressed the need "to prevent, at all costs, the rise of new sovereignties intermediate between the individual and the state." There seem to be echoes of Rousseau when Mosca lauds the liberal regime of the Victorian past because it had made possible "a strong state," capable of harnessing all social energies.[76]

If this Mosca is so little known today, part of the blame—but only part of it—belongs to his *terribles simplificateurs;* his work remains confusing because he, like others, could not overcome a basic hesitation between the two theories of power.

In the 1950's as the undemocratic profile of the "corporate economy" emerged more clearly, such terms as *elite* and *power structure* became popular with the American intelligentsia. Squads of research workers got busy to refute the proposition that the organized few at all times and in all places rule the many—Mosca's and Pareto's main contention. An enormous mound of data, mostly based on local studies, was accumulated. The supreme achievement of that school is probably Professor Robert Dahl's New Haven survey.[77] It was he who most succinctly formulated the American complaint against the theorists of the elite: their hypothesis was "cast in a form that makes it virtually impossible to disprove. . . . But a theory that cannot even in principle be controverted by empirical evidence is not a scientific theory." [78] Such a theory fitted preindustrial or recently industrialized societies in which the class structure was stable and uncomplicated, whereas the superdiffuse and mobile modern society makes the formation of elites extremely difficult, if not impossible.[79] Elites exist, but elite control is either temporary or else limited to specific cultural or economic spheres. Nowhere in the United States did one consolidated ruling class exist. There were, according to Sereno, rulers, but they were not—*pace,* Mosca!—*organized.*[80] Ralf Dahrendorf, not an American but very influential with American sociologists,

---

[75] David Riesman, *The Lonely Crowd* (New Haven: 1950), pp. 246 ff.
[76] Mosca, *op. cit.,* pp. 481, 475.   [77] Robert Dahl, *Who Governs?* (New Haven: 1961).
[78] Robert A. Dahl, "A Critique of the Ruling Elite Model," *American Political Science Review* (June 1958), 463.
[79] See Karl Mannheim, *Man and Society in an Age of Reconstruction* (London: 1940), pp. 86 ff.
[80] Renzo Sereno, *The Rulers,* pp. 139 ff.

likewise rejected Mosca's great discovery, remarking that "the distinction between ruling and subjected groups is but one element of society." He also rejected Mosca's claim that ruling groups determine the cultural level of a people.[81]
But Mosca knew that

> . . . the ruled mass remains the humus out of which grow leading groups; the ruling class must never be considered as an isolate. Its ideology remains, if not epiphenomenal, an aspect of the total social process until, at some point of class differentiation, the myth of the ruling class obstructs the evolutionary flow and becomes a mere "class ideology." [82]

To Mosca, then, the dominant minority is merely the visible cap of the iceberg; once it sets itself apart, it will soon join, in Pareto's celebrated phrase, the "graveyard of aristocracies." [83]

What many of the opponents of Mosca and Pareto overlook is their indebtedness to the first builders of the model which they are so anxious to tear down. Without it, quite a few of them might be out of a treasured pastime.

While the campaign against the un-American mystique of the elite continued, the two founders of the school became almost respectable—much as aged rebels are incorporated into the Establishment as "elder statesmen." Thus Pareto became integrated into the Parsonian system. Mosca too gained ground, but—another irony—vicariously: Mosca's main acolyte, Robert Michels, became the darling of political sociologists, and a few rays of reflected glory fell upon the teacher. Joseph Schumpeter evolved a synthesis of democratic and elitist principles which echoes Mosca's saying that "the representative is not elected by the voters but, as a rule, has himself elected by them." [84] Another influential textbook, the collaboration of a social scientist and a philosopher, supplied the student with a splendid catalog of definitions, many of them going back to Mosca.[85] Mosca's conviction that "a whole metaphysical system must

[81] Dahrendorf, *op. cit.*, p. 198. "Mosca in particular has fallen victim to a Marxian overestimation of class analysis" (*ibid.*). Similarly negative: Suzanne Keller, *Beyond the Ruling Class* (New York: 1963), pp. 11-14, 79.

[82] Meisel, *op. cit.*, p. 17. See also Meisel, "Power Source and Power Flow," reprinted here. For the evidence, consult Mosca, *The Ruling Class*, pp. 415 ff.

[83] *Trattato*, Sec. 2053.

[84] Mosca, *Teorica . . . , op. cit.*, p. 85. Schumpeter, *Capitalism, Socialism, and Democracy* (New York: 1942, 1947), Chap. 22. The author does not mention Mosca.

[85] Harold D. Lasswell and Abraham Kaplan, *Power and Society* (New Haven: 1950). Mosca took a sympathetic interest in Lasswell's early work, according to Sereno, "Note on Gaetano Mosca," *American Political Science Review*, XLVI: 2 (June 1952), 605.

be met with a whole scientific system" at long last seemed to have struck a sympathetic chord in the American mentality.[86]

But it was left to a young cultural historian, H. Stuart Hughes of Harvard, to write the first depth study of Mosca.[87] Another author's more extended monograph came next.[88]

In 1956, the *enfant terrible* of American sociology made bold to "bury," in one mighty heave, the two contending creeds. The view of C. Wright Mills was that America could no longer be called a democratic country, and the theory of the elite had to go, too, inasmuch as it was nothing but the ideology of the discredited middle class. A new power elite to end all elites had taken over: a triune directorate of civil, military, and big corporate administrators. A small group of men made the decisions over life and death. No longer responsible to popular control, theirs was the rule of "higher immorality." [89]

How did these men acquire their power? Unlike Mosca's and Pareto's old elites, they do not represent specific residues or social forces. Neither are they simply Burnham's managers. *Power elite* is defined by Mills "in terms of institutional position." [90] Office, not social power, makes the man. Nor is it necessary to prove that the high and mighty are an organized minority: they habitually draw together, for their interests and social backgrounds tend to be similar.

Mills died too soon to show his many young admirers the way out of the new labyrinth. He vaguely talked of the responsibility of intellectuals to mobilize new democratic "publics" against the new Caesars. If he were alive today, he might point at the end of what had been called, prematurely, the end of ideology: the unemployed, the Negro revolution, automation, Appalachia.[91] He might tell us that his Minotaur was meant to be both less and more than real, an inverted myth, a warning, not unlike the negative utopias of contemporary science fiction. In the end,

---

[86] Mosca, *op. cit.*, p. 327.

[87] Reprinted in this volume. Both in this and in his later work, *Consciousness and Society, op. cit.*, Hughes speaks, like Livingston and Burnham, of the "heirs of Machiavelli."

[88] Meisel, *op. cit.*

[89] C. Wright Mills, *The Power Elite* (New York: 1956), Chap. 15. See also Mills' "Notes on Mosca" reprinted here.

[90] Mills, *The Power Elite, op. cit.*, p. 366, n. 6.

[91] Daniel Bell, *The End of Ideology* (New York: The Free Press of Glencoe, Inc., 1960), deals with the "Exhaustion of Political Ideas in the Fifties." See the sharp attack on Bell by Henry David Aiken, "The Revolt Against Ideology," *Commentary*, XXXVII: 4 (April 1964), 29-39.

Mills, the humanist and moralist, may loom larger than Mills, the social scientist. If so, he will no longer be so far from Mosca, the Cassandra of an older generation. Midway between the two angry men, Mills and Pareto, stands Gaetano Mosca, the less spectacular, more modest figure. He refused to be dogmatic about his own theory. If anything, he did not give it enough scope and missed quite a few opportunities to reinterpret the past in light of his new method. But this very caution makes him also much less vulnerable. Controversy will still rage around Pareto at a time when Mosca may well be remembered as a latter-day John Stuart Mill.

GLORIOUS AND ODIOUS PARETO

One of Friedrich Nietzsche's last works had a chapter heading: "Why I am Such a Good Writer." [92] Being at the time all but unknown to his contemporaries, he resorted to the desperate device of advertising himself to posterity. In Nietzsche's case, posterity agreed.

When fame comes to a man in his own lifetime, as it did to Pareto, later generations may reject the claim precisely because it had been accepted by their forebears. How, the argument runs, could they have been so credulous? Is not fame in most cases merely a misunderstanding in reverse? Is not success, no less than failure, the result—not of true merit—but of those deceptive reasonings for which Pareto coined that odd term, *derivations?*

How would he have analyzed his own considerable fame? No one knows, but it is possible to speculate.

When Pareto's *magnum opus* first reached America in the four-volume English version (1935), there was instantaneous and almost unanimous recognition that sociology had been enriched by an important, even epoch-making work. Some critics echoed what Professor L. J. Henderson had said of the *Trattato* eight years earlier: "This . . . may possibly be the commencement of a new era in the history of thought. . . . One need not hesitate to call this theory magnificent . . . unique." Not even Henderson could overlook the fact that the great work showed signs of being "apparently incoherent and without plan," that it is "hardly at all a quantitative research and even qualitatively . . . but an extremely rough approximation," therefore hardly scientific, as Pareto had claimed. Yet, the writer is convinced that it is "an example of the most powerful and sustained logical thinking. . . . However unsatisfactory

[92] Subtitle in *Ecce Homo.*

the result, when compared with the achievements of the exact sciences, a truly dynamical conception of society emerges at last." [93]

Professor Henderson was not the first American to sing Pareto's praises. In 1921, long before the *Trattato* was translated into English, James Harvey Robinson had discovered the existence of

> . . . an Italian sociologist, Vilfredo Pareto, [whose] term, *derivations*, seems to be the precise way of expressing what we have called the "good" reasons, and his "residues" correspond to the "real" reasons. . . . His aim is to reduce sociology to the "real" reasons. . . . This conclusion may be ranked by students of a hundred years hence as one of the several great discoveries of our age. . . .[94]

But Arthur Livingston disputes Professor Robinson's priority as the American discoverer of the *Trattato:* "My first moves toward the introduction of this work to the English-speaking world go back to 1920. . . . I had published what I believe to be the first American note on Pareto December 3, 1915 ([*The*] *Nation*) and the second in 1916 (*International Yearbook*). These two articles were anterior to Professor Robinson's now famous footnote. . . ." Arthur Livingston claims that his essay in *The Nation* (May 1926) was "the beginning of the Pareto vogue in America." [95]

Professor Talcott Parsons, who absorbed Pareto's method into his own system, sounds an early warning: the *Trattato* "does not constitute a finished sociological theory but rather an approach to one. . . ." [96] He amplifies this statement later:

> Pareto, though he is not alone . . . marks a major turning point in sociological thought. . . . [His] work is not . . . a perfected system. It is a pioneer work. But it is throughout dominated and guided by the logic of systematic theory and goes far toward building up such a system.[97]

Even those unfriendly to Pareto are respectful . . . Franz Borkenau, who shared with Arthur Livingston an active interest in Mosca as well as in Pareto (he wrote a book about the latter, excerpts of which will be found below, and translated Mosca's *Elementi* into German), be-

[93] L. J. Henderson, "The Science of Human Conduct: An Estimate of Pareto and One of His Greatest Works," *The Independent*, CXIX: 4045 (December 10, 1927), 575-77, 584, *passim*.

[94] James Harvey Robinson, *The Mind in the Making* (New York and London: 1921), p. 47.

[95] Editor's Note in *The Mind and Society*, Vol. I, p. v.

[96] Talcott Parsons, "Pareto's Central Analytical Scheme," *Journal of Social Philosophy*, I: 3 (April 1936), 244. See pp. 71-73.

[97] *The Structure of Social Action* (1937), Second Edition (Glencoe, Ill., 1949), pp. 299, 300.

lieved that "there [is] hardly any reason . . . to number Pareto under the important sociologists. But as a matter of fact, he is very important . . . as a precursor of the political and social changes we behold in our days. . . ." [98] Professor Hughes agrees. He goes so far as to accuse Pareto of the intellectual treason of which Julien Benda[99] wrote and exclaims:

> We may well ask: Why bother with Pareto at all? Why, despite all his failings, do we still come away from reading him with a sense that he has at least partially established what he undertook to prove? . . . [It is because] Pareto's central assumption has stood firm. Again and again political scientists and sociologists have returned to his major principle that political movements could never be more than the work of active minorities. . . .[100]

And the same note of bafflement is sounded by a recent German critic, who reminds one of Professor Hook's remark when saying that

> . . . paradoxically, Pareto . . . advanced sociology and, in particular, the study of elites, through a series of errors. He directed our attention to the right problems. In doing so, he often gave wrong or unsatisfying answers. But attention remained focused on those problems.[101]

This leads to another peculiarity of the phenomenon, Pareto: disagreement about his specific claims to glory is as general as the agreement on his over-all importance. Professor Hughes put the main emphasis on Pareto's theory of the elites: "this last section, by general consent, ranks as the most satisfactory part of his sociology, indeed the only part that has exerted much permanent influence." [102] Runciman flatly dismisses as a "failure" all that precedes it.[103] But this is the same as saying that the blossom of a flower is the important thing, and all the rest—the leaves, the stem, the soil which feeds the roots—a mere mistake. Some comfort may be derived from Professor Werner Stark, who says that "the heartpiece of Pareto's *Trattato* is in [Sections] 2060-2104, which deal with 'the elements that serve to constitute society' and 'the state of equilibrium.' " True Paretians will be gratified to read this, only to be let down on the next page, on which Professor Stark asks:

> But do societies . . . [really have] an inherent tendency to equilibration? Pareto does not prove it. He simply assumes that they do, that they must. . . . Here, where he really **reveals** his central conceptions, Pareto speaks with

[98] Franz Borkenau, *Pareto* (New York: 1936), p. 168. See pp. 113-14.
[99] Julien Benda, *The Treason of the Intellectuals* (New York: 1928).
[100] Hughes, *op. cit.*, pp. 515, 254.
[101] Urs Jaeggi, *Die gesellschaftliche Elite* (Bern: 1960), p. 45.
[102] Hughes, *op. cit*, p. 268. [103] See pp. 14-15 and n. 53.

the voice, not of the sociologist, but of the mechanician. In his early years, he had been an engineer, a bridge-builder. . . .[104]

Pareto's seminal distinction between logical and nonlogical action has been questioned—even ridiculed—as the discovery of one who had not done his homework in psychology. Emory S. Bogardus, another of the early critics of Pareto in the United States, wrote: "He must have had an 'error complex,' for he discovers so many errors in the thinking of the common people, of leaders, and of scholars, that one wonders whether or not it is possible to avoid error in thinking." [105] Floyd N. House wrote a long essay to prove that Pareto was, in almost all his findings, trailing behind others—notably Americans. Among those who anticipated "the idea that human behavior is always and everywhere in large part non-rational, the author mentions Darwin, William James in his *Principles of Psychology* (1890), and William McDougall in *An Introduction to Social Psychology* (1908). "Even more striking anticipations of Pareto's treatment of the 'residues,' and of 'nonlogical' behavior generally, in the works of sociologists whom he does not mention in his *Treatise,* are found in Sumner's *Folkways* (1906) and Graham Wallas's *Human Nature and Politics* (1908)." [106] Accordingly, House comes to the conclusion that "the contribution of Pareto to the development of sociology and social psychology in the United States, up to recently, has been very small." Yet, he goes on to say, "if others had made much the same points, they did not at any rate succeed in impressing their colleagues in the fraternity with the significance of their point of view." Apparently, Pareto did just that, in the reviewer's judgment. Without trying to explain exactly why that should be so, he ends on a reluctantly admiring note:

. . . coming generations of sociologists will accord to Pareto's *Treatise* an important place in the history of their science, though possibly not as high a place as enthusiastic admirers have lately claimed for him.[107]

Lack of originality was also stressed by Ellsworth Faris. After having read "these bulky volumes" he found: "What in them is sound is not only not new, but is much better stated by authors long familiar to American scholars." One expects him to add "And what in them *is* new is not sound." That is, indeed, the gist of what follows. Faris, too, seems

[104] Werner Stark, *The Fundamental Forms of Social Thought* (London: 1962), pp. 127, 128-29.
[105] Emory S. Bogardus, "Pareto as Sociologist," *Sociology and Social Research,* XX (November 1935), 167-68.
[106] Floyd N. House, "Pareto in the Development of Modern Sociology," *Journal of Social Philosophy,* I: 1 (October 1935), 85.
[107] *Ibid.,* p. 89.

to resent the foreigner who had been "ignorant of Sumner," who was, like Pareto, an economist by training.[108] Another witness for the prosecution, the most irate of them all, William McDougall, also points to the "out-of-date character of Pareto's thinking and knowledge." He calls it "mid-Victorian," granting that "this may be untrue of his mathematics and his engineering. But of his psychological sociology and psychology it is a fair description." And he lists, in a long footnote, twenty-three important authors—among them, Freud and Jung—to whom Pareto makes no reference at all.[109] On the next page, he adds a twenty-fourth: McDougall. The delightful (*sub specie posteritatis*) savagery of his attack has been unequalled since, except perhaps by the brief piece in which Benedetto Croce hurls his own thunderbolt against his great compatriot.[110] It is not easy to decide who is the real target of McDougall's ire: Pareto, or his "eulogists"—among whom McDougall lists L. J. Henderson, G. H. Bosquet (Pareto's biographer), and Bernard de Voto.[111]

As a professional psychologist, McDougall was especially offended by Pareto's vague and arbitrary terminology. In a memorable passage he subjects Pareto's cryptorationalism to a withering critique:

> Pareto has become obscurely aware that there are at work in the human mind certain obscure forces or dynamic factors which often disturb the course of reasoning. He does not yet see that these are the springs of all activity; he still imagines, with the writers whom he derides, that the man of science (and Pareto especially) possesses an intellect which works automatically and independently of these dynamic factors—sometimes at least.[112]

This is McDougall's subtle way of hinting at Pareto's frequent disregard of his own logico-experimental—that is, scientific—method, aiming at objective truth (not the utility of its discoveries). He then reproaches Pareto for "having glimpsed as, it were, one aspect only of the work of these dynamic factors: namely, their disturbing and quasi-pathological aspect, and having so variously and confusedly named them[,] . . . he proceeds to study not the dynamic factors themselves but their manifestations: the 'residues.' "

To make his meaning perfectly clear, he adds in a footnote:

> It is as though an engineer of the eighteenth century should come alive today and set about the study of all the "manifestations" (lights, sounds, movements of trains, and cars, and machines) of electricity . . . while rigidly abstaining from all endeavors to achieve any understanding of electricity, its

---

[108] *Op. cit.* (see n. 47), pp. 658, 661.   [109] McDougall, *op. cit.*, p. 37 and n. 2.
[110] See pp. 33-34.   [111] McDougall, *op. cit.*, p. 36, n. 1.   [112] *Ibid.*, p. 39.

nature, distribution, modes of operation and relations to other forms of energy.[113]

So much about the engineer Pareto. His refusal to be more precise about the residues—"we know only the derivations" (Section 2083)—presents no further problem for McDougall, for Pareto's "crude terminology and thinking" is incapable of dealing with "the subtle psychological problems of belief and its relations to feeling, to conation, to action. . . . [T]he word *residues* cannot be defined. It stands merely for a muddle in the mind of its author." [114]

One of the participants of the crusade, Professor Faris, stabbed McDougall in the back by likening him to—Pareto: As Pareto "finds the institutions of Athens and Sparta to be due to differential residues, manifesting differential inherited instincts ([Section] 2419)"—Athens the Instinct of Combinations; Sparta, that of the Persistent Aggregates—just so "McDougall accounts for the Protestant Reformation by asserting that the Nordic Protestants had different instincts from those of the racial groups that remained true to the Catholic Church. . . ." Pareto and McDougall both explain "a social fact by applying a biological label" and assuming "biological constants, which are obtained by first describing the conduct that is to be explained and then inventing a residue that would account for the conduct." [115] (Coincidentally, two of the younger critics put it in exactly the same terms: Professor Stark declares that a residue is "no more than a label affixed to an action after it has been done";[116] Professor Aron's comment will be found on p. 117.) Faris concludes by saying that McDougall's disagreement with Pareto is the typical case of "two writers who have assumed a common erroneous premise." They had inverted the problem, for "the sentiments, the emotional aspects of the attitudes, are powerful and nonlogical but they are the effects of social participation, not of innate constants." [117]

By rigidly insisting on both attributes, Pareto joins the junto of the Great Reductionists. Like Hobbes and Nietzsche (passion, will to power), and like Marx and Freud (relations of production, sex), Pareto reduces the mechanics of the social process to a number of preponderant and archetypical responses to the collectivity of social stimuli. Pareto's catalog, a crude attempt at sorting out these elementary reactions (which, of course, can hardly ever be found unadulterated), lists six basic types, but only the first two play an important role in his empirical investigation. These two residues, and their human representatives: the speculators

---

[113] *Ibid.*, p. 40, n. 6.   [114] *Ibid.*, p. 43.   [115] Faris, *op. cit.*, pp. 664-65.
[116] Stark, *op. cit.*, p. 136.   [117] Faris, *op. cit.*, p. 665.

(foxes) and the *rentiers* (lions) are what may be called Pareto's *independent invariables*. Or, as Professor Hughes puts it, more elegantly:

> The residues represent what was unvarying, or at least what changed only very slowly, in human conduct; the derivations, the constantly varying explanations and rationalizations of such behavior.[118]

This essay is an attempt to review, not to refight, the ancient war against Pareto. Because it may have given disproportionate attention to his disapprovers, it seems fitting to conclude this section with F. Creery, who takes issue with McDougall, House, and their confederates. By turning the Paretian searchlight on their own more or less hidden derivations, he attempts to show that, far from contradicting the professional psychologists, Pareto actually corroborated their discoveries: "In the same period during which Freud and the psychiatrists were arriving at certain conclusions by the study of the individual, Pareto was arriving at the same conclusions from the study of society." There is no use denying "the peculiar character of the classification of the residues." But then, Pareto knew what he was doing:

> [He] is constantly insisting that his method is inductive, his classifications being based on his facts and I believe this is exactly true. . . . It should be remembered in addition that Pareto was endeavoring (among other things) to make a scientific study of the causes of bias in social science and perhaps in general. This is perhaps the explanation of his neglect to consult psychological literature. He wished to build up his system independently so that after it was built up comparison with psychology could be made and it would be found that his researches supply a new and different line of evidence as to the facts of human nature. Where they agree with the conclusions of psychology, both are confirmed. Where they disagree, further research is indicated.[119]

There will always be those very special people who prefer the first overture to Beethoven's *Fidelio* to the more elaborate third version, or the early short stories of Hemingway to his later novels. Are those people merely snobs? Not necessarily, but there is definitely something odd about the urge to trace the great ideas of a master back to their first, tentative appearance in an early work and for that reason alone, in the joy of recognition, to extol the sketch and throw out the finished canvas.

These remarks are necessary because lately it has become fashionable to deny that the *Trattato* is Pareto's masterwork. "He said the same

---

[118] Hughes, *op. cit.*, p. 257.
[119] F. Creery, "Residues and Derivations in Three Articles on Pareto," *Journal of Social Philosophy*, I: 2 (January 1936), 179.

things better, and more briefly in his *Systèmes* and in his *Manuel*," one can hear.[120] The fact that no translations of these two older works are available endears them still more to the happy few, but their contention will not bear close scrutiny. Nobody will object to the plain statement that *Les Systèmes* is "at the bottom of the inductive studies culminating in the *Treatise*," [121] nor to Hughes' pronouncement that *Les Systèmes* "early established itself as the classic refutation of Marxian economics and sociology. Legend has it that it caused Lenin graver worry than any other anti-Marxist writing. . . . ." Equally incontrovertible is Hughes' next claim that "with the completion of *Les Systèmes socialistes*, Pareto had already formulated in rough outline [all his] theories of social organization. . . ." And one might acquiesce in Hughes' considered judgment that

> . . . it was [in that work] . . . rather than in the *Trattato*, that Pareto's superb critical intelligence appeared to the best advantage. For in his book on socialism he combined most effectively the analytical tightness that characterized his original economic views with the literary verve that his subsequent sociological work was to display.

Hughes justly observes that *Les Systèmes* "had a narrower theme than the *Trattato* . . . ," but that "perhaps for this very reason it accomplished its purpose better. . . ." [122]

Fair enough—provided that the narrow scope and the rough outline of the older work is fully recognized.

At first sight, a preference for the early Pareto and a total rejection of the *Trattato* would appear to be a much more radical response than merely to discard three fourths of it and concentrate exclusively on the circulation of elites. But that impression may well be deceptive. To single out the final part, disregarding what goes before it, is risky business. It can be done—it has been done—but it will be rewarding only if it helps to explain and to reconstruct the theory of history developed in the first three volumes. Actually, it ought to be called a theory of antihistory, for Pareto militates both against the historicism of his age, and the philosophy of progress. There is some justice in the saying that he "has succeeded all too well in his attempt to abolish history." [123] Without a clear awareness of this background, the discussion of elites will bog down in empirical detail and end up with the verdict, already referred to,[124] that the monster is imaginary.

[120] Schumpeter, *op. cit.; Manuel:* the French edition of the *Manuale di economia politica* (109, 1927).
[121] G. H. Bousquet, *Pareto, le savant et l'homme* (Lausanne: 1960), p. 106.
[122] Hughes, *op. cit.*, pp. 78, 82, 267.   [123] Stark, *op. cit.*, p. 137.   [124] See pp. 20-21.

Recognition of the theory of the elite as an inherent part of the Paretian system, which in turn owes its existence to a certain method, is in evidence, for instance, in the statement that Pareto's concept of the circulation of elites is

. . . an interpretation of history according to which social change is brought about by the struggle between groups for political power, and there are alternating periods of harsh rule by a vigorous and newly triumphant elite, and of mild, humanitarian rule by a declining elite. The theory rests upon the assertion of biological differences between groups in society . . . and is supported by little historical evidence. . . .

The author of these lines, Professor Bottomore,[125] would differ from Professor Hughes, who thinks that "the assessment of how much of each residue characterized the successive elites of history . . . called forth Pareto's most pungent and telling commentary." [126] But neither of the two would question that

. . . the theory of the circulation of elites is, in the last end, a passionate protest against historicism and its belief in the uniqueness and individuality of each society and epoch. Its sociological mathematics is at the same time directed against all optimism of progress—in particular and explicitly against the utopian hopes of the Marxist philosophy of history. It thereby turns against the nineteenth century, and falls back on the skepticism of the eighteenth. On the other hand, Pareto's pessimism is quite modern: actually, his world is governed, not by the elites, but by the residues with their irrationality. By this persistent process of reduction faith in history is radically changed to a belief in naked power.[127]

The historic process, as Pareto saw it, is the subject of a recent study by Professor Guy Perrin. The salient points of the Paretian universe are these:

A theory of the "undulatory process of social phenomena" inspired by a metaphysic of "recurrence"; a critique of the idea of progress, condemned by the very logic of the undulatory process as well as by its pretentious attempt to inject a rational order into the course of history. And finally, the elevation of force to the dignity of a decisive social value. The combined effect of these analyses is to rob history of all its meaning by infusing it with the [assumed] irrationality of social nature.[128]

---

[125] T. B. Bottomore, *Sociology* (London: 1962), p. 274.   [126] Hughes, *op. cit.*, p. 269.
[127] Hans P. Dreitzel, *Elitebegriff und Sozialstruktur* (Stuttgart: 1962), p. 59.
[128] This and the following is a brief summary of Guy Perrin, "Thèmes pour une philosophie de l'histoire dans le *Traité de sociologie génerale*," *Cahiers Vilfredo Pareto*, I (Geneva: 1963), pp. 27-38. By permission of the publisher. (Pertinent paragraphs in the *Trattato*: 2330, 1694, 2391.)

The ancestry of this philosophy of social evolution is, according to Perrin,

> . . . embarrassingly metaphysical. . . . The influence of Plato and of Vico
> . . . is unquestionable, but to see which parts of that tradition were rejected
> by Pareto is as interesting as to find out what he kept of it. . . . From Plato,
> he preserves the theory of cycles founded on the notion of the psychological
> antipathy existing between generations, but he does not recognize the ele-
> ments of harmony and divine rationality informing each returning cycle. He
> equally neglects to use what had been Vico's most original idea . . . [when he]
> gave a rational direction to each cycle, so that every society would go through
> a succession of three ages: of the gods, the heroes, and of men. . . .[129]

What Pareto does with the Platonic and Viconian universes is to empty them of their idealistic, theological, and rationalistic contents, retaining only "a psychological formalism which permits him to link the undula-tory process to the alternation of the two main residues." Quite unlike Vico, he sees no internal progress within each historic cycle: the curve may either ascend or descend. Over a long period, however, an ascending orientation is accepted and explained by the increasing rationalization of behavior (Section 2393). A gain of logical over nonlogical action? Was Pareto getting ready for a possible reconciliation of progress and recur-rence? No, because an increasing rationalization of behavior, far from integrating with the social system, would—according to Pareto—contra-dict it in a major aspect: rationalization presupposes domination, in the long run, of the Class 1 residues over those of Class 2, and that would disrupt the long-range balance of the psychological constants—something which Pareto is not ready and not able to concede.[130] So he opposes "to the ideology of progress his own ideology of violence . . . which plays a double function, positive and normative, in his philosophy of history." When it restores the upset equilibrium, violence—a simple fact of life—becomes an absolute necessity.[131] But it is not just useful to society in balancing the scales—violence has supreme human value in and by itself: it "remains superbly alien to the values which it is supposed to serve. . . . Force is its own justification. . . ." But the notion of utility is not absent even here, because force has a regenerative quality which raises man above himself, enabling him to follow the irrational commands of

[129] *Ibid.*, p. 30.
[130] *Ibid.*, pp. 31, 32-33. On p. 34, n. 26, Perrin refers to Morris Ginsberg's criticism of Pareto's progress phobia. (See pp. 106-7, below.)
[131] *Ibid.*, p. 35. Perrin cites Sec. 1858 of the *Trattato:* ". . . the use of force is indis-pensable to society; and when the higher classes are averse to the use of force . . . it becomes necessary, if society is to subsist and prosper, that that governing class be replaced by another which is willing and able to use force."

his own nature without false concessions to fantastic derivations: "This ethical purification applies equally to the rebellion of the slave as to the backlash of the master." Little does it matter to Pareto what the struggle is about, because it has an ethical significance all of its own. The influence of Georges Sorel, but without Sorel's proletarian bias, is much evident.[132]

The final consequence of this philosophy, Perrin concluded, is an "impoverishment of history" and a denial of all rationality in the historic process. "Extremely anti-intellectualistic, the mystique of violence shunts the Paretian train of history far from the positive [positivistic?] roads along which it was meant to travel. . . ." [133]

Pareto's cult of violence has always been the focus of critique. As Talcott Parsons puts the case with scholarly detachment:

> Persons of liberal antecedents are often impressed, perhaps more strongly than in any other way, by a kind of Machiavellian element in Pareto's thought. This takes the form of laying great emphasis on the social importance of force and fraud. . . . The role and significance of both has undoubtedly been very seriously minimized by the "liberal" theories of progress and linear evolution. . . .

There is no denying that "force frequently attends the 'creative' process by which a new value system becomes established in a society in part through the accession to power of a new elite." But Parsons wonders "whether this is the whole story. Some new values, like Christianity, have come in by rather a different process. . . ."

So much for violence. "Fraud, on the other hand, attends the later stages in the breakdown of the persistence of aggregates . . . and may become an important factor in the state of instability which necessitates a reintegration."

But, Professor Parsons insists:

> Pareto nowhere delivers any attack on . . . liberal values. He is not a lover of brute force, a glorifier of the beast of prey. . . . He is, to be sure, a scoffer at bourgeois morality, especially antialcoholism and sexual puritanism, but this only goes with the aristocratic bent of his liberalism and is an authentic element of the liberal tradition.[134]

Parsons is unquestionably right about Pareto's liberal credentials. But the liberals were fretting about something more than just an intellectual

---

[132] Perrin, *op. cit.*, p. 36-37. About Sorel, see Hughes, *op. cit.*, p. 40, and J. H. Meisel, *The Genesis of Georges Sorel* (Ann Arbor: 1951), pp. 292-97.

[133] Perrin, *op. cit.*, p. 38.

[134] Parsons, *op. cit.*, pp. 289-90, 291, 293 (n. 3).

pedigree; they were concerned about the possibility that there was more
to the Paretian theory than met the eye: that it contained a manual of
Machiavellian practice. Benedetto Croce, who took a dim view of the
sociologist, Pareto—"I do not intend to detract from the merits of Pareto's
other work as an economist"—can name "only one aspect in which [the
Trattato] presents any real interest. It is [the] constant assertion of force
as the creator of political facts, against democracy. For this reason, the
book, in the political struggles of our day, will please not a few people." [135] Benedetto Croce was, apparently, not one of them. Norberto
Bobbio, writing about Croce, Mosca and Pareto, quotes "some famous
sentences from the Introduction to *Les Systèmes socialistes*" (1902):

> A human being who is afraid to return blow for blow and to spill the
> blood of his enemies places himself by this attitude at the mercy of his enemy.
> . . . It is with force that social institutions are established, and with force
> they are maintained.

But the same article contains these lines from Benedetto Croce:

> The vigorous minds killed and had themselves killed. This is history, and no
> one can change it. . . . Only a false ideology, a sophism concocted by petty
> *littérateurs*, tries to substitute the ideology of right and wrong, of just war and
> unjust war for the simple and rigorous concepts of power.[136]

These two sentences were written in 1909 and during World War I,
respectively. When Fascism enacted his belief in power, Benedetto Croce
went the way of Gaetano Mosca: he recanted and recoiled from Pareto's
"violence."

But what about Pareto himself? He was and is still regarded as a sympathizer—if not the patron saint—of Mussolini's creed. That this conviction was particularly strong all through the decade which preceded
World War II is not surprising, and the essays by Aron and Borkenau
do not conceal the antifascist animus.[137] But there is scant agreement
even about basic facts. Aron, for instance, mentions that Pareto was given
a seat in the Fascist Senate, while Timasheff maintains the order was
tendered but declined.[138] Sereno reports the appointment but says nothing about the refusal;[139] Hughes has it that Pareto "accepted the senator-

[135] Benedetto Croce, "The Validity of Pareto's Theories," *The Saturday Review* (May
25, 1935), 13.
[136] Norberto Bobbio, "Liberalism Old and New," *Confluence* (1956), 244, 242. The
Pareto quotation is from *Les Systèmes socialistes, op. cit.*, pp. 38, 40.
[137] See below.
[138] Raymond Aron, "La sociologie de Pareto," *Zeitschrift für Sozialforschung*, VI
(1937), p. 516 (below, Ch. 7); N. S. Timasheff, *Sociological Theory*, p. 158.
[139] Sereno, *The Rulers, op. cit.*, p. 43.

ship that the Duce offered him—although he never actually took his seat—and during the ten months that elapsed between the March on Rome and his own death he ranked as at least a qualified supporter of the Fascist regime." [140]

In opposition to these views, Professor Schumpeter, no blind admirer of Pareto, finds his liaison with Fascism

> not problematical in the least. . . . Mussolini honored himself by conferring senatorial rank on the man who kept preaching moderation and who stood throughout for the freedom of the press and of academic teaching. . . . To his last day Pareto refused to embrace this *ism* as he had refused to embrace any other. There is no point whatever in judging his action . . . from the standpoint of Anglo-American tradition.[141]

Schumpeter concedes, however, that Pareto may have had some hopes that Mussolini would become his lion, superseding the discredited Italian foxes, whose demise Pareto had long since predicted. In the same vein, his own biographer, Bousquet, calls him "the prophet, not the apostle of Fascism," [142] while Borkenau says that "Pareto is a precursor of Fascism, but he certainly is not a Fascist or an agent of Fascism." [143] Professor Hook, one of the harshest critics of Pareto, treats the accusation with contempt and snorts: "Sheer poppycock!" [144]

Of course it is! But, then, as the philosophers would say: it had been the wrong question all along. As soon as one turns from Pareto's personal and public life to the implicit meaning of his work, he may discover what Raymond Aron found out with quiet rage: the "fascist" clues scattered throughout the Paretian system. Writing when he did, Aron showed a Weberian grasp of the essential in analyzing the two existent models of the fascist system. His 1937 essay on Pareto remains an impressive feat of foresight which anticipates, by twenty years, the internally contradictory *Gestalt* of the "authoritarian personality." [145] Like any pioneer, Aron is groping through the wilderness of the new intellectual territory, nameless still. "Through a glass darkly" he beholds the brave new world, the supersystem of the Machiavellian engineer. The term, or an approxima-

---

[140] Hughes, *op. cit.*, p. 271.   [141] Schumpeter, *op. cit.*, p. 118.

[142] Bousquet, *op. cit.*, pp. 193-94, n. 4. The author cites a *fascist* writer.

[143] Borkenau, *op. cit.*, p. 174.

[144] Hook, "Pareto's Sociological System," *The Nation*, CXL: 3651 (June 26, 1935), 747. See below, Ch. 2.

[145] See below, Ch. 7; T. W. Adorno, *et al.*, *The Authoritarian Personality* (New York: 1950); R. Christie and M. Jahoda (eds.), *Studies in the Scope and Method of "The Authoritarian Personality,"* (New York: The Free Press of Glencoe, Inc., 1954); Else Frenkel-Brunswik in *Totalitarianism*, edited by Carl J. Friedrich (Cambridge, Mass.: Harvard University Press, 1954), pp. 187-189.

tion of the term, *totalitarian,* does not yet occur, but the new version of nonterroristic mass control is already intuited in the first intimations of the power elite—even of the Gaullist brand, which is, however, not up to Aron's Paretian standards, lacking, as it does, an ideology (beyond the veneration of De Gaulle) and a firm power structure.

The Aronian theory of the elite did not shed altogether the chrysalis of the fascist prototype. This is a pity, because an elitist rule may well develop without any fascist attributes. Hughes might be right when saying, in a recent essay: "Fascism became unnecessary when populations began to behave in a politically apathetic and disciplined fashion under regimes which remained democratic in form." [146]

The theory of the elite, both in Pareto's and in Mosca's version, was found equally intractable by democratic doctrine and empirical research. Or more precisely: "In each single case, elites can be empirically verified, whereas the fact of an elite society as such eludes research." [147] Two possibilities remain, to vindicate the theory. The first requires its psychologization: the elite concept becomes a myth, employed defensively by ruling groups, aggressively by rising strata (in our day, the interclass intelligentsia). For the many, their suspicion of the few fills an imaginative vacuum. It is a role-assigning myth; the question of whether there is such a cabal in reality becomes irrelevant. Precisely because it is difficult, if not impossible, to verify a ruling class in a complex industrial order, the compulsion to assume it becomes all but irresistible. As power tends to become more and more impersonal, repersonalization takes place inside the collective mind. From an object of suspicion, *they* are transformed into a reality.

Another rescue of the theory of the elite has been attempted by Professor Dreitzel. He interprets it in terms of an "ideal type." Dreitzel first makes a distinction between two types of elites: those active in production, and those who reflect—or are expected to reflect—the goals of leisure and consumption (a fast-growing sector in contemporary mass society). Professor Dreitzel's "leisure hero" is none other than our culture hero, modelling the images of popular demand in fashion, on the screen, and in the sports arena. In a rare case, he may even be an artist or philosopher with whom the masses can identify.[148]

There is no need here to go into the old problem: Are the top people the best, or are they only thought to be the best because they happen to

---

[146] H. Stuart Hughes, "Mussolini," *The New York Review of Books,* II: 11 (July 9, 1964), 9.

[147] *Dreitzel, op. cit.,* p. 153.   [148] *Ibid.,* p. 147.

be at the top? In Pareto's scheme, under conditions of complete social mobility, the best would automatically rise to pre-eminence. Since these conditions are not present under ordinary circumstances, the elite cannot be anything but props to be held up, and to be held out to all, as the accepted target points of the collective will.

Today, these signals all point in the same direction: the accepted goals of mass society are based on the "performance principle." [149] This is, of course, no new discovery; a quarter of a century ago, Karl Mannheim had already indicated that the old criteria—noble birth and wealth—were giving way to the achievement test, a mixed blessing which strengthened the dynamic element but contributed to the decline of social continuity. And without some degree of continuity, elites cannot consolidate; they need time to conceive and to transmit their message. In democratic mass societies, therefore, there will be too many elites and none will endure.[150]

The theory of the elite could be redeemed from its chimeric existence only by a slowdown of mobility. It would permit the growth of model groups suggesting, if not realizing, excellence. Thus understood, the theory would take on teleological significance, deriving its vitality from the perennial "tension between the ideal and reality. . . ." [151]

To paraphrase a famous saying of one of Pareto's predecessors in the eighteenth century: If an elite did not exist, it would be necessary to invent it.[152]

Most of the argument concerned Pareto's method and to what extent he followed or ignored it; whether his conception of reality was accurate and to what consequences it was leading him. Sometimes the argument was heated and *ad hominem:* few writers managed to antagonize their public quite as much as he. Pareto has a secure place among the great enragers of mankind. As Schumpeter observed,

> The naïve lover of modern social creeds and slogans must feel himself driven with clubs from Pareto's threshold. . . . The problem is not to explain why Pareto did not exert influence more widely; the problem is rather to explain how he came to exert as much as he did.[153]

[149] *Ibid.,* p. 153. [150] Mannheim, *op. cit.,* pp. 86 ff. [151] Dreitzel, *op. cit.,* p. 154.
[152] Giuseppe La Ferla wrote a study of *Vilfredo Pareto: filosofo volteriano* (Florence: 1954), and Professor Hughes, who refers to it, remarks that the "impression of Pareto as a belated French *philosophe* is confirmed when we learn that Bayle's *Dictionnaire historique* was his favorite bedside reading" (*op. cit.,* p. 266). Professor Bobbio says about Pareto: "It has been justly said that from selected excerpts from his works, the new *Dictionnaire philosophique* of the twentieth century could be compiled" (*op. cit.,* p. 243).
[153] Schumpeter, *op. cit.,* p. 112; Runciman, *op. cit.,* p. 71: "The ruthless iconoclast of illusions."

The same idea has been well expressed in the American vernacular by Talcott Parsons: "One possible reason for the prevailing hostility to Pareto in this country is that he was a 'knocker,' not a 'booster.' " [154]

But rejection was too avid to be quite sincere. One frequently detects a note of morbid fascination in the studies dedicated to the proposition that Pareto was, if not the devil incarnate, then certainly a charlatan.[155] What malevolent delight they took in panning the *Trattato*, which, according to Sereno, "marked a date in the history of American social thought . . . [and] changed not only views or conceptions but the very nature of social studies. . . ." [156]

To say that there are minds which stimulate by committing intellectual mayhem, as it were, and that this was Pareto's role in the United States, is only one part of the explanation. For a better answer to the question— Why was he so famous?—one must remember how Americans reacted, in the 1930's, to the temporary breakdown of their economic system: "The depression had made them depressive. . . . There was a defeatist attitude among social scientists." That attitude, however, antedated the Great Depression:

> Early twentieth-century American sociology had been biased in favor of find-ing fixity, stability, and laws of permanence. . . . This seemed odd because . . . the history of the United States since the turn of the century, when sociology began sorting itself out in our universities, has above all indicated continual social change.

The author who evoked these lines was Gunnar Myrdal, but the words apply with equal reason to Pareto.[157] In his system, not a few American sociologists found fixity—but with the built-in element of motion. They discovered a philosophy of history which reassured them, because there was to be recurrence (read: restoration of the status quo ante) and, in the long run (with some minor fluctuations), social balance. It was a philosophy which linked renewal to decay, and flux to the perennial stasis of the culture. Why, then, did it so enrage Americans? The reason was that the full consequence of the Paretian system frightened them. The price to be paid was too high. Its "oscillations," after all, were real revolutions; its elites denied the democratic truth. Because it could not be

---

[154] Parsons, *op. cit.*, p. 293.

[155] *E.g.:* "Why did such a ponderous work gain such great fame? The answer is a familiar one; here again, a whole system of thought was advanced *under the guise* of being scientific. . . ." George L. Mosse, *The Culture of Western Europe* (Chicago: 1961), p. 294. Editor's italics.

[156] Sereno, *The Rulers, op. cit.*, p. 45.

[157] Naomi Bliven, writing on a reissue of *An American Dilemma* in *The New Yorker* (April 18, 1964), 196.

separated from its toxic elements, Paretianism was rejected totally. But it has retained its subterranean attraction to this day, as the selections here presented prove. Pareto's shrill, Voltairian laughter, his interminable grumbling against human foibles, hurts our ears. But then again, he surprises us with a gentleness, a smiling wisdom—as in these words of Olympian unconcern:

> The politicians have no knowledge of the distant consequences of their measures. . . . Richelieu, by humbling the nobility, Louis XIV, by reducing them to servitude, did not suspect that they were sharpening the cleaver which would sever the head of Louis XVI. In Russia, Nicholas I said: "There are no Russian grandseigneurs, except him to whom I speak, and only as long as I am speaking to him." Which explains why no one could be found who would defend Nicholas II. In France . . . the Revolution and Napoleon I prepared, without suspecting it, the unification of Germany. . . . The Tolstoyans and other deliquescent intellectuals made, in part at least, Kerensky possible, and he, in turn, made Lenin. . . .

This is the Pareto who delights in sampling and lampooning human ignorance and folly, turning history into a giant jigsaw puzzle which will never come out right. But then the tone abruptly changes, and another, less well-known Pareto has his say:

> We spoke ill of the intellectuals; now let us turn the page. The human sentiments, obscure, confused, and therefore by themselves not too effective, are made more precise, more efficacious by the intellectuals. Athenian democracy owes much to Pericles. Roman law, one of the most sublime conceptions of humanity, has its source in the sentiments of the Roman people, but it was the intellectuals who have given it its form and immortality. The Renaissance is much indebted to the great intellects of antiquity. If the French Revolution is something more than an explosion of brutality, it owes this to the intellectuals, and their works will have readers as long as our civilization lasts. Who knows, perhaps our present intellectuals, without knowing it, will manage to distill some useful lessons from the very movement which now threatens to unleash a storm upon humanity? [158]

A NOTE ON THE CONTRIBUTORS

This volume could not possibly include every worthwhile study ever made of Mosca and Pareto. The process of sifting the many possibilities led to the conviction that the critical extremists ought to be eliminated. Accordingly, the "boosters" and the "knockers" have been discussed in

[158] Vilfredo Pareto, "Réponse à René Johannet," from *Les lettres*, January 1, 1920, in *Cahiers Vilfredo Pareto*, II (1963), 328, 329. Reprinted by permission of the publisher.

this introduction. This, however, does not mean that the essays selected are uncritical; on the contrary, some of them will be very critical indeed, but animosity will play a minor part in the criticism—just as there will be friendly comments without adulation.

Some studies were unavailable—for example, the seven lectures on Pareto recently delivered by Raymond Aron at the Sorbonne.[159] That distinguished author, however, is represented by an earlier examination of Pareto's work which, in addition to reflecting vividly the temper of the period, has all the freshness of discovery.

The time factor excluded T. B. Bottomore's most recent study of elites which, at this writing, has not yet been published in the United States. One of his interesting comments deals with the attempts to integrate elitist views into the democratic frame:

> The theorists of elites defend, by . . . various means, the legacy from the inegalitarian societies of the past, while making concessions to the spirit of equality. They insist strongly upon an absolute distinction between rulers and ruled, which they present as a scientific law, but they reconcile democracy with this state of affairs by defining it as competition between elites. . . .[160]

Another much regretted omission is the work of Renzo Sereno. Excerpts from his recent book, *The Rulers,* would have charmed the readers with its erudition and euphonious style. But he and other noted figures are not altogether missing from this introduction.

On the whole, critical appraisals of more recent date have been preferred to earlier examinations. That decision, too, was influenced by the desire to present judgments not passed hastily, but from a later vantage point and, therefore, one hopes, more judicious. The objective was not to achieve consensus, for that would have been utopian. But on one point agreement exists: the questions posed by Mosca and Pareto are still worth debating, even though their answers remain open to argument. The best their critics can do is to keep the argument alive.

There are, in all, fourteen contributors, representing the United States and most of western Europe.[161]

[159] They are going to be published by Basic Books, Inc., New York.

[160] T. B. Bottomore, *Elites and Society* (London: 1964), p. 141. The author mentions Schumpeter (*op. cit.,* pp. 10, 11), while Professor Runciman refers to Schumpeter and Maurice Duverger (*op. cit.,* pp. 75-77); for an earlier discussion of exactly the same two "democratic revisionists," see Meisel, *The Myth of the Ruling Class, op. cit.,* pp. 348-53.

[161] Georg Lukacs's general indictment of "prewar imperialist sociology," already briefly noted, includes Weber and Pareto, indirectly Mosca, whose disciple, Michels, is singled out for special castigation as a Bernsteinite revisionist. (*Die Zerstörung für Vernunft,* pp. 315, 187. The late, distinguished Polish sociologist, Stanislaw Ossowski,

The discussion of Pareto is led off by Werner Stark, with an article written in 1963. Stark brings Pareto's personality alive, drawing on the well-documented study by Dr. Eisermann, who has assimilated the most recent work done by Pareto specialists.[162] Stark's piece is placed first (in disregard of chronological considerations) in order to establish, once for all, the mood of disengagement from what, after all, is almost ancient history today. His essay shows less of the tendency to "get" Pareto than did his earlier works.[163]

The untiring analyst of words, Pareto, is himself analyzed by Professor Hook, who manages to state the author's propositions in deceptively clear terms. Today, he might be more relaxed about Pareto; in the 1930's violence seemed indicated.

The philosopher yields place to the sociologist, N. S. Timasheff, who puts the main accent on Pareto's equilibrium theory. In this he follows his great teacher, Pitirim Sorokin, one of the first to give Pareto a fair deal.[164]

Next comes Talcott Parsons, with his study of "Pareto's central analytical problem"—which leads up to the chapters in *The Structure of Social Action* (mentioned above).

With the contributions of Professors Hook and Parsons, we are brought back to the 1930's. There they are joined by three other authors: Ginsberg, Borkenau, and Aron. Morris Ginsberg concentrates on the elusive residues and questions the distinction between logical and nonlogical action. He ends on a note of wry amusement: "If a choice is to be made between persistent aggregates and combinations, I see no reason for not choosing combinations." (Professor Creedy had already said that "Paretian analysis seems to be the only branch of science having a humorous side. Why this should be, I do not know." [165])

The late Franz Borkenau is best known as a European authority on Communism. That he also wrote a good book on Pareto is a fact almost forgotten. We take pleasure in presenting various excerpts from that study dealing with the theory of the elite and closing with a general evaluation of Pareto's work.

The short selection from Raymond Aron's 1937 essay cannot give more than a faint idea of the scope and sweep of his argument. Aron himself

---

discussed Pareto (as well as Durkheim and Weber) briefly but with great fairness in *Class Structure in the Social Consciousness* (London: 1963).

[162] G. Eisermann, *Vilfredo Paretos System der allgemeinen Soziologie* (Stuttgart: 1962). Some of his sources will be listed in the *Index*.

[163] See pp. 25-26 and n. 104, above.

[164] Pitirim Sorokin, *Contemporary Sociological Theories* (New York: 1928), pp. 37-62.

[165] Creedy, *op. cit.*, p. 179.

said: "Today I would say some things differently." [166] He is no longer sure, as he was in 1937, that the logic of Pareto's thought makes him a Fascist:

> Pareto is not necessarily, as it is thought and sometimes said, a doctrinarian of authoritarianism. In truth, he makes a case for many creeds if not for all, and he can be interpreted in the most various ways.
> Whether in or out of power, you can always invoke Pareto.[167]

Various lines run from Aron to other authors of this text. He shares with both Perrin and Borkenau an interest in the Paretian theory of antihistory.[168] Like Borkenau, he stresses the contemporary meaning of Pareto's work, its hints of things to come and to beware of. And to Ginsberg he is linked by at least one remarkable agreement: in a passage omitted from this text, Aron declares Pareto's theory of interest (defined as a distinctly logical pursuit) "astonishing":

> How can we tell whether an individual acts from interest or sentiment? Does not the action prompted by desire give pleasure and thus enter into the same category as the actions caused by interest? Are not the sentiments analogous to just those tastes and dispositions which are basic to all economic reasoning?

Compare this to the argument in Ginsberg:

> It is not easy to see why . . . it is more logical to pursue honor and consideration than to satisfy other social impulses, or let us say, the desire for knowledge. Or is the pursuit of interests regarded as logical not because of

[166] Written communication, April 2, 1964. In a subsequent letter to the editor, dated September 25, 1964, Professor Aron has this to say:

"It is not without some misgivings that I grant you the authorization of reproducing the selection of some paragraphs from an already too short and too condensed article published in 1937.

From a certain point of view, your selection is justified. But taken out of context and argument the paragraphs you have put together might give to the reader the impression of a Pareto style attack against Pareto. Neither the article taken as a whole nor the lectures on Pareto which Basic Books [, Inc.,] will publish are as vulnerable to criticism as the present extracts.

As you seem to be convinced that, in spite of their fragmentary character, these pages contain some valuable insights, I give in to your friendly insistence, but I hope you will be kind enough to publish the present letter as a footnote."

Torn between editorial necessity and profound sympathy with the distinguished author's viewpoint, we publish his cry *de profundis* with our sincere apologies, proud to have him among the contributors to this book.

[167] Raymond Aron, "La signification de l'oeuvre de Pareto," *Cahiers Vilfredo Pareto,* I (1963), 15.

[168] Cf. Aron with Perrin (p. 33). See also Borkenau, p. 112.

the particular ends involved, but because in achieving them men can be shown to act with greater circumspection. . . ? [169]

Pareto, the sociologist, and Pareto, the economist, with his theory of equilibrium, are inseparable. It is only proper that he should be judged here by another great economist-turned-sociologist. Professor Schumpeter's assessment is too long to be reprinted in *extenso*, but the final section may be read as an incisive summary of Pareto. It is also a study in contrast: where some of the other writers seemed to struggle through a maze, Schumpeter marches on triumphantly, with magisterial self-assurance, to the end.

The transition from Pareto to Mosca is made by Professor Franco Ferrarotti of the University of Milan, who views both authors in the context of Italian intellectual history. The name of Benedetto Croce reappears, and we are made to understand that Croce's diatribe against Pareto was not just politically motivated but arose from a fundamental difference in their philosophies. The dispute between Croce's metaphysics and Pareto's antimetaphysics remained unnegotiable.

Professor Ferrarotti also makes clear why Croce could afford to be more lenient towards Mosca. Although he found Mosca's methodology as faulty as Pareto's, he conceded that there was "much sturdy common sense" in Mosca's work; he could agree when Mosca argued: "If it is objected that it is . . . virtually impossible to make experiments where social phenomena are involved, one might answer that history, statistics, and economics have by now gathered such a great store of experimental data [as] to permit us to begin our research." [170]

There is no lack of good Italian studies dealing with Mosca, but they treat him, on the whole, as an exclusively Italian figure.[171] For this reason, non-Italian writers dominate this part. Professor Hook's short essay was written four years after his study of Pareto. It is followed by the article by Professor Hughes, which is the central piece of this whole section. "Notes on Mosca" lets us peep into the workshop of the late C. Wright Mills, while the next entry, by the present editor, examines Mosca's version of the circulation of elites.

The brief excerpt from Carl J. Friedrich's recent inventory of elitist thought makes it quite clear that he still rejects, as a good democrat, the

---

[169] See Raymond Aron, "La Sociologie de Pareto," *Zeitschrift für Socialforschung,* VI (1937), p. 499, and p. 91, below.
[170] Croce, *La Critica,* XXI (November 20, 1923), 377; Mosca, *The Ruling Class, op. cit.,* p. 337.
[171] See Bibliography, under *Mosca.*

theory and does not think much of the proof so far submitted to substantiate its correctness. "There is," he writes in a passage omitted from this text, "in the search for some kind of hidden governing elite a strange fascination which makes the argument asserting its existence one of infinite regress. . . ." And he cites, with obvious approval, Dahl's now-famous squelch:

> If the overt leaders of a community do not appear to constitute a ruling elite, then the theory can be saved by arguing that behind the overt leaders there is a set of covert leaders who do. If subsequent evidence shows that this covert group does not make a ruling elite, then the theory can be saved by arguing that behind the first covert group there is another, and so on.[172]

No doubt. The windmills of research will keep on turning and unhorsing the elitist Don, who forthwith will remount his Rosinante and, with his splintered lance, come back for more.

[172] Carl J. Friedrich, *Man and His Government*, p. 325; Dahl, *op. cit.*, p. 463.

ONE

IN SEARCH OF THE TRUE PARETO

WERNER STARK

If a man is genuinely intent on reaching his goal, he must keep his eyes
on the road ahead and not look sideways over his shoulder. Unfortunately,
this is precisely what far too many sociologists have done and are still
doing. Instead of asking what methods will help them most to master the
problems offered by social life, they watch what methods are being applied
in the physical sciences and then try to apply them, by hook or by crook,
to their own chosen field; instead of deciding what forms are most appropriate for the embodiment of sociological truths, they set mathematical
and mechanistic propositions up as their models and squeeze what insights their labors will yield into that narrow mold. Down to the seven-
teenth and then again in the nineteenth century, it was biology that was
aped; in the eighteenth and now in the twentieth century, it is rational
mechanics. The results of this pathetic endeavor have often been down-
right ridiculous. Even great men, like Bishop Berkeley with his *Principles
of the Moral Attraction,* have fallen into deep absurdity—not to speak
of lesser men like Spencer and Schäffle or Fourier and Carey. Vainly have
the greatest social philosophers, from Vico to Max Weber, pointed out
that one kind of science cannot possibly cover two kinds of reality; that
the social world which men have made is different, in essence, and hence
a different challenge to the mind in pursuit of knowledge, from the physical world which men have not made; that the social sciences, admittedly
inferior in other respects, are superior to the physical sciences in that they
can not only "know about" their object, but also "understand" it—the
naïve imitation of physics and physiology goes on. Indeed, it has become
steadily worse. Some of the assertions of the would-be social physicists and
physiologists of yesterday were so outrageous that they will not be repeated
again: who would dare nowadays to suggest with Spencer that Sheffield is

"In Search of the True Pareto," by Werner Stark. From *British Journal of Sociology,*
XIV (June 1963), 103-12. Reprinted by permission of Routledge & Kegan Paul, Ltd.

an iron-secreting organ in the social organism of Great Britain, or with Carey that Ireland is a country in which the socioelectric batteries are wrongly connected up? But just because these inanities have become impossible, the imitation of the natural sciences has assumed less obvious and more sophisticated forms; and the underlying trend continues. The task of exposing this truth-inhibiting factor has become correspondingly more difficult.

Of course, there is no merit in opening a gap between the physical sciences and the social, if this can be avoided. Who would not rejoice if one formula could be found which would explain all facts in one go? And, quite apart from such utopian hopes, who would not like to wield Ockham's razor, if it would lead to a simplification of our world view? But a razor must not be handled by the ham-fisted. If it is, it may kill, not clean. Where the data themselves demand distinctions, distinctions must be made. If they are not made, contact with reality is lost, and a pretended science becomes its own caricature.

The great, the unique, importance of Vilfredo Pareto consists in the fact that he was the most outstanding intellect among all the adulators of the natural sciences who have set up to be social scientists. Others have been narrow, often to a regrettable degree, and their narrowness shows as a rule on the very first pages of their books. Pareto was as close to being a polyhistor as any man in this century. Not only was he endowed with a superb intelligence, he was also in possession of far-flung, well-nigh encyclopedic, knowledge. His command of the ancient languages and literatures, and of the facts of the ancient civilizations, is particularly noteworthy. The longer one reads in his *Trattato,* the more one sees that he was *not* narrow—not, at any rate, insofar as his factual equipment was concerned. For that reason, he is a commanding figure; we cannot pass him by. Whatever our last judgment about his effort may be, that effort is massive and impressive. Perhaps he is only a roadblock in our way; but, if so, it is imperative that he be removed.

It cannot, as yet, be said that sociologists as a whole have found a clear-cut attitude to Vilfredo Pareto, as they have, more or less, to Max Weber and Émile Durkheim. On the contrary, there is an abiding ambiguity: they would have him, and at the same time they will not have him. He is treated much in the way in which David Ricardo is treated by the economists. On the one hand, there is admiration for his intellect, for his integrity, and for his scholarly ideal; on the other, there is a realization, not to be kept down, that his system does not fit the realities of social life. It is high time that we should all make up our minds about him.

But that we cannot possibly do unless we know the man better than we have known him so far. It is true that Bongiorno and Livingston have given us, in *The Mind and Society*, an admirable English version of his greatest work. But that is not enough. Some of his other writings are as important. To quote but one example: his *Introduction à le Capital de Marx*, though under ten pages, is a critique of Marxian economics so incisive that one would vainly look for its equal in the literature. It is the great merit of Professor Eisermann's latest book, *Vilfredo Paretos System der allgemeinen Soziologie*,[1] that it helps us to see the man in all his width and depth. There is nothing that seems to have escaped Eisermann's Argus eyes. He has, above all, made good use of Pareto's invaluable *Lettere a Maffeo Pantaleoni*, now available in a fine three-volume edition. But his aim is not only to complete the picture: it is as much and more to restore it to its pristine colors. A thick layer of legend, Eisermann tells us, has formed around this figure, even though it is only about forty years since he died. These incrustations must be removed before a sound judgment can be formed. Eisermann has gone in search of the true Pareto, and we shall do well to accompany him on his journey of exploration.

II

What is it that we find? Already the bare biographical detail is revealing. It throws light not only on the man, but also on the mind.

Perhaps one can most quickly unravel the enigma of Pareto's personality by saying that his was the psychology of the disappointed lover. As a young man, he was an intransigent liberal in the Mazzini tradition of his country: "popular sovereignty and freedom were his highest ideals, and at the same time the universal remedies for all social ills." But liberalism *à la* Mazzini was not so much a political as a religious movement. It was a late, and particularly fervent, form of that general deism which is everywhere connected with the incipient struggle of the middle classes for liberation and world domination. In other countries, this religious tinge of liberalism had worn thin or worn off by 1882, which seems to have been a crisis year for Pareto: in Italy it was still in full vigor, partly because national ambitions had only recently been fulfilled, and partly because an internationalist church continued to irritate the nationalist-minded intellectuals. To them, Italy was still what it had been to Mazzini, God's chosen country, and the Italian nation the "herald-people" of God. Filled with such ideologies (*derivazioni*, as he was to call them later on), Pareto

---

[1] Eisermann, *Vilfredo Paretos System der allgemeinen Soziologie* (Stuttgart: Ferdinand Enke Verlag, 1962). The bulk of the volume consists of annotated translations from the *Trattato*.

offered himself as a parliamentary candidate—and was defeated. The herald-people would have none of him. It is perhaps difficult for an Anglo-Saxon (or even a German!) to appreciate what this meant; nor can there be many anywhere with an emotional life intense enough to be able to feel fully with this supremely passionate man. For Pareto, at all events, this experience was a decisive turning point: from then onward he burnt what he had adored, and adored what he had burnt. The cloudy religiousness of Mazzini's *Faith and the Future,* summed up in Garibaldi's slogan "God and the People," gave way to a radical rationalism; belief in democracy turned to scorn for it; the representative of *umanesimo italiano* became a *filosofo volteriano;*[2] the man who had pressed forward into public life now retired from it, and, as he did nothing half, tended to become a proper hermit, brimful with contempt for the human race. It is significant that, later in life, he never spoke of politicians, but always only of politicasters.

But a second, not dissimilar, blow was to fall. Already well over forty years of age, Pareto married in 1889 a much younger woman, Russian in origin, Alessandra Bakounine. One day, returning from Paris, Pareto found his house empty: Madame had flown with the cook, who had obviously been more to her than a cook, taking thirty cases and boxes of valuables with them. But this was not all: being still an Italian citizen, though living at the time in Switzerland, Pareto was bound by the canon law, according to which *matrimonium ratum et consummatum separari non potest.* All that he could achieve was separation of bed and board, and his later remarriage to Jeanne Régis, sixty-one days before his death, was only possible through some none-too-savory lawyers' machinations. We may receive with sympathy Pareto's declaration that he would not marry again, if he were to return to earth for another life; but what matters to us here is the second psychological root and reinforcement of that hate of humanity which was thenceforward one of his most prominent character traits. In that attitude—at any rate, in its intensity—he has had only one equal in the social sciences, Eugen Dühring, to whose misanthropy Theodor Lessing once devoted a most enlightening study.[3] Surrounded by Angora cats, Pareto expressed some of his reactions to contemporary events in imaginary conversations with these beasts. His diaries would have been most interesting reading for a psychiatrist! Unfortunately only one of them has survived. The rest were destroyed by Madame Pareto II, not without good reason, we can be sure.

[2] The former is a description of Pareto by Paolo Arcari, the latter by Giuseppe La Ferla.

[3] Theodor Lessing, *Dührings Hass* (1922).

Though seeing him, in spite of everything, in the most favorable light, Professor Eisermann cannot help referring repeatedly to Pareto's "almost unsurpassable pessimism, hopelessness, deep-rooted bitterness, depressed state," etc. etc., and he has to quote some of the language which he used of others: a band of brigands, eunuchs, *canaille.* . . . He tells Pantaleoni that he does not desire children under any condition, and adds: "If only my mother had thought like that! How excellent that would have been!" Understandable perhaps, but a bad background to the study of human relationships.

Surely, we have in these life experiences the key to the explanation of the philosophical anthropology which became basic to Pareto's *Trattato* and all his mature work. It can be summed up by saying that for him man was marked by two contradictory, but related, features: his actual animality and his potential rationality. Mercilessly to expose the former, maximally to promote the latter, was Pareto's twin aim. He devoted himself to it with all the passion which, in other mortals, finds fulfillment in less intellectual pursuits.

III

It is as the bigot of rationalism, then, that Pareto stands before us, and he proved himself in practice not one whit less partial and partisan than any of the others who deserve that hard name. Above all, he was as oblivious as the rest of them of the source of error that was working in the depth of his mind. Full of smugness, he writes as follows to his friend Pantaleoni:

> Not because of any merit of my own, but because of the circumstances in which I found myself, I have no prejudices of any kind . . . which hinder others to do scholarly work in this field. I am not tied to any party, any religion, or any sect; therefore I entertain no preconceived ideas about the phenomena.

Strictly speaking, this is true. But error lurks not only in preconceptions about the *facts* which a science has to investigate; it lurks as much or more in preconceptions about the *results* to which the investigation of the facts is expected to lead. The truly scholarly man is as free from wishful thinking in the latter respect as in the former, but Pareto was not. His social science *had to be* something like mechanics, whether the facts warranted this conceptualization or not. There is another letter to Pantaleoni, written in the last years of his life, in which Pareto's domination by, and obliviousness of, this prejudice comes to the surface:

My *Trattato di sociologia* is a—very imperfect—attempt to introduce into the social sciences that relativity [Pareto means *that positivism*] which, in a much more perfect manner, is now being introduced into the natural sciences. . . . Galilei, Copernicus, and Newton have made tremendous advances; a further step forward is just being made by Einstein. Who knows, in a century from now, if a copy of the *Sociologia* should escape being chewed up by mice, some scholar will perhaps find out that there was an author at the beginning of the twentieth century who wanted to introduce the principle of relativity into the social sciences, and he will ask: "How could it happen that this was not understood, while the same principle made so much headway in the natural sciences?" I believe that he himself will give the following answer: "Because the social sciences were then far behind the natural sciences in development."

Pareto's naïve assumption is that for a social science to be little advanced means to be unlike astronomy, to be far advanced means to be like it. If this conviction had been the end result of his study of society, it would not have been so bad; but it was the unconscious metaphysic with which he set out; it was, to be blunt about it, the initial prejudice—prejudice in the fullest and narrowest sense of the word—which spoiled his work as irretrievably as other prejudices spoiled the work of other writers. Pareto was simply the last of the many "Newtons of the Moral World," at least one of which appears in every generation; and a "Newton of the Moral World" is no less of a nuisance in sociology than a "Lamarck of the Moral World" or a "Plato of the Physical World" in astronomy—a figure for which Pareto has nothing but ridicule and contempt.

As the present reviewer has just shown in another place,[4] Pareto's strategy consisted in replacing the social system as it really is (which is not amenable to treatment in mechanistic terms), by an artificially constructed model (which is amenable to such treatment). The results are, to say the least, artificial. But Pareto has not only failed significantly to advance our knowledge of social life; because of his unreasoned and unreasonable adherence to the self-contradictory image of a social science that would in effect be a physical science, he has also inhibited the advancement of our knowledge of economic reality; and this is particularly interesting, because in economics his fame is as secure as it is insecure in sociology. A side glance at this matter will be highly instructive; it can teach us something about the historical relationship between the two

[4] Werner Stark, *The Fundamental Forms of Social Thought* (1962), Chap. 9 (pp. 124-39). Cf. also Chap. 13 (pp. 184-99 especially *ad finem*), where Pareto's theories, and other mechanicist doctrines are analyzed from the point of view of the sociology of knowledge. What is said there must be combined with the psychological analysis attempted here in order to get a full picture of Paretianism.

sister sciences, which has not, so far, realized all the potentialities inherent in a possible cooperative effort.

It goes without saying that one of the tasks a science of economics has to fulfill is the analysis of the factors which determine demand. Yet for many decades next to nothing was achieved in this field: demand was simply taken as a datum. The underlying idea was that demand was ultimately determined by rationality, and that irrationality was only a secondary and disturbing factor. Then Veblen appeared and proved that the direction of demand was decisively and abidingly influenced by irrational strivings; his concept of "conspicuous waste" opened up a true and deep insight into the mind of *homo oeconomicus,* or rather *homo non oeconomicus.* One should have thought that the economists would have welcomed this contribution to the understanding of one of the main springs of economic conduct; but they did not; they turned a deaf ear; they passed Veblen by. And why? Because theirs was the Pareto spirit. What Veblen offered was the truth, but it was the kind of truth which refused to blend with a mechanistic-rationalistic conception of economic life in general and market dealings in particular.

Very similar was the reaction to Tönnies' contribution. Tönnies showed that the two great types of social ordering—community and association—produced also two dissimilar types of market. In an associational society, the contracting parties are first and the price forms only afterward, by their higgling and haggling; in a society of the community type, on the other hand, the market value is prior to their negotiations, part and parcel of an antecedent and continuing tradition, and the contracting parties are expected, and often constrained, to accommodate themselves to the "just price." Again, one should have thought that economists would have taken over and elaborated this insight; but this was far from being the case. And when some of them, later on, led by the facts themselves, developed the concept of "market indifference," they failed to recognize that market indifference (i.e., indifference of the price mechanism to individual items and agents of offer or demand) is so great in some economies, and comparatively so weak in others, that their contrast is one in essence rather than merely one of degree. Again, it was their mechanicism and rationalism—driven to its highest point by Pareto—which prevented them from utilizing, or even comprehending, this salient truth. A pair of scales always operates in the same way; how then could a market operate differently at different times?

Potentially even more valuable was what Durkheim had to contribute. The classical economists had maintained that material progress in general, and the unfolding of the division of labor in particular, were due to an inborn and ever-active desire on the part of men "to better their condition." This crude assumption became increasingly untenable when comparative anthropology proved that in most societies there prevails an amazing readiness to be content with conditions such as they are. Durkheim demonstrated that men's inertia is broken through only when the population increases so that competition intensifies, and that specialization is one of the methods by which they ward off, and indeed overcompensate, the consequences of this intensification of the struggle for existence. Before Durkheim, the "maximum theorem," so basic to economics, was no more than a surviving piece of utilitarian pseudopsychology; he made it into a well-defined and well-supported scientific explanation of progress, that crucial process of the modern economies. Yet it would be difficult to find traces of Durkheimian influence in economic literature.

All three suggestions—Veblen's, Tönnies' and Durkheim's—were rejected because the pan-mechanistic Paretian mind cannot comprehend historical, or merely local, variation. And this is the reason, too, why those economists who were out-and-out mechanicists could not even make anything of Max Weber's demonstration that the regularities of human action (in the narrower sense of the word) are regularities confined to concrete societies, and not, like physical facts (in the narrower sense of the word), ubiquitous and unchanging. Properly understood, this doctrine of Weber's was as much a confirmation of mechanicism as a critique of it. For in a capitalist society (which was, after all, what those economists were concerned with), individual action is, in principle, free and the social order (including the ordering of the market) is an order emergent, and not an order pre-existent; and because this is so, there is sense in comparing the action of the parties to mechanical pushing and pulling (trying to push the price up or to pull it down) and the fixation of the point of contract-making to the establishment of an equilibrium position. All this would have been perfectly reconcilable with Paretian economics; but his disciples, carrying on the master's pan-mechanicism, took no notice at all of Weber and continued to teach that all societies function in the same manner, and that the laws of economics are exactly like the laws of physics: once true, true forever.

It is precisely at this point that Pareto's weakness can be seen in its most glaring colors. For there is "Pareto's law"—almost the perfect example of a proposition which is *not* a law, which is merely a false pretense. According to this supposed "law," the income pyramid is the same in all societies. The most elementary acquaintance with the facts of history proves beyond the shadow of a doubt that this is not so. Some societies show a steeply rising gradient—in other words, much inequality; others, a far flatter surface—i.e., little inequality. How much truer than Pareto's doctrine was John Stuart Mill's, advanced in the very year when Pareto was born!

> The distribution of wealth [he wrote] depends on the laws and customs of society. . . . The rules by which it is determined, are what the opinions and feelings of the ruling portion of the community make them, and are very different in different ages and countries; and might be still more different if mankind so chose.

But, then, Mill really wanted the truth, the whole truth, and nothing but the truth; Pareto wanted merely such truths as would fit into a preconceived scheme; and truths, like men, do not take kindly to a Procrustean bed.

IV

Some of the most authoritative interpreters of the history of our subject, notably Talcott Parsons in *The Structure of Social Action* and Nicholas Timasheff in *Sociological Theory: Its Nature and Growth,* have suggested that it is permissible to see it in terms of convergence, unanimity gaining progressively the upper hand over disagreement. Happily, there is much to substantiate this view. It can, for instance, be applied to Max Weber and Émile Durkheim and their respective successors. For Durkheim, society was one rather than many; his definition of it was holistic or realistic in the sense of the philosophical doctrine called realism; society, in other words, was to him a real entity. For Weber, society was many rather than one; his definition of it was atomistic or nominalistic in the sense of the philosophical doctrine called nominalism; society, in other words, was to him essentially a term of summation. But both developed sociology as a theory of action. Both started from the conviction that human conduct is basically free and becomes ordered if and when certain socially approved and supported norms form and force it into definite, largely harmonized patterns. Seen from this vantage point, the initial philosophical disagreement between the two great theorists shrinks to a simple difference in emphasis. Durkheim thought of the patterning agencies as ontologically prior and more potent; Weber took the opposite view. Durkheim's sociology became more a theory of institutions; Weber's, more a theory of spontaneous behavior; but both were agreed that a society is essentially a system of norm-controlled human conduct.

Pareto, too, developed a theory of action, and that is why he, too, has been regarded as a strand or stream in the great movement of convergence. But with regard to him, the optimistic idea of increasing unanimity in social theory is more difficult to uphold. The decisive thought-pattern of Weber and Durkheim is enclosed, as it were, between two fixed poles: human freedom on the one hand, normative control on the other. Both conceptions are rejected, if not indeed ridiculed, by Pareto. Man is not free; his conduct is determined by the "residues"; residues are body-born and body-borne drives; whatever else they may be or may not be—Pareto is less explicit than he should have been—they are not something which sociocultural life has thrown up; they are physical, animalic, at any rate genetic, not properly human, in their origin. Everybody is made the way he is made; and he will act accordingly. In Parsons's terminology, Pareto may have a theory of action, but it is not a theory of voluntaristic action, and that is decisive. And normative control means little to Pareto either. To Weber and Durkheim, societies are different because their normative rules are different: a society with monogamy is one thing for them, a society with polygamy another. Pareto, blinded by the timelessness and universality of mechanical regularities, denies that the differences are real. He asserts that in *every* society those who can afford such luxuries have many wives, and those who cannot, have only one. What he is really concerned with, is mating, not marriage as an institution; and a sociologist who treats institutions as unimportant is not much more than a contradiction in terms. All the difference between polygamous and monogamous societies reduces itself for him to a matter of words, or rather cant: presence of hypocrisy in the latter case, absence in the former. This is profoundly unrealistic, for the existence of co-wives is right in the one society and wrong in the other. But this does not mean anything to Pareto, however much it may mean in life. Once again we see him enslaved to the arch-error which is so palpable in "Pareto's law"—the error of believing that everything is the same everywhere; that everything is, as it must always be. His whole attitude amounts to denying the form-giving, fact-forming influence of norms; and for this reason Pareto's theory cannot be brought into line with Weber's and Durkheim's, however hard we may try. He missed the all-decisive point which they grasped. They, indeed, were students of human sociality: he was merely an exponent of human nature—indeed, of man's lower nature—whose transformation by sociality he did not manage to understand.

Professor Eisermann has served Pareto well. He has shown us the light and pleasant hues in the portrait which he has lovingly restored to its original and authentic state. But, as Goethe says in *Götz von Berlichingen,* where there is strong light, there also are deep shadows, and these are less prominent than they ought to be in the image of the man with which we are presented. By all means, let us admire the fearless fighter who never failed to stand up for the truth as he saw it; but let us not forget that he saw it through spectacles which distorted it until it became unrecognizable by natural and normal eyes.

TWO

PARETO'S SOCIOLOGICAL SYSTEM

SIDNEY HOOK

WERE PARETO ALIVE today he would undoubtedly interpret the noisy reaction provoked by the publication of his work as a confirmation of one of his theorems. It is impossible, he holds, for most people to distinguish between an attempt to acquire knowledge of social processes and action which seeks to modify them. Like most of Pareto's theorems, this states a truth at the cost of a more significant truth. So long as we do not confuse the objective implications for practice which a theory has in its relevant field with the subjective purposes in behalf of which it has been projected, the tendency to raise questions concerning the practical import of doctrine is quite healthy. For in that way the meaning of a theory is amplified, and leads are derived by which it may be put to experimental test. But whatever the practical implications of Pareto's doctrines are, they have as little to do with the theory and practice of Fascism as the psychology of Pavlov, for example, has to do with the politics of the Russian government at whose hands its author has received honors and rewards. Many of Pareto's doctrines cannot be defended in Italy or Germany without bringing their professors into concentration camps. No matter how many honors Mussolini may have heaped upon Pareto *in absentia,* any talk about Pareto being the ideologist or prophetic apologist of Fascism is sheer poppycock.

Pareto's work represents the most ambitious attempt of the twentieth century to construct a scientific system of sociology. "My wish is to construct a system of sociology on the model of celestial mechanics, physics, chemistry." In this brief notice I wish to state Pareto's chief claims and to raise some questions. Although I believe his work represents a brilliant failure, his errors and limitations are more instructive than many a lesser man's truths.

"Pareto's Sociological System," by Sidney Hook. From *The Nation,* CXL: 3651 (June 26, 1935), 747-48. Reprinted by permission of the author and *The Nation.*

1. *Operationalism in sociology.* Pareto's most abiding contribution to social thought is his demand that the experimental or operational theory of meaning be applied to a field in which for centuries sonorous phrases have concealed the absence of clear ideas. Whether it is an appeal to "natural law," "the spirit of the times," "the forces of progress," or other shibboleths of the academy or marketplace, Pareto mercilessly exposes their multiple ambiguity, vagueness, and emotive connotations. He does not deny their enormous social influence. But their failure to denote specific existential patterns of behavior makes them experimentally meaningless. Although they may induce action, they cannot conduce to understanding. Every critical reader will enjoy the deftness with which Pareto lances the inflated proper nouns that figure in most sociological constructions. Unfortunately, Pareto himself does not adhere rigorously to his own principle. His theory of residues suffers, among other things, from his inability to isolate out of different social situations anything that fulfills the definition of a residue as an invariant predisposition to action or belief.

2. *Conception of scientific method.* A considerable part of Pareto's treatise is devoted to a fervent plea that the social sciences adopt the methods of the physical sciences and to an illustrative analysis of those methods. This raises two questions: whether such methodological reduction is possible, and whether Pareto's conception of the nature of scientific method is adequate.

Extending a method which he helped introduce into mathematical economics, Pareto argues for the abandonment of a simple cause-effect relation between configurations of events. Instead of saying that certain relations of production are the "cause" of a system of morals or that a determinate form of religious worship is the "effect" of a given geographical milieu, we are to replace the concept of causality with that of interdependence or functional correlation. Since the form of a society is determined by all its elements, if we can assign quantitative indices to these elements and solve the equations describing their interdependence, this would give us exhaustive knowledge of the system. Pareto admits that we cannot assign quantitative indices to the elements, and that even if we could, the equations could not be solved. He would also have to admit that if we were to make any further progress in social studies than the truism that a society is determined by all its elements, we must restrict ourselves to limited phases of social interaction, operate with specific hypotheses, and be content with piecemeal knowledge. But where shall we begin? With what hypotheses? And in what direction and at whose cost shall we experiment to test the validity of our hypotheses? And it is precisely at this point that the normative element in social theory, which Pareto is so anxious to extrude, enters. At the heart of every social theory, some ideal, value, or preference is to be found which determines not the truth of any body of doctrine but the selection of the central hypotheses whose truth is to be "experimentally" tested in fateful, because irreversible, action.

What strikes one over and over again in Pareto's discussion of scientific method is his underestimation of the nature and role of hypothesis. He asserts that "no study that aims at discovering some uniformity in the relation of social facts can be called useless." He holds that any historical analyses which conjecture "what would have happened had a certain event never occurred are altogether fatuous." He maintains that the assumptions of scientific method about the intelligibility of the world order do not involve any metaphysical presuppositions. These as well as many other beliefs betoken a rather smug and nearsighted empiricism. It would not be difficult to show that for purposes of solving a specific problem some uniformities between facts must be dismissed as irrelevant; that unless we could say what would probably have occurred if certain events had not taken place, we cannot pretend to understand those events; and that if we probe the basic assumptions of scientific method we uncover a whole nest of metaphysical propositions.

3. *Residues.* According to Pareto, the elements which determine the form of a society may be roughly classified into three groups: physical, historical, and internal. Chief among the elements of the third group are residues—a fancy synonym for *instincts.* They are the most constant elements in human behavior. Specific forms of conduct (derivatives) may vary; so may the theories and beliefs which attend them (derivations). But changes both in conduct and belief are primarily determined by com plexes of residues (sentiments) which remain comparatively invariant throughout history. The sociological moral to be drawn is that whoever desires to control human behavior and to make people receptive to new beliefs must appeal not to logic but to sentiment. The only thing new about this celebrated theory of residues is its ponderous classificatory subdivisions and the extravagant claims made for it. Its whole significance is summed up in a sentence tucked away in a long footnote: "The centuries roll by, human nature remains the same." Dewey's *Human Nature and Conduct* is, I suppose, the definitive refutation of this favorite theme song of all Tories. It is important to observe, however, that in constructing his theory Pareto violates all the scientific cautions he urges upon others. Every residue is "inferred out of" a specific social and historical milieu. If they are reduced to a schedule of biological impulses, the specific social

forms they take go begging for explanation. If residues are not biological drives, then since they are never found in a pure form but always expressed in various historical traditions, it is extremely hazardous to assert that they have the same role and significance as we go from culture to culture. It is very questionable, for example, whether there is anything in human beings which corresponds to a love of power as such. Even if there is, a love of power expressed in a desire to win a laurel wreath in Greek society is—in origin, form, and effects—sufficiently different from a desire to win a prize in the Irish sweepstakes to make us chary of classifying them under the same invariant sentiment. For all his historical erudition Pareto never took an historical approach to the social facts he considered. This is the fundamental weakness of all his work. He saw that history without social theory is blind. He failed to see that sociology without history is empty.

4. *Derivations. Derivations* is the technical term Pareto uses for what is popularly known as *rationalization*. Applied to social classes, it is what Marx called *ideology*. Pareto's insight into the social role of these vital lies goes deep. He attacks as the commonest fallacy of moralists and reformers the assumption that people act as they do because of the beliefs they hold. It is far truer to say that they believe as they do because of the way they behave. Truest of all, according to Pareto, is the proposition that both conduct and belief spring from the same residual root. Derivations are always present except when behavior is purely instinctive or purely logical—and that means almost all the time. Pareto's contention that most of human behavior is nonlogical is sound enough. But I cannot help believing that he has underestimated the importance of the fact that men seek, find, and accept "derivations." Pareto admits, but apparently only as an afterthought, that man is a reason-finding animal, too. It should not be hard, with only a fraction of the effort Pareto consumed, to establish cases of the opposite sort, to accumulate evidence showing how "reasons" influence human behavior when physical conditions are irrelevant, historical tradition is silent, and interests and residues are deadlocked.

5. *Circulation des élites.* Pareto regards the homogeneity of society as a myth for simpletons. The simplest division Pareto recognizes is the source of one of his most interesting theories. Every society is divided into two classes—a nonelite which embraces the lower strata of the population and an elite which includes all who enjoy the fruits of recognized excellence. The elite, in turn, divide into a governing elite and a nongoverning elite. The governing elite we always have with us. Whenever its members lack qualities of vigor, will, discipline, and readiness to use force, it recruits into its ranks the stronger members of the nonelite. If it fails to

do so, the reins of power are torn from its hands by a revolution. "History is the graveyard of aristocracies." But aristocracies there will always be. Power may be taken in the name of all; its very nature is such, however, that it must be wielded by a few. Pareto seems to enjoy a grim satisfaction at the prospect. If this theory is not interpreted as an innocuous truism to the effect that there will always be leaders, it calls for at least two comments. Certain "experiments" remain to be tried which may require us to reinterpret this alleged law. These involve the separation of economic and political power, the destruction of the monopoly of higher education, and the introduction of democratic processes of control into industry. Under such conditions leadership may not involve exploitation or government rest upon special bodies of armed men. Secondly, even if the elite—the lions and foxes together—will always prey upon the sheep, there may be certain institutional safeguards regulating the number of sheep to be sacrificed and the manner of their selection. And perhaps the sheep will console themselves with the reflection that the wolves, which are sure to be around, may be worse. . . .

THREE

THE SOCIAL SYSTEM, STRUCTURE, AND DYNAMICS

N. S. TIMASHEFF

PARETO'S MOST IMPORTANT contribution to sociological theory is his conception of society as a system in equilibrium. This formulation allows sociology to forsake crude organicism without abandoning certain of organicism's sound propositions.

If society is a system, it is a whole consisting of interdependent parts; change in some part affects other parts and the whole. The "material points or molecules" of the system, according to Pareto, are individuals who are affected by social forces which are marked by constant or common properties. The state of a social system at any given time is determined by the following conditions: first, the extrahuman environment; second, other elements exterior to the society at the time, including other societies and the given society's previous states; and third, inner elements of the system—namely, interests, knowledge, and residues and derivations which are manifestations of sentiments. Of these determining conditions, only the residues and derivations are submitted to a detailed study by Pareto.

In this general formula of equilibrium, no place seems to be given to such cultural phenomena as law, politics, religion, or art. But lack of explicit treatment does not mean that Pareto failed to recognize their importance. They all play their part in maintaining social systems, but, in his view, only inasmuch as they manifest basic sentiments. The role of sentiments is, then, essential in the maintenance of social equilibrium.

For Pareto, society is a system in equilibrium. This means that there exist, within every society, forces which maintain the form (or configuration) which the society has achieved or which guarantee even and uninterrupted change; in the latter case, the equilibrium is dynamic. An important corollary follows: if the social system is subject to pressure of outward forces of moderate intensity, inner forces will push toward the restoration of equilibrium, returning the society to its undisturbed state.[1] These inner forces consist chiefly of the sentiment of revulsion against anything that disturbs the inner equilibrium. Without this sentiment, every incipient alteration of the social system would meet little or no resistance and could grow with impunity. This situation may in fact occur, but its likelihood is minimized by the sentiment of resistance regardless of the number of individuals directly affected positively or negatively by the proposed changes.

This theorem of the restoration of equilibrium of social systems has been confirmed, to some extent, by the study of social reaction to crime, of the outcome of revolutions, and of the impact of war on societies. In these cases, as well as others, a large amount of evidence indicates the frequently temporary nature of social upheavals and the persistent quality of fundamental social arrangements.

The analysis of inner forces is based on the distinction between logical and nonlogical action. According to Pareto, an action is logical if its end is objectively attainable and if the means used are objectively united with the end in the framework of the best knowledge available; all other actions are nonlogical (which does not mean that they are illogical, or contrary to logic). Presumably logical actions are rather rare. In Pareto's treatise appear only a few examples, including the formulation of scientific theory, economic action (which by no means, in fact, is always logical), and the behavior of trial lawyers. But even judicial activity is nonlogical because the role of the judge involves more than the mere logical application of abstract legal rules to concrete cases. Pareto argues that judicial decisions to a great extent manifest the sentiments of the judges (which they share with other group members) and that reference to written law is an ex post facto explanation of a decision gained in another way. "Court decisions," he writes, "depend largely on the interests and sentiments operative in a society at a given moment; and also upon individual whims and chance events; and but slightly, and sometimes not at all, upon codes or written law" (No. 466). This illustration is one of many used by Pareto to demonstrate his basic theorem: the predominance of nonlogical action in social life.

Nonlogical action is related to residues and derivations. Both of the latter are manifestations of sentiments which are indefinite but seemingly basic biopsychic states. Although Pareto admits that these states are not

---

[1] More exactly, in Pareto's theory, equilibrium is defined by the presence of forces eventually restoring it.

directly knowable, he indicates the presumably specific nature of their expression in residues, derivations, and human conduct. Pareto seems to believe that the sentiments are instincts or innate human tendencies; for example, he names one of the most important sentiments *the instinct of combination*. On the other hand, he admits that residues are correlated with the changing conditions under which human beings live, that actions in which the sentiments express themselves reinforce such sentiments and may even arouse them in individuals lacking them, that sentiments are engendered or stressed by the persistence of groups and, in their turn, may help such groups to survive. These qualities are not properties of innate and immutable instincts but, rather, characteristics of learned behavior. The theory of learned behavior was just being developed in psychology in Pareto's day—a fact, no doubt, accounting in part for the ambiguity of his terminology.

Some of the sentiments, according to Pareto, urge men to justify their actions by formulating nonlogical theories which their advocates consider to be highly logical. Examination of these "theories" reveals the distinction between deep, constant, and therefore important elements —the residues—and superficial, variable, and therefore less important elements—the derivations. Residues can be discovered by studying diverse statements bearing on the same subject and abstracting from them the constant elements. Knowledge of the residues, which are closer to the sentiments than the derivations, permits deeper penetration into the causation of human actions. Yet residues are also manifestations, and ultimately causation must be sought in the depths of the sentiments. However conjectural or questionable this particular formulation, we must agree with Pareto that to explain actions by accepting at face value what men say about their behavior is, of course, a procedure void of scientific validity—a principle long recognized by students of human life.

Pareto emphasized the difference between his view of human actions and rationalistic explanation. The latter assumes that men first think, first formulate ideas or theories, and then act accordingly. In Pareto's opinion, behavior follows the reverse process: commission precedes rationalization. For example, he concludes the discussion of popular doctrines of the emergence of private property by declaring: "A family, or some ethnic group, occupies a piece of land. . . . The fact of the perpetuity of occupation, of possession is in all probability antecedent . . . to any concept of law of inheritance" (No. 256). For Pareto, there is no direct causal relationship between theory and action. Both are caused by basic sentiments which are revealed in action in a rather constant manner, but in theory or justification, sentiments are manifested almost at random.

Every mode of conduct is justified by some theory, to be sure, but in each concrete case the theoretical justification is determined by the accident of invention and therefore is of no great importance in analyzing behavior. This conclusion is another major theorem of Pareto's sociology.

According to Pareto, there are six classes of residues (and several sub-classes in each): one, the instinct of combination, the faculty of associating things; two, the residue of the persistence of aggregates, the conservative tendency; three, the residue of the manifestation of sentiments through exterior acts (among them, the formulation of justifications; in simple terms, self-expression); four, the residue of sociability, or the drive to compose societies and to impose uniform conduct; five, the residue of personal integrity, leading to actions that restore lost integrity, such as those forming the source of criminal law; six, the sexual residue. In social life, these residues may combine in different ways. For example, through a combination of the residues of equilibrium and of group persistence, compound forces of great social importance are built up, corresponding to vigorous and powerful sentiments of the type vaguely designated by the term *ideal of justice.*

Pareto's classification of residues is nowhere explained or justified. Class six, the sexual residue, is heterogeneous and logically would seem to re-quire a complement, like hunger. Classes three to five are related to the tendency of social systems to remain in or to restore a state of equilibrium. Classes one and two are shown in their distribution among people, as indicated below. A great admirer of Pareto concedes that this classification was "the spade work of a pioneer." [2] Although additions and improve-ments to this spade work have been suggested, it seems improbable that scholars will attempt to develop this phase of Pareto's work because of its conspicuous shortcomings.

Pareto's classification of residues is, in part, based on his study of material taken predominantly from classic authors. He held that a great literature roughly reflects actual life, that concentration on classic litera-ture precludes bias, and that since the residues remain constant universal propositions can be derived from careful analysis of classic literature. (Not-withstanding these claims, newspaper releases were interspersed among selections from the classics.) Each item selected from these sources was first interpreted as the manifestation of a particular sentiment; then the individual items were compared and large numbers of similar items were formed into classes and subclasses. This procedure (hardly a forerunner of present-day content analysis used in the empirical study of communica-

[2] L. J. Henderson, *Pareto's General Sociology: A Physiologist's Interpretation* (1935), p. 58.

tions, though similar in purpose) is the closest approximation of the inductive method to be found in Pareto's work.

Pareto's analysis of derivations is less detailed than his treatment of residues. Derivations, as pointed out above, are conceived as surface manifestations—as explanations—of underlying forces in social life. Pareto first considers derivations from the viewpoint of the subjective character of such explanations and thereafter outlines four principal classes of derivations: one, derivations of assertion, including affirmations of fact and sentiment; two, derivations of authority, whether of individuals, groups, custom, or divinities; three, derivations that are in accord with (and therefore serve to maintain) common sentiments and principles; four, derivations of verbal proof, for example, various metaphors and analogies. Pareto's many illustrations of these different kinds of verbal explanations of conduct show the categories to be overlapping. However, there is no close connection between the classes of residues . . . and [those] of derivations; each cross-cuts the other.

THE CIRCULATION OF ELITES

In Pareto's view, although the residues are common to all societies and times, they are unevenly distributed among individuals, and their relative frequency in various societies and epochs is subject to change. Social change, as it is related to the first two classes of residues (the instinct of combination and the persistence of aggregates), is discussed at length. This study results in the formulation of the theory of the circulation of elites, which forms one more basic theorem in Pareto's sociology. Elites consist of individuals of highest performance in their respective fields. There are two principal classes of elites: a governing elite, comprising individuals who directly or indirectly play an important role in the manipulation of political power; and a nongoverning elite, consisting of capable men not in power positions. The differential distribution of residues among the members of elites is much more important for social affairs than their distribution in the masses.[3] Depending on the dominance of residues, respectively, of Class 1 and Class 2, two types of men are depicted, designated by the terms *speculator* and *rentier*.[4] When the governing elite is dominated by speculators, society is subject to relatively rapid change; when *rentiers* dominate, change takes place slowly. Pareto holds that a natural tendency exists for the elites of the two types to rotate in positions

---

[3] This is a point of view which especially appealed to the Fascists.

[4] *Rentier* connotes in French a person seeking security and therefore investing his savings in bonds (*rente* in French).

of political power. When an elite of one type has ruled for some time, superior elements accumulate in the governed classes and, conversely, inferior elements develop in the ruling classes. Consequently, an elite consisting, say, of speculators commits mistakes which open the way to ascent of *rentiers*; but after the latter are consolidated in power positions, they also commit mistakes, opening the doors for the speculators.

A cyclic theory of social change is thus introduced, the two phases of the cycle being characterized by the dominance respectively of conservative or of progressive attitudes. History, therefore, asserts Pareto, "is a grave-yard of aristocracies" (No. 2053). This theory, which closely resembles Saint-Simon's view of the necessary recurrence of organic and critical periods, is illustrated from ancient history and classical literature. But illustration . . . is not systematic demonstration. In absence of the latter, there seems little reason to ascribe universal validity to this theory on the basis of Pareto's work itself.

SUMMARY AND APPRECIATION

What, in summary, are Pareto's answers to the fundamental problems of sociological theory? He conceives society to be a system in equilibrium, the material reference points of which are individuals who are exposed to a limited number of so-called forces. These forces, first of all sentiments and residues, determine the condition of the social system. In this conception, the role of culture seems to have little place.

The basic unit for sociological analysis, in Pareto's scheme, is a single manifestation of these persistent underlying forces. Analysis should be primarily concerned with residues, themselves manifestations of unknowable biopsychic phenomena.

For Pareto, the problem of the relationship between individual and society is an aspect of the general problem of the relation between part and whole in any system. His viewpoint on this question is essentially functional: any changes in parts of a system affect the whole, and vice versa.

The latter view is consistent with Pareto's rejection of any version of sociological monism which would reduce explanations of social life to single factors or causes. Nevertheless, he outlines a limited number of factors which he believes determine the state of society and social change. In the case of change, he stresses the nature and distribution of specified residues, or tendencies to act in certain ways, in the ruling elite. Changes in elites seem to occur by immanent necessity.

Pareto does not define the relationship between sociology and the other social sciences. But he insists that sociology must be based on the logico-experimental method, a method requiring disciplined observation and logical inference from such observation. His strong admonitions in this respect are weakened by his own inclination to substitute the collection of others' statements about facts for observation itself and to forsake inductive procedure for seemingly intuitive classification schemes.

These characteristics help to make the study and interpretation of Pareto's theoretical writings exceedingly difficult. His *Treatise,* to be sure, contains a large number of plausible propositions about various phases of social and cultural reality which represent a source of suggestion and hypothesis in present-day study of social structure and change. Yet relatively little use has been made of Pareto's work in this respect, a notable exception being the landmark research in industrial sociology, *Management and the Worker* by F. J. Roethlisberger and W. J. Dickson.[5]

Pareto's main contributions are the insistence (though not the practice, as we have seen) that sociology must be governed by strictly scientific canons and the conception of society as a system in imperfect equilibrium. With respect to the latter conception, Pareto's propositions concerning the tendency of social systems to restore disturbed equilibrium, the various factors contributing to the condition of social systems, the significance of nonlogical action in social life, and the intermittent nature of social change, marked by successive periods of slow and rapid alterations, are suggestive formulations which approximate observable conditions.

Much less useful is Pareto's analysis of inner forces operating in social life, especially the reduction of these forces to residues. In the final account, Pareto's explanation (a derivation itself?) of social facts rests on a biopsychic theory of something closely akin to instincts. Today we know that any such explanation of individual or social behavior is misleading because of the ubiquitous role of cultural and institutional factors in human conduct.

But even if we identify Pareto's sentiments and residues with learned behavior rather than with instincts, his procedure in establishing these forces is highly questionable. In the first place, to quote the philosopher F. S. C. Northrop, "instead of being the firsthand psychic states given immediately to the trained introspective psychologist," Pareto's psychic traits are "second- or thirdhand characteristics assigned to people . . . who, at the time Pareto makes his 'observations,' exist only in his imagina-

---

[5] This study of a Western Electric Company plant at Hawthorne, Illinois, makes use of Pareto's equilibrium theory especially; see particularly pp. 272 (n.), 567-68.

tion. . . . Not once in getting his 'facts' does Pareto leave the armchair in his study." [6]

In the second place, Pareto set for himself the difficult task of sifting presumably fundamental residues from innumerable and admittedly deceptive derivations. The accomplishment of this task requires the identification of derivations associated with "the same subject"; yet criteria for distinguishing subjects are nowhere made clear. Nor are the procedures used in determining the particular residues manifested in the derivations specified. Obviously, Pareto's own work falls far short of the scientific demands he himself voiced so strongly and clearly.

His treatment of residues and derivations, which occupies a large part of his *Treatise,* is, then, the weakest aspect of his work. Yet diffused throughout this part of the work are many penetrating insights and suggestive leads for further investigation. And, as we have seen, the remainder of Pareto's theoretical formulation, particularly his conception of the social system as a dynamic equilibrium, remains an important contribution to the cumulative development of sociological theory.

[6] F. S. C. Northrop, *The Logic of the Sciences and the Humanities* (1947), p. 270. See all of Chap. 15 in this volume for evaluation of Pareto's work.

FOUR

PARETO'S CENTRAL ANALYTICAL SCHEME

TALCOTT PARSONS

THERE HAS RECENTLY been much discussion of Pareto's sociology apropos of the appearance of the English translation. A large part of this discussion seems to me to have suffered from being at cross purposes. Each participant has tended to pick out things which seemed to him particularly praiseworthy or objectionable, as the case might be. If one were to subject this critical literature to an inductive analysis, I for one think it would be exceedingly difficult to arrive at any clear conclusion as to what the common reference to "Pareto's theory" really is.

If this be true, it must be explicable in one of two sets of terms. Either Pareto's *Treatise* is really a hodgepodge and does not contain a coherent theory at all, or the critics have failed to penetrate to the deeper levels of the work. In my opinion the truth is nearer the latter . . . alternative. There is in Parento's work a definite analytical scheme of which, with few exceptions,[1] one does not get a clear conception from the secondary discussion. At the same time it does not constitute a finished sociological theory, but, rather, an approach to one.

It is my strong conviction that a clear understanding of the theoretical issues raised by Pareto's work cannot be attained until this scheme is clearly worked out. The reasons for Pareto's use of it and the way in which unsolved problems emerge from it must be grasped before a judgment can be ventured. It is to this task of elucidating Pareto's central analytical scheme, and this alone, that the present paper will be devoted. It is not a general critical evaluation of Pareto's work.

"Pareto's Central Analytic Scheme," by Talcott Parsons. From *Journal of Social Philosophy*, I: 3 (April 1936), 244-62. Reprinted by permission of the author.

[1] The principal exception is Professor L. J. Henderson's *Pareto's General Sociology* which, however, is largely confined to the methodological side.

There are two elements in Pareto's personal background which are of decisive importance in understanding his approach to sociology: physical science and economics. He was himself trained in physical science and mathematics, and spent many years as a practicing engineer. He was also, later, an economic theorist of distinction and a professor of economics at Lausanne.

The first significance of the background of physical science is methodological in a specific sense. Pareto wished to base his work in both economics and sociology on essentially the same methodological foundation which had made the phenomenal success of the physical sciences possible. In this ideal he was, of course, by no means alone, having perhaps the majority of social scientists outside Germany, at least since Comte, with him. But there is an important difference. Most previous social scientists following the natural science ideal have carried over the dogmas connected with an illegitimate "reification" of some elements of the classical physics. This is certainly far less true of Pareto, whose views of scientific methodology are much more skeptical and sophisticated.

As readers have doubtless been told ad nauseam, he reduces the essentials of science to the two elements he indicates in the name *logico-experimental*. Science consists essentially of observation of fact (with or without experimental aid) and logical inference from fact. Logic by itself is capable of yielding only tautologies[2]—hence, though logic is an indispensable tool, the central content of science lies in the factual element.

It is noteworthy that in his discussion of fact Pareto is extremely cautious, and nowhere to my knowledge commits himself to a definition which would draw an arbitrary line. Above all, two things are to be noted: first, he does not commit himself to any such formula as "sense data," which is so common among natural science methodologists; second, he does not exclude data concerning the subjective states of mind of persons other than the observer. In particular his treatment of propositions as observable facts[3] clearly implies that not merely the physical properties of objects but also the meaning of symbols is capable of observation. This is, as we shall see, a matter of far-reaching importance. In fact, one may lay down only two very general criteria of what constitutes fact for Pareto—one that a factual observation must involve a "thing" or "event" or aspects of it, which is "given" in the sense of being independent of the subjective wishes, whims, or sentiments of the observer, and second, as a check

_____

[2] Vilfredo Pareto, *Traité de sociologie générale*, Sec. 28. All references are to the French edition. The sections are uniform through the Italian, French, and English editions.

[3] *Ibid.*, Sec. 7. The general methodological discussion occupies the whole of Chap. 1.

on this, that by a combination of "pointing" and rational argument any two "reasonable" men may be brought to agree in the essentials of their description of it.[4]

There is one other highly important point. It is quite clear that Pareto does not mean by *fact* necessarily a concrete thing or event; indeed, it is questionable whether a completely concrete description exists at all.[5] But, however that may be, most "facts" of science fall far short of the empirically possible degree of concrete completeness—they state only certain aspects or elements of the concrete situation in hand.

It is only with this in mind that we can appreciate the meaning of Pareto's conception of scientific law as the statement of a uniformity existing in the facts.[6] This is not a repudiation of the role of abstraction in scientific theory. But Pareto does not set concept over against fact— the one abstract, the other concrete. This position, short of the radical empiricism which repudiates abstract concepts altogether, issues in the "fiction" theory that concepts are useful fictions, but somehow not "true." Contrary to this view, the element of abstraction is included in his concept of fact as such.

Then any concrete phenomenon is to be regarded as resulting from a concatenation (an *entrelacement,* as Pareto says[7]) of a number of different laws meeting in a given concrete situation. The failure of any particular law to provide a satisfactory account of the *total* concretely observable facts of the situation is not prima facie evidence that the law is wrong but, rather, that the elements formulated in it need to be supplemented by those formulated in other laws.

On this crucial methodological point Pareto's experience with economics was of decisive importance for his view of sociology. . . . There seems to be no doubt that his principal personal motive for venturing into sociology lay in his dissatisfaction with the concepts of economic theory as adequate tools for the solution of concrete problems, even . . . [those] generally regarded as [of] a predominantly "economic" character, such as that of the effects of protectionist measures. But from this inadequacy, which he realized more and more vividly, he did not conclude (as does, for instance, the "institutionalist" school of economists) that the proper course was to discard the economic theory to which he himself had greatly contributed but, rather, to supplement its abstractions with other sociological theories applicable to the same concrete phenomena. It is highly significant that it is just this example which he gave to

[4] Pareto himself clearly recognized the relativity of this last criterion. There is no space here to enter into the methodological issues.

[5] Pareto, *Traité* . . . , *op. cit.*, Sec. 106.   [6] *Ibid.*, Sec. 99.   [7] *Ibid.*, Sec. 101.

illustrate the abstractness of scientific theory in his own methodological discussion.[8]

We may, then, take Pareto as, with all his insistence on logico-experimental method, representing an undogmatic, relatively open-minded view of science and its method [9] which, above all, leaves room for the admission to scientific treatment of subjective phenomena, and which avoids the pitfalls of radical empiricism with an explicit vindication of the role of theoretical abstraction in science. Whatever its shortcomings from the point of view of completeness, it is, in my opinion, a sound foundation on which to build.

With these methodological considerations in mind, we may now turn to Pareto's substantive theoretical structure, the distinction between "logical" and "nonlogical" action. This is, as Pareto explicitly says, not a classification of concrete actions but of elements in concrete action.[10] Moreover, there can be no doubt that the concept of logical action is framed with the concepts of economic theory primarily in mind, though it is a broader category than the economic, containing other elements.[11]

It is defined as consisting of "operations logically united to their end" from the point of view both of the actor and of an outside observer "with a more extended knowledge of the circumstances." [12] From the context, it is made clear that the "more extended knowledge" in question is the best available scientific knowledge. That is, action is logical insofar as it may be thought of as guided by a scientifically verifiable theory of the intrinsic relations of means to the end in question. The standard of "logicality" or rationality is thus derived from science. In another place Pareto says that logical action may be thought of as determined by a "process of reasoning" [13]—that is, of scientific reasoning.

Nonlogical action, on the other hand, is not positively defined at all, but is a residual category. It comprises all the elements of action not falling within Pareto's explicit definition of the logical element. This is a fact of the first importance which must be kept continually in mind if Pareto's thought is to be understood.

The "sociological" theories of which Pareto spoke as constituting the necessary supplement to economic theory in understanding concrete action[14] are predominantly those dealing with the nonlogical elements

---

[8] *Ibid.*, Sec. 34.   [9] In rather marked contrast to the dogmatism of some of his followers.
[10] Pareto, *Traité* . . . , *op. cit.*, Sec. 148.   [11] *Ibid.*, Sec. 152.
[12] *Ibid.*, Sec. 150. Pareto also gives another definition, where the objective and subjective ends coincide (Sec. 197). I do not take this up explicitly because it would complicate the discussion without contributing sufficiently to justify it.
[13] *Ibid.*, Sec. 161.   [14] *Ibid.*, Sec. 38.

of action, and these are the only ones which he attempts to develop by an explicit analysis in his own sociological treatise.

Having abstracted the logical elements of action from his immediate concern, Pareto proceeds to develop an analytical scheme for the study of the nonlogical, predominantly on an inductive basis. There are two essential steps in this development which have not generally been clearly understood in relation to each other. The first is the setting up of a scheme the essential purpose of which is to attain a clear statement of the problem and to decide what concrete data to select for intensive study.

It takes the form of a discrimination between three elements of the problem.[15] Two of them are roughly distinguishable sets of concrete data bearing on nonlogical action, those of "overt acts," designated as B, on the one hand, "linguistic expressions" or "theories," called C, concretely associated with them, on the other. Human beings, unlike animals, both "act"—that is, their organisms go through changes which may be interpreted as spatiotemporal events, and also express explanations and justifications of their actions in linguistic, i.e., symbolic, form. Casually connected in a state of mutual interdependence with both these sets of concrete data is a third entity which Pareto designates as A, the "state of mind" of the actor or, more frequently in his later usage, his "sentiments," which is not directly observable in the same sense as B and C. But insofar as B and C [are concerned], the observed phenomena are not determined by the external situation of the actor, the forces which determine nonlogical action, and hence in the last analysis the state of society,[16] will be found in A.

It should be noted that A is not specifically defined, but is rather left as indefinite as possible. Indeed, there is good reason for this, since its investigation is the problem of the study, and to define it rigorously at this stage would be to beg the question. All that can be said about it at the outset are three things: that since the whole scheme is concerned with *non*logical action, it excludes the prime determinant force of logical action—that is, scientific knowledge; that Pareto's phrase *state of mind* (*état psychique*) indicates he intends to approach the problem primarily in "subjective" terms; and that it is roughly distinguishable from the concrete categories of fact, B and C, (indeed, it cannot be a concrete category at all, but must be an analytical element—its "factualness" is on the analytical plane, like that of logical action).

---

[15] *Ibid.*, Sec. 162. Pareto illustrates this scheme graphically by means of a triangle with the apexes denominated A, B, and C, respectively.

[16] Only insofar as it is dependent on *non*logical forces, of course.

Now, both B and C, being in a state of mutual interdependence with A, may be regarded as, in part, "manifestations" of it. But of the two, for *non*logical action, C is the more closely tied to A because it is less affected by the external circumstances of action. Hence Pareto decides to confine his analytical attention to the study of C, the "theories" associated with nonlogical action,[17] and leave B aside until he comes to his synthetic treatment in the last three chapters of the work. The essential function of this ABC scheme which, to differentiate it from another introduced presently, we may call *the triangle scheme,* is to state his inductive problem in this way—it is not his final analytical scheme at all. This is the first step in the inductive process.

The second step is the substantive study of theories themselves. But since he is concerned with studying nonlogical action only, he is confronted immediately with a problem—it is not concrete theories he wants to study, but only the nonlogical elements in them. But how are these to be identified? The answer to this question takes Pareto back to the original starting point: the concept of logical action. Its principal distinguishing feature, it will be remembered, was that means were intrinsically related to their end in a scientifically verifiable way. Then, insofar as logical action is guided by a "theory," it will be a theory which meets the requirements of logico-experimental science. True to the residual character of nonlogical action, then, any departure from this standard will suffice to mark the theory in question as relevant to nonlogical action, as a datum for Pareto's problem.

His first concern, then, is an exhaustive critique of theories associated with action according to the scientific standard.[18] His second is an inductive study of the nonscientific elements found. The result of this second procedure is the distinction of two types of nonscientific elements, a fundamental, relatively constant one and a contingent, much more highly variable one. These two are the residues and derivations, respectively.[19] It must never be forgotten, as it generally has been, that these much discussed concepts of Pareto both designate elements of nonscientific *theories.* Above all, the residues are still not elements of the A of the earlier scheme, but only manifestations of A.

In fact, the theory of the residues as such is not a substantive sociological

---

[17] Cf. Pareto, *Traité* . . . , *op. cit.,* Secs. 798, 851.

[18] This is why the criticism of theories from a scientific point of view is so prominent in Chaps. 4 and 5. It is not a continuation of the methodological discussion of Chap. 1 but a part of his *positive* analytical procedure.

[19] Defined as the elements (a) and (b) respectively of his *second* analytical scheme, which is wholly different from the ABC triangle. Cf. Pareto, *Traité* . . . , *op. cit.,* Sec. 803.

theory at all, but only a conceptual framework in terms of which the task of developing a theory may be approached. It is rather a method than a theory. It does not even tell us what order of forces are predominant in determining the state of society except negatively—it is not those involved in logical action so far as the residues are important, for they are elements of nonlogical action. But nonlogical action is a residual category, and this character is shared by that of residues. It all depends on what they "manifest," and there is no reason whatever why the simple inductive distinction of residues and derivations should exhaust the question.

This is the point at which Pareto's own explicit analytical scheme stops. Even it is not, in the terms in which it is put forward, without serious difficulties. Indeed, the scheme as stated contains an embarrassing ambiguity which, until the analysis is pushed further, threatens to develop into a serious contradiction. It is worth a brief exposition in order to show the importance of the further development which is implicit, as I shall show, in Pareto's later synthetic treatment.

The difficulty reaches back into the concept of logical action. There Pareto's mode of treatment had two outstanding features—his definition was exclusively in terms of the character of the means-end relationship, it was the case of "operations logically united to their end"; but at the same time there is, in the conceptual scheme itself, no reference to systems of logical action, but only to a logical element in the particular act. The effect of this is to leave the status of ends indeterminate. For the determination "by a process of reasoning"—that is, by a scientific theory—may be meant with or without the qualification *"given the end."* The importance of this lies in the fact that logical action is thought of as a causal element, and hence the whole great question of the causal role of ends is involved.[20]

In these terms two lines of thought tend to open out. In the one case it may be assumed that the logical element includes a given end. Then the latter takes the central role in logical action, and the tendency is to think of nonlogical action as determined by factors other than a subjective end. This leads to the interpretation of the sentiments manifested in the residues as psychological drives to which the subjective aspect of the "theories" is irrelevant except as an index of forces of a different order.

If, on the other hand, a scientific theory be taken as the complete determinant of action (without the end being "given" apart from the theory), the trend of thought is entirely different. Instead of the question at issue between logical and nonlogical action being the role of subjective

---

[20] That is in one sense the question of teleology. But this slippery concept must be handled with great caution.

ends as such, it is the character of the theories in terms of which the
subjective aspect of action is expressed. At least the ultimate ends of
action do not have a place in a scientific theory, because they do not
constitute elements of knowledge of the situation—that is, "facts"—to the
actor, but are "subjective," are "manifestations of sentiments." [21] Then,
insofar as action is determined by ultimate ends or values which cannot
as such be "justified" by a scientific theory, the action is insofar nonlogical, no matter what the character of the means-end relationship. This
clearly brings quite different considerations into the picture from the
other trend of thought. If the residues constitute or manifest the ultimate
values, the major premises on which systems of action are based,[22] the
term must be something quite distinct from a "fancy name for instinct."

Moreover, whatever his original bent may have been, Pareto was
strongly pushed in this direction by the procedure he chose for the study
of nonlogical action. For, having selected theories as the factual material
to study, he was, in order to identify his data, forced to lay special stress
on the scientific standard in connection with logical action and hence,
ipso facto, to emphasize the nonscientific character of the theories in the
nonlogical case, rather than to question the general importance of the
subjective elements expressed in them. It is no mere coincidence that the
secondary writers who have interpreted Pareto as primarily putting forward a new version of instinct theory have uniformly overlooked the fact
that his central analysis, issuing in the concepts of residue and derivation,
was concerned with theories and not with total complexes of action.[23]

The effect of this dichotomy is to bring into the foreground a distinction between two entirely different categories of nonlogical elements in
action which cuts across the residue-derivation distinction so that both
of them are "manifested" in the residues. The combination of the residual
way of conceiving nonlogical action, with Pareto's inductive method of
its study, made it impossible for him to develop the distinction systematically without going beyond the point to which he pushed his own analytical scheme. The distinction is that between the elements of heredity and

---

[21] It is to be noted that Pareto speaks of the residue as always the "manifestation of
certain sentiments." Cf. Pareto, *Traité* . . . , *op. cit.,* Sec. 868.

[22] As Pareto put it at one point "le principle qui existe dans l'esprit de l'homme."
Cf. *ibid.,* Sec. 798. An instinct is not a principle. To be sure a residue "corresponds to"
and "manifests" instincts, but curiously enough *so do all the other major sociological
categories.* Cf. *ibid.,* Sec. 851.

[23] Thus for instance Professor Sorokin, perhaps the most eminent sociologist who has
written on Pareto, interprets them as elements of the ABC triangle schema: Cf. Sorokin,
Contemporary Sociological Theories, p. 50. We are here concerned with Pareto's explicit
conceptual scheme. His actual usage is often forced by the latent ambiguity just discussed in the direction of an instinct theory.

environment on the one hand and what may be called *value elements* on the other.

Its significance is best brought out in terms of its relation to the means-end schema which is, after all, Pareto's own starting point and is central to any tradition of thought in which the concept of rationality of action has a place. Analysis[24] will show that, if the means-end scheme is to have more than descriptive—that is, causal—analytical meaning, ends as a factor in action must be conceived as containing an element independent of the conditions of the situation of action, including the "given" features of the actor's own hereditary equipment.

If this general proposition be accepted and its implications applied to the understanding of systems of logical action defined as Pareto does it in terms of the character of the means-end relationship, we get somewhat the following picture: such a system will be found to involve a series of inter-related "chains" of means-end relationships. But the postulate of the causal independence of ends implies that there will at one extreme be elements which constitute "ultimate means and conditions" of action; at the other, "ultimate ends" which are, in terms of the chain, "ends in themselves" and not means to any further ends.[25] In between will lie an "intermediate sector" of elements which constitute both means and ends, according to the point of view.[26]

Both the ultimate-condition element and the ultimate-end element are nonlogical in the sense that they do not constitute or involve means-end relationships. In fact, Pareto's definition of logical action will be found to apply quite satisfactorily to the intermediate sector of the intrinsic means-end chain. But this very fact indicates the great importance of the distinction between the two categories of nonlogical factors. Objectively —that is, from the point of view of an outside observer—the one element is to be attributed to the agency of the actor, the other not. Subjectively,[27] from the point of view of the actor, the difference is equally marked. The conditions of action[28] manifest themselves in the "theories" guiding action in the form of "facts" of the situation known to the actor. His ultimate ends, on the other hand, are not "reflections" of an external

---

[24] For the details of which, unfortunately there is no space in the present paper. See my *Place of Ultimate Values in Sociological Theory, International Journal of Ethics* (April 1935).

[25] This whole analysis has reference to *elements* and not to concrete entities, acts or otherwise.

[26] Thus money is an end of acquisitive activities but, in turn, a means of purchasing goods and services.

[27] This is a highly important distinction which Pareto himself makes use of. Cf. Pareto, *Traité* . . . , *op. cit.*, 199.

[28] At the rational pole. See below for the main qualifications of this proposition.

reality in the same sense, but are subjective—are, as Pareto says, "manifestations of sentiments." It follows from this that to conceive concrete action as guided entirely by a scientific theory is to eliminate the role of ends altogether, in fact to eliminate action itself, by making its subjective aspect merely a reflection of the facts of the situation.

This dichotomy of nonlogical elements is not, as has been pointed out, present in Pareto's original explicit analytical scheme. It does, however, make its appearance in a most interesting manner in the later synthetic portion of his work. In connection with his discussion of social utility he formulates two abstract types of society.[29] One is that where "reason" does not enter in at all but where action is determined exclusively by the sentiments and the external conditions of the society—or, if we add the determination of the sentiments by the external conditions, "the form of the society is determined if the external conditions alone are given." [30] The other is one where action is determined "exclusively by logico-experimental reasoning." [31] But in this case the form of the society is "by no means determined when the external conditions are given. It is necessary to know in addition the end which is to be pursued by means of logico-experimental reasoning." [32] Pareto then goes on to say that the essential reason why a society based exclusively on reason "does not and cannot exist" [33] is not that men's "prejudices" prevent them from acting reasonably; it is not that it is impossible to know the conditions accurately and to act upon the knowledge, but that data essential to the solution of the problems presented by action to reason are lacking. These essential data are the ultimate ends of action.

Thus Pareto, when he has come to consider action systems as a whole instead of isolated acts, has clearly seen what is, in his terms, the nonlogical character of ultimate ends, and at the same time the clear distinction of this nonlogical element from the conditions of action. The "sentiments" of the first abstract type of society . . . clearly [can] not be those manifested in the ultimate ends of action, for Pareto does not hesitate to think of the former as determined by the external conditions, while for ends as a factor in action to be so determined would be a contradiction in terms. Conversely the ends which constitute the missing data equally cannot be mere reflections of the conditions—there is no bar in principle to the latter constituting data of a scientific theory which can serve as a guide to action. Thus we see one essential reason why the theories associated with action always contain nonlogical elements.

[29] Pareto, *Traité* . . . , *op. cit.*, Sec. 2041.   [30] *Ibid.*, Sec. 2142.   [31] *Ibid.*, Sec. 2143.   [32] *Ibid.*   [33] *Ibid.*

I now wish to call attention to two further important features of Pareto's treatment of action which are not explicit in his main analytical scheme but which emerge from a careful study of the synthetic parts of his work.

The first concerns the way in which his thinking finally breaks with the "atomistic individualism" which has been a conspicuous feature of the utilitarian climate of opinion of orthodox economic theory and has constituted an important element in the background of his own thought. We have already seen how the distinction between logical and nonlogical action, in the way in which he formulated it, involved by implication—in order to avoid otherwise insuperable difficulties—the conception of a complicated web of means-end chains instead of a mere aggregation of isolated acts. Only these considerations give a clear determination of the relation of the logical element to the two orders of nonlogical: heredity and environment and the value element.

There emerges, however, in the theory of social utility, a further differentiation of the modes in which the latter are related to action. In spite of the fact that this treatment is couched in normative terms, it has highly important theoretical implications. Its point of departure is the normative aspect of economic theory in the form of the traditional economic doctrine of maximum satisfaction. This is the proposition that, under certain rigidly defined conditions (the most important of which are rationality of action, mobility of resources, freedom of competition, and independence of wants from the processes of their satisfaction), the pursuit by each individual of his own economic self-interest will result in the maximum possible satisfaction of the wants of all the members of the community.

Pareto starts by noting that dropping certain of these conditions pertaining to equality in the terms of exchange, a distinction emerges between two types of maxima of satisfaction, or utility, which he calls maxima *for* and *of* a collectivity, respectively.[34] The first is a point in a given process of change up to which the utilities of all the members of the collectivity without exception are affected in the same direction. This is the only type of maximum which can be treated on an economic level of analysis,[35] for the economic level is concerned with means only and precludes the comparative evaluation of the wants—that is, of the ultimate ends of different individuals. Going beyond this point involves, because it would benefit some individuals and groups to the detriment of others no matter what the numbers on each side, extra-economic con-

---

[34] *Ibid.*, Secs. 2128-29.   [35] *Ibid.*, Sec. 2130.

siderations precisely because it cannot dispense with such extra-economic evaluation.

The economic point of view is inherently distributive; it concerns the allocation as between competing wants of scarce resources. But the reason why this allocation, when the claims are conflicting, cannot be settled on economic grounds alone is that it involves the ethical consideration of relative claims of different individuals. But this is still a distributive question. It becomes meaningful on a sociological level just because the sociological level for Pareto does include the factor of ethical values, or ultimate ends, while the economic does not. But just because this is a distributive question, on the sociological level it becomes one of utility *for* the collectivity, not *of* it.

But on the sociological level this other set of considerations of utility does arise: that involved in defining a maximum *of* a collectivity.[36] Here the question is no longer distributive, a matter of settling relative claims of different individuals and groups within the community; it involves the treatment of the collectivity "if not as a person, at least as a unity." [37] This concerns value elements, at the rationalized pole ultimate ends, *common* to the members of the community, in a phrase which crept into the French edition of the *Traité: the end which a society should pursue.*[38]

What is the significance of this rather curious distinction, as it may seem to many? It concerns the senses in which the ultimate values of different members of a community are related to each other—the ends of the different means-end chains. The underlying, often implicit, assumption of much individualistic thought has been that they are random and relative to each other. Such has come to be more and more the explicit assumption of certain economic theorists, and is expressed in the theorem of the incomparability of the wants of different individuals.

Pareto's first qualification of this assumption of randomness may be interpreted to mean that the rational pursuit of purely "private" ends, unintegrated with those of others, is only possible as an aspect of a social system within the framework of a distributive order, a system of rules and practices which settle the relative claims of different individuals to

[36] *Ibid.*, Sec. 2133 ff.   [37] *Ibid.*, Sec. 2133.
[38] *Ibid.*, Sec. 2143. This phrase does not occur in the original Italian nor in the English translation, which was made from the Italian. Its occurrence in the French cannot, however, be regarded as a mere error of translation since first the translation was itself approved by Pareto who, himself as much French as Italian linguistically, would surely not have let such a thing slip at so crucial a point had he not meant it. Even more important, it fits very definitely with the line of his thought at this point.

desirable but scarce goods.[39] Pareto's statement that an "hypothesis" is necessary to render these claims comparable may, in its empirical application, be interpreted to mean that every functioning social system actually embodies such a system of rules which more or less effectively settles these claims. And, since such an hypothesis rests on judgments not of fact but of ethical value, in relation to different traits, achievements, and positions of status, a social order insofar involves a nonlogical element of the value order.

But this distributive aspect does not exhaust the question. There are equally involved in a social order certain common ethical elements which do not involve such a distributive aspect at all. By virtue of these a collectivity is not merely, as it were, "coerced" into unity in the sense of repressing potential internal conflict, but it constitutes a unity in a more positive sense, it involves the promotion of common ideals and ends—its members share a common "faith," as Pareto frequently says. The place in sociology of a maximum of utility *of* a collectivity indicates the empirical role of this common value element which is also nonlogical for the same reasons that the distributive standards are.

This element still further transcends the "atomism" of the predominant strain of individualistic thought, conceiving social unity as conditioned by an integration of values. It completes the elaboration of the total implications of the means-end schema at the intrinsic rational pole indicated by Pareto's initial concept of logical action.

Pareto's use of the phrase *if not as a person, at least as a unity* suggests the theoretical significance of this element. It is unquestionably an important version of what is sometimes called *the organic theory of society,* or better *the sociologistic theorem.* It is this element which constitutes society, in Durkheim's phrase, *a reality sui generis* not reducible to terms of its individual constituent parts, in this case the "private ends" of the individuals which make it up.

We may now turn to the second emergent theoretical element. . . . It concerns the significance of a fact which must strike any careful reader of Pareto forcibly—the very great prominence in his empirical examples of the nonlogical of a special type of actions which may roughly be called *ritual.* Almost the first case by which he illustrates the distinction of logical and nonlogical is that of the Greek sailors who, as a means of getting to port, on the one hand row and navigate, on the other make sacrifices to Poseidon (the latter is, of course, the nonlogical element).

---

[39] Which, for reasons which cannot be gone into here, focus on the two categories of wealth and power.

Similarly the first large-scale case in terms of which he illustrates his method of arriving at the residues is also a ritual case, that of magical practices aimed at control over the weather.[40]

Since ritual is so very prominent empirically in the work, the question naturally arises as to its theoretical significance in Pareto's scheme. But, beyond the mere fact that it is predominantly nonlogical, he gives no explicit answer. There is one highly interesting point at which he makes a distinction between ritual and nonritual acts, but curiously enough he drops it and does not develop its implications further.[41] One possible view is that ritual constitutes merely illogical action, that it is a manifestation of certain instinctive tendencies of men which simply have nothing to do with whatever modicum of rationality they may possess.

The first objection to this is the curiously close connection between theory and overt act in the case of ritual. In the case of action in pursuit of a specific end by rational means, the gap between the rational norm and the actual issue is often too conspicuous to be ignored. And to account for it, factors resistant to the realization of the norm must be posited. But in treating of the "theories" associated with ritual acts, Pareto often[42] goes so far as to include the means employed in the derivations which are ostensibly elements of theories, not of overt acts. In fact, in connection with ritual, what impresses Pareto is not the difficulty men find in living up to the prescriptions of their theories, not the difficulty of carrying out the sacrifices to Poseidon correctly according to the prescriptions of the ritual tradition. On the contrary, it seems to be assumed that this is very generally achieved. What impresses him is, rather, the arbitrariness of the "combinations" of means and end laid down in the prescriptions of the theories themselves. In other words, the peculiarities of ritual which make it nonlogical lie in the nature of the whole complex of action, "theories," and overt acts taken together, not in the relations of the theories to the acts.

A second possible interpretation is that the theories are simply erroneous, that with the progress of knowledge they will gradually be transformed into scientific theories and ritual actions will become "logical." There are several things in Pareto which argue against this as the principal interpretation. In the first place he warns in general that *"nonlogical* is not to be taken to mean *illogical,"* [43] and error is surely a case of illogicality. Secondly, with reference to nonlogical action in general, the main tenor of his argument is definitely against any progressive tendency for the nonlogical elements to be eliminated with the progress

---

[40] Pareto, *Traité* . . . , *op. cit.*, Secs. 186 ff.   [41] *Ibid.*, Sec. 167.
[42] For instance: *ibid.*, Secs. 863, 865.   [43] *Ibid.*, Sec. 150.

of science. He surely does not deny the existence of the latter, but at the same time his general emphasis is strongly on the relative constancy of nonlogical elements—which would argue that the nonlogical basis of ritual is not primarily error but, rather, something positive. Third, there are a good many specific statements which repudiate this interpretation in particular instances.

A third interpretation is possible. So far the ultimate value element has been dealt with only in its direct relations to "logical" action or, as I prefer to say, the intrinsic means-end schema. In the latter context it appears primarily in the role of ultimate ends. And, considering his starting point from the concept of logical action, it is not surprising that it is only this aspect which Pareto brought to explicit formulation at all in his theory of social utility. But there is no reason why this should be the only type of relation of the value element to action.

Perhaps the best starting point is a consideration of the connotations of the term *manifestation,* of which Pareto makes such frequent use. Such a proposition as "a residue is the manifestation of certain sentiments" seems to me to be open to two interpretations which fall in with the general dichotomy which has formed the main theme of this discussion. One is suggested by the analogy of the thermometer reading which Pareto himself used.[44] The thermal properties of mercury are such that when some of it is placed in a narrow vacuum tube and the end of the tube placed in a substance, the elevation of the mercury in the tube may be taken as an index of the thermal state of the substance. This is because the mercury in the tube and the substance in question both form part of the same system of physical causation or mutual interdependence —there is a causal interrelation between the two. Similarly, for instance, certain mental symptoms, as financial irresponsibility, may be taken in paresis as evidence of certain syphilitic lesions of the brain. Insofar as residues, which are propositions, are taken to be manifestations of instincts, the relation between manifestation and thing manifested is of this character.

On the other hand, the relation may be that between a symbol and its meaning. Insofar the causal relation is always "arbitrary" but the symbolic relation is nonetheless important to human life.[45] Thus a residue which, being a proposition, is after all a complex of linguistic symbols, may manifest sentiments in the sense that it is a symbolic expression of

[44] *Ibid.,* Sec. 875.
[45] Once a given symbol is accepted it of course comes to form part of a causal system but this depends on the phenomenon of "acceptance" which is foreign to physical systems.

a "state of mind." I think it a fair inference that insofar as the non-logical elements of action are value elements and not those of heredity and environment, the manifestation involved is predominantly of this and not the other character. There is, of course, no reason why the symbolic relation should be confined to such media as language, and altogether excluded from overt action.

What characterizes logical action in this respect is that the systems of symbols involved in it refer to or express systems of intrinsic relation-ships in the external world. Their "function" is that of intrinsic altera-tion of the external world in the service of an "end." But there is no reason why there should not equally be systems of symbols—i.e., "theo-ries" whose reference is not "objective" in this sense but "subjective," which manifest sentiments in the sense of forms of expression. Insofar as these theories imply and determine overt action, the action itself also becomes a form of expression, the function of which is not modification of the "real" world but something quite different.[46] In this case the theories, just because of their subjective reference, must necessarily be nonscientific and the action, hence, nonlogical.

Ritual, I should consider as one[47] of these modes of expression of values, of value attitudes in overt action. And indeed there are certain types of situations where the urge to such expression is particularly strong because of a combination of a strong interest in the value con-cerned and limitations on doing anything about it by intrinsic means. On the one hand, there is the type of situation where we have available certain intrinsic means of attaining an end but their inadequacy is such as to leave an important margin of uncertainty of success even with their most efficient possible employment. This is the situation which typically calls forth magical ritual, as in such activities as love and war. On the other hand, there are equally situations which bring us hard up against the absolute boundaries of human comprehension and control but where circumstances are such that we cannot remain indifferent—perhaps the most typical is death. It is this type of situation which occasions religious ritual.

Ritual, however, is not necessarily merely a mode of expression if by that is meant something functionally unimportant to action. The total action-system of a society is integrated in a way which makes it extremely unlikely such a prominent part of it could simply be dropped out with-

---

[46] The empirical line between these two types may well be quite indistinct with a gradual shading off.

[47] The other principal ones I should consider art and play. Limitations of space forbid entering into the distinctions here.

out repercussions on the rest. And indeed concrete studies of ritual, including Pareto's own, tend strongly to show that it is functionally highly important. Wherein then lies its function since, by definition, it cannot be intrinsically effective? The answer seems to be largely in relation to "effort." Ritual is largely important as a social mechanism for the maintenance of the tone of effort of a society.[48]

The theoretical scheme we have outlined, of course, by no means exhausts Pareto's sociological work. In particular he had a great deal to say about many more empirical subjects, highly interesting and important in themselves, but for which there is no space in the present discussion. At the same time this scheme and its ramifications are central to the work. I do not think it possible to get very far in the interpretation of any part of it without these questions becoming involved. Hence it has seemed worthwhile to devote the present article to the lucidation of this scheme and the theoretical problems growing immediately out of it.

. . . The problem of the rationality of human action undoubtedly forms one of the few main foci of modern social thought. The two aspects of the problem which constitute Pareto's main starting points, the role of scientific knowledge on the one hand, the "economic" problem on the other, constitute with equal certainty vitally important modes in which the more general problem has been involved in our intellectual tradition. Since these problems are the main focus of Pareto's theoretical scheme, I think there can be no doubt of the interest of his work to general social theory.

Within this general stream of thought his importance seems to me to lie mainly at two points. Outside Germany at least I think it is safe to say that the treatment of the problem of rationality has been in the main "positivistic." More specifically, it has been placed in the dilemma of accepting the theories of economic individualism as literally and concretely true, or insofar this position was rejected to fall back on psychological anti-intellectualism, above all some version of the "instinct" theory.

Pareto was one of the first to transcend this dilemma in a thoroughgoing way. In the first place he treated "logical action" as an element of concrete action, not as a class of acts. He thereby escaped the objectionable "reification" with which so much of orthodox economic theory has been burdened. Secondly, he treated nonlogical action as a genuine

---

[48] The general view of ritual presented here and, admittedly to a considerable extent read into Pareto, is closely related to that developed by Durkheim and some of the anthropologists especially of the "functional" school. See Durkheim, *Les formes élémentaires de la vie religieuse;* Malinowski, *Magic Science and Religion;* and Radcliffe-Brown, *The Andaman Islanders.*

residual category. The door was open for its content to emerge as a result of empirical study. For both of these results, a large share of the credit is due to his skeptical "natural science" methodology.

From this starting point, Pareto did not develop a satisfactory general theory of human action. His residue and derivation analysis is, however, properly understood, a highly useful analytical tool for certain purposes. At the same time we have shown that underlying his empirical work in the later parts of the *Treatise* are to be found emerging several further categories which can be given a place in an analytical theory of human action.

I submit that the aspect of Pareto's sociology to which this discussion has been devoted constitutes, in spite of its incompleteness, a major contribution to social theory. Both for understanding the rest of Pareto's work, and for the further development of the theory of action, a clear grasp of it is essential.

FIVE

THE SOCIOLOGY OF PARETO

MORRIS GINSBERG

PARETO's SOCIOLOGY falls naturally into two parts. The first is devoted to an analysis and classification of the elementary constituents of human nature as manifested in social life. The second is concerned with the interactions of these elementary traits and the changes which occur in their distribution in the different classes of society. The method followed is inductive and comparative—that is to say, it starts with empirical facts such as beliefs actually held in different societies, maxims of conduct accepted by them, and the like, and it seeks to analyze . . . the constant and variable elements in these forms of behavior and to discover the laws or uniformities which determine their mutual relations. Incidentally, Pareto discusses at great length the nature and importance of what he calls *the logico-experimental method* in social science, but he hardly lives up to his own requirements. The definitions given of fundamental terms are obscure, and they are not, as they might be expected to be, gradually clarified by "successive approximations." Further, what appears to me the most interesting portions of the treatise—namely, those devoted to the dynamics of social change—are very inadequately supported by empirical evidence, the facts given being hardly more than illustrative of the hypotheses put forward. The plan of the work is conceived on an imposing scale and it is carried out with great independence and a wealth of learning. It is therefore worthy of the serious consideration of sociologists.

The analysis of the fundamental forces of social life is carried out mainly by means of a classification of human actions into logical and nonlogical, and by a more detailed account of the nonlogical acts which

From *Reason and Unreason in Society*, by Morris Ginsberg. (First published in the United States by The Macmillan Company, 1960. The essay originally appeared in *The Sociological Review*, XXVIII: 3 [July 1936], 221-45.) Reprinted by permission of The Macmillan Company, Heinemann Educational Books, Ltd., and *The Sociological Review*.

brings out their overwhelming preponderance in human affairs. In this account Pareto pays no attention to the work of psychologists, but proceeds to put forward independent hypotheses suggested, as he thinks, by direct inspection of the facts. His neglect of psychology has resulted in an extremely vague use of such terms as *sentiments, instincts, interests,* which has made a proper understanding of his views more difficult than it needs to be.[1] But shed of technicalities and expressed as a first approximation, his conclusions are hardly revolutionary. They amount to this: that people perform and always have performed many acts without knowing why they do them (i.e., by habit and instinct); that the real drives of action are often quite different from the purposes which the agents consciously entertain; that in the pursuit of given conscious ends people often attain quite other ends than those aimed at, either because they adopt the wrong means, or because they do not foresee the remoter consequences of their acts; that men, having a hunger for logic or reason, will try to give a reasoned explanation or justification of acts they do from obscure or unconscious motives. The bulk of the treatise is devoted to an analysis of the nonrational elements in human conduct and of the fictions which are invented to give a flavor of rationality to conduct that is really the result of feeling and impulse.

The classification of acts into rational and nonrational or, in Pareto's not very happy terminology, *logical* and *nonlogical,* turns upon the distinction between means and ends which he assumes without further inquiry to be applicable to all human behavior. Briefly, acts are nonlogical (1) when they serve no end subjective or objective, e.g., futile or nonadaptive instinctive acts, if such there be; (2) when the agent thinks a particular end is being realized but nothing is in fact achieved through the act as judged in the light of wider knowledge, e.g., in magical operations; (3) when there is an objective end but the subject is not consciously aiming at it, e.g., in theoretically "pure" instinct; (4) when an end is actually achieved which differs from the end the subject sets to himself, whether the objective end would or would not have been acceptable to him could he have foreseen it. Briefly, acts are nonlogical when the subject acts without explicit knowledge of the purpose of his action, or, having such knowledge, chooses means which in the light of better grounded information are either not likely to achieve the purpose, or to achieve something else. By contrast, acts are logical when the consequences anticipated by the subject are identical with the consequences that might reasonably be anticipated in the light of wider knowledge. So

---

[1] Cf. William McDougall's criticism, "Pareto as Psychologist," *Journal of Social Philosophy,* I (October 1935).

far logic, or rather rational reflection, is not concerned with ends at all, save perhaps that in order to act rationally you must know what you want. Logic is concerned, rather, with the appropriate linking of means and ends. But this position is not consistently maintained. Unfortunately, Pareto makes no attempt to classify the ends of conduct or to relate them to the fundamental drives. These are said to consist of sentiments, tastes, proclivities, inclinations, instincts, residues, and interests. The residues are said to include neither the simple appetites or instincts nor the interests, but to "correspond to" instincts or appetites. By this, as we shall see later, appears to be meant that there is a residue when an appetite or instinct does not act itself out simply but finds expression in an indirect or disguised form. Thus sex conceived as mere union of the sexes is not a residue, but it is residual, for example, in the behavior of people who preach virtue as a way of lingering in their thoughts on sex matters. If this is the correct interpretation, the residues are not themselves drives, but rather ways in which the fundamental drives disguise themselves, and they are thus nonlogical in the sense of obscuring the nature of the impulses really at work. So far it would seem that the adequate fulfillment of *any* impulse, provided it is conscious and direct is logical. But there are many passages in which it seems to be suggested that it is more logical to act in accordance with one's interests than in accordance with other drives. What, then, are the interests? They are said to consist in impulses to acquire material goods, whether "useful" or merely pleasurable, and to seek consideration and honor (2009). It is not easy to see why these goods are singled out as rational—why, for instance, it is more logical to pursue honor and consideration than to satisfy other social impulses or, let us say, the desire for knowledge. Or is the pursuit of interests regarded as logical not because of the particular ends involved, but because in achieving them men can be shown to act with greater circumspection than in other activities in the choice of appropriate means?

The difficulty may be illustrated by reference to the frequent description of economic activity as typical of logical behavior. It is easy to see that economic activity contains a logical element insofar as the means chosen are technically appropriate to given ends. But economic behavior is clearly nonrational insofar as men acting economically are not aware of the motives which impel them. A man's choice of profession may be as an intention clearly envisaged. But the motives of the choice are often obscure and even unconscious. It may be influenced by all Pareto's residues, for example, by authority and prestige, by sociability, by the persistence of abstractions and what not. Further, it is clear that men, in seeking economic satisfaction, attain ends which they did not foresee and do not want. Men do not want war, but their behavior leads to it. Businessmen and workers do not want unemployment, but the outcome of their linked activities is to produce it. If success in the fulfillment of impulses is the criterion of logical behavior, economic activity must be largely nonlogical, since it fails to secure for the masses of men the conditions of a purposeful life. In short, without an examination of the ends of human endeavor and of their relations to each other as well as to the means available for their realization, it is impossible to throw much light on the rational elements in behavior, or on the relation of economic to other activities in human life.

There is a further complication which must now be considered. In the later portions of the treatise a person is said to act logically insofar as he tries to secure a maximum of individual utility. This means action in accordance with what is "advantageous" or "beneficial" to him and involves a comparison of different satisfactions in accordance with some norm. Presumably a logic is required for making these comparisons, but this line of thought is not pursued. In economics it would seem the individual is assumed to be the best judge of his own interests or utility and to act rationally in regard to it. But outside economics there may be an infinite number of norms and therefore an infinite number of possible maxima of utility. The choice of the norm itself is arbitrary and nonlogical. Thus we cannot say whether it is to the advantage of the individual to suffer physically for the sake of a moral satisfaction, or whether it is better for him to seek wealth or to apply himself to some other pursuits. Despite the elaborate discussion of utility, there is extraordinarily little to be gained from it. Since the norm is arbitrarily chosen, we can only determine the maximum utility for an individual from the line of conduct that he actually adopts. That is the maximum which in fact appears to him to be such and that appears to be the maximum which in fact he pursues. Or is it possible for the individual to make mistakes regarding what is to his advantage apart from the mistakes he may make in the choice of means? If so, a logic of ends is required which would enable the individual to distinguish apparent and real advantage, and that would soon lead to an ethics of the teleological kind which Pareto despises along with all other brands of ethics. In brief, Pareto's treatment of the logic of behavior leaves out of consideration what to most people will appear essential to it. Rational behavior no doubt requires us to know what we want and to choose means in a manner which will stand the test of empirical verification. But a logic of behavior would also have to discover whether the norms that individuals adopt in relation to the ends that they pursue are self-consistent, and whether they form part, or can be made to form part, of a systematic and ordered whole. Such a logic obviously could not be confined to the norms governing the acts of particular individuals, since it is equally or more important to inquire how far the norms of different individuals or groups are or can be made to be compatible and perhaps harmonious. Pareto makes no attempt whatever to deal with these problems and asserts as a self-evident dogma that norms are just the expression of "sentiments." There is, for example, no criterion save sentiment for choosing between a society based on large inequalities of income and one based on approximately equal incomes. If we admire supermen we will assign zero utility to the lower classes; if we love equality we will prefer the type of society which secures to the lower classes an equal share in the goods of life. Is reason really helpless in the face of such a problem?

It may be suggested that before dealing with the ultimate problems of valuation here involved there is a good deal that reason can do by way of clarifying the issues and settling questions of fact. Pareto, together with other anti-egalitarians, assigns a meaning to the principle of equality which egalitarians are not concerned to defend. The principle does not assert either that men are equal in endowment or that they should be treated equally. It is concerned, negatively, to exclude arbitrary assignments and, positively, to base distribution on a general rule impartially applied. If for the sake of argument it be agreed that this rule is that distribution should be in proportion to the needs of individuals with a view to the realization of such capacity in them as they have, it will be seen that this does not involve equality of treatment. Certain questions of fact then become very important. First, what is the extent of the differences in capacity between individuals, and are these so great as to justify us in regarding some of them as supermen and large numbers of the masses of men as having zero value? Second, how great are the differences in external conditions which are really required in order to enable the alleged supermen to fulfill their capacities, and can these differences in conditions only be assured them by a system of private property, involving the amount of inequality that now prevails? Third, we need to know what effects upon the total available for distribution will be produced by adopting the principle of equality, and this raises questions not only of economics but of psychology also, since we need to know how incentives work in different economic systems. Ultimately, no doubt, when these questions of fact have been answered, value judgments will have to be discussed, but it may be doubted whether they would then loom so large in the minds of the disputants. Pareto, at any rate, does not discuss the nature of value judgments, but merely asserts dogmatically that they express nothing but "sentiments." He is impressed by the fact that in moral judgments, for example, people are swayed by superstitions and prejudices which deceive themselves and others. But this applies to all human thought and action and, if seriously pressed, would lead inevitably to the conclusion that there can be no logical thought or action at all. Pareto also makes much of the argument that if ethical judgments permitted of rational examination, ethics would have made greater progress than it appears to have made since the days of Aristotle. This, however, is not substantiated by any examination of ethical systems. Moreover, it would apply with equal force to, say, economics right up to the eighteenth or nineteenth century, since it is by no means certain that any great advances were made in it in the interval between these periods and Aristotle's discussion of economic problems. Curiously enough, Pareto thinks that ethical discussions, though logically futile, have had great influence on social life: "they are forever shaking the foundations of the social order" (2002). A philosopher might say that this was no mean achievement for mere "derivations."

The difficulties in Pareto's theory of nonlogical actions are due ultimately to his failure to inquire more fully into the nature of logical or, as I should prefer to say, rational action. The function of reason is, according to him, exhausted in linking means and ends appropriately. But even Hume, who held a similar view, admitted that thought can influence action by disclosing the hollowness of objects of desire which before reflection excited lively passions, and it is clear further that many of our most passionate devotions are only possible on the reflective level. Thought and impulse cannot, in fact, be sharply dissevered and the ends of life cannot therefore be relegated to the sphere of impulse alone. Ends and means again profoundly affect one another, and it is impossible to deal logically with means without clarification of the nature of the ends. Reason, too, is concerned with the relations of the various ends to each other, with the possibility of their mutual consistency or harmony, and in cases of conflict with the grounds of preference. An element of generality in preferences cannot surely be denied. We prefer not only particular things to other particular things, but kinds of things to other kinds, and our orders of preference have a certain constancy; the business of reason is to reflect on the standards which are implicit in these intuitive judgments. If action can be rational at all, such reflection on values and standards of values must be able to claim validity. If, on the other hand, our choices and preferences are utterly arbitrary, there can be no sense in speaking of any action as rational or as logically justifiable. All that we could then do in a theory of conduct would be to describe and classify human actions as sheer matters of fact, and at most to inquire into the relations which men subjectively set themselves and the ends which are in fact attained by them. In such a theory of human conduct the belief that some acts are "logical" would only be one fact among others, and to deal with it "logico-experimentally" would mean to inquire whether it in fact satisfies the queer hunger for logic that men appear to have, or whether it is useful as a means to other ends. Its power to satisfy the demands of logic, at any rate, does not seem to be very great.

The theory of nonlogical actions is further elaborated by Pareto in his doctrine of the residues and derivations. Formal definition of the residues is lacking and we can only rely upon an analysis of the very numerous examples given and the classification offered of the principal types. To begin with, the residues are not identical with what psychologists call *instincts*. They are expressly said not to reflect all the instincts, and to include neither the simple appetites, tastes, or inclinations, nor what he understands by interests. Yet the residues "correspond to" the instincts, and it is pointed out that there may be residues corresponding also to other impulses, though these are not further dealt with. The meaning seems to be this. Insofar as the fundamental impulses are realized directly without diversion or substitution of object, they do not give rise to residues. Animals who are supposed to act on pure instinct can have no residues, and in human beings the simple satisfaction of food or sex impulses is not residual. The sex residue becomes important when we recognize its influence in such phenomena as asceticism. Only creatures capable of theorizing, and therefore of deceiving themselves, can have residues. A classification of the residues would thus be a classification of the different ways in which the fundamental impulses realize themselves in human behavior, excluding, on the one hand, fully conscious and experimentally directed behavior, and on the other, behavior which is based on simple and direct impulse. If this is the right interpretation, the ultimate dynamic elements in human nature are not to be found in the residues but rather in what Pareto calls the *sentiments*. The residues are the patterns or principles in accordance with which the sentiments work, and they can only be discovered by an analytic and comparative study of complex acts, in which the influence of the sentiments may not at first sight be at all obvious. In studying them Pareto is thus trying to discover the different ways in which the sentiments unconsciously affect belief and action.

Pareto does not undertake, as might have been expected, an analysis of such processes as repression, projection, aim inhibition, substitution or sublimation, symbolization, dramatization, and the like. Of the work done in this connection he appears to have no knowledge. Yet, despite his repudiation of psychological methods, what he here attempts to do is psychological and not sociological. He does not endeavor to study the social influences affecting belief and behavior, but on the contrary finds the explanation of social behavior in the permanent underlying psychological elements and their varying combinations in different societies, and his conclusions must be therefore tested from the point of view of their adequacy in the light of psychology. Thus regarded, his account is not very impressive. He gives six classes of residues with numerous subdivisions; namely, combinations, persistent aggregates, sociability, activity, the integrity of the individual, and sex.

The residue of combinations is of such wide scope that it really includes the whole synthetic activity of the mind, the operations of science and of constructive imagination, and, indeed, all forms of association. Behind all these there is apparently a single drive to combine elements into aggregates. That the mind has a tendency to combine or synthesize is true, though it is equally true that it has a tendency to break up or analyze, and no account of mental activity can be given unless both these tendencies are taken into consideration. But in any case the resort to such general tendencies takes us but a little way, and it is important to discover the principles in accordance with which the various forms of analysis and synthesis are effected. As far as the underlying motive is concerned, it cannot be assumed that it is just an urge to combine. This is certainly not the case either in purely theoretical or practical activity. When Pareto comes to distinguish the different types of combination he is far too ready to rely on his assumed general tendency just to combine. This leads him to stress unduly the arbitrariness of the combinations, as in his account of magical operations, or to adopt familiar principles of association such as of similars or opposites which permit of more refined psychological analysis. Magical practices, for example, do not rest upon a general tendency to combine anything and everything, but upon a readiness, under the stress of practical needs and in the absence of a critical method, to rely on coincidences. There is always an element of experience behind them, though this is too readily generalized and no adequate means are available for disentangling the subjective and objective factors. The tendency to generalize on a slender basis has a much better claim to be called a residue than the tendency to arbitrary combinations. No doubt the experiences underlying a particular belief may be difficult to detect, and Pareto is undoubtedly right in stressing the difficulty of tracing the historical origins of ancient or primitive magical beliefs. Yet occasionally what appears to be an arbitrary association can be shown by historical analysis to be based on intelligible—though, of course, not scientifically founded—associations. To say "five" in order to avert the evil eye may seem hopelessly arbitrary. Yet in Morocco, according to Westermarck, this is a remnant of the ancient practice of throwing the hand forward with outspread fingers and saying "five in your eyes"; which has now become attentuated to just saying "five" or even "Thursday." Here the original practice requires examination in accordance with the psychology of the magic of gestures, and is in line with much else of the pantomimic or dramatic in magic. In all cases an analysis of the objective and subjective conditions determining belief in particular connections is necessary. It is mere evasion of the issue to appeal to purely general tendencies capable of explaining all connections, and therefore not specially helpful in dealing with any of them.

Under the heading of the persistence of aggregates Pareto brings together a number of interesting facts, but here again the analysis is not very illuminating from the psychological point of view. At least two rather different things are here confused. One is the tendency for sets of psychological dispositions which have grown up between a person and other persons or things to cohere and persist in time. This requires analysis in terms of Shand's doctrine of the sentiments and the theory of complexes. The other is the tendency to individualize or to regard as single entities groups of experiences in relation to which sentiments have grown up, and to attribute to these entities, real or imaginary, any further attributes which our emotional attitude to them requires. The phenomena here included have usually been studied under the headings of animism, animatism, personification, and the like, and to their elucidation, I should say, Pareto makes very little contribution, except perhaps in the stress he lays on the influence of personified or reified abstractions on social life.

Under the residue of activity Pareto discusses facts which are usually treated by psychologists under the heading of the expression of the emotions and other drives and the pleasure taken in the exercise of faculty. He rightly stresses the part played by fantasy or imagination in providing symbolic expression of the emotions, but does not further analyze symbolism, nor does he inquire into the reasons why symbolic substitution is needed. The principal examples that he uses are taken from the phenomena of religious exaltation, such as revivals, mystical ecstasies, and the like. But his interpretations of these phenomena are of very doubtful value. There is much to be said for the view that ecstatic manifestations are due not so much, as he thinks, to a sheer need for activity as to the need for relaxation from the strain and monotony of ordinary life and for release from repression and conflict. In political agitation, which is another of his examples, the feeling that "something must be done" is hardly due to a desire for activity as such. On the contrary, in the case of leaders and agitators it is rooted in deep conflicts, and in the masses the readiness to yield to leaders who claim to get things done is a reflection of their own apathetic anxiety and the disinclination or inability to do anything effective themselves. The whole discussion is extraordinarily vague. It is not at all clear whether the residue of activity is a specific tendency to act, or whether it is a collective term for the need of expressing all the emotions and impulses in outward acts. In any event, to find the residual—that is to say, the constant and invariable—elements in religious manifestations in bare activity without any attention to the nature of the emotions and needs which are at work can hardly be said to constitute a profound contribution to the psychology of religion.

The residues of sociability include a number of tendencies, principally the desire for uniformity; the desire to impose uniformity on others; the hatred of the new, counterbalanced by interest in novel combinations; the tendency to pity, balanced by cruelty; the tendency to share with others, to suffer for them even to the extent of self-sacrifice; the need for the approval of others; the compound of submission, fear, respect, pride, and domination which constitutes the psychological basis of hierarchical organization, and others. The account given of these tendencies, and especially the discussion of asceticism, is of great interest, but it is not very precise or systematic, and there is too great a readiness to invent instincts ad hoc. The desire for uniformity, for example, is hardly to be accounted for in terms of a general instinct to imitate. Psychologists are not agreed that such an instinct exists, and, in any case, the respect for rules qua rules is very complex. There is a rational element in it based on the recognition that for societies to cohere there must be a readiness on the part of individuals to conform to rules without insisting on a reasoned justification on every occasion of their application. Such recognition may not be very clearly present to the minds of all members, but there is always present a feeling that order must be maintained and that there must be rules. Whether rational or not, the feeling of respect for accepted rules does not rest on sheer imitativeness, but on deeper social bonds. The purest form of the tendency to imitate Pareto sees in fashion; but here again the analysis strikes me as superficial. Fashion is not based on a tendency to imitate anything and everything, but rather upon an identification with those who have social prestige, and thus involves at least as much desire to be distinguished from others as to be like them. In regard to his account of the other social tendencies, it may be noted that Pareto owes much of his recent popularity to the cynical account he gives of humanitarianism. Anything more remote from logico-experimental evidence can hardly be imagined. He imputes all sorts of motives to humanitarians without the slightest attempt at proof, and indulges in vast historical generalizations without anything like adequate inductive verification. It is one of his favorite generalizations that repugnance to suffering and the tendency to pacifism are characteristic of élites in decadence. One might counter this by formulating ad hoc the parallel generalization that brutality and war-mongering are characteristic of élites uncertain of their power. For neither generalization is there adequate evidence of the "logico-experimental" kind that Pareto considers essential for a scientific sociology.

The treatment of asceticism as a residue of sociability is striking. Pareto interprets ascetic behavior as, in the main, due to a hypertrophy or perversion of the social instincts, or—as it might perhaps be better put —as an exaggeration of the need to control and master the self-assertive impulses. The interpretation is worked out with much insight, but perhaps insufficient attention is paid, especially in the elaborate discussion of flagellation and allied phenomena, to the sado-masochistic elements in asceticism.

The residue of the integrity of the individual broadly includes all reactions tending to maintain equilibrium or to restore a violated equilibrium. It is not at all clear whether this is a specific tendency, how it is related to what psychologists call *the self-regarding sentiment,* and whether it is not merely a collective term for a group of reactions. In a sense all responses whatever may be brought under it, since they may all be interpreted as the result of a disturbance due to inner or outer stimuli. The examples that Pareto gives here are mainly derived from ritual. Thus purificatory rites are regarded as efforts to restore the integrity of the individual which has been disturbed by pollution. But here, as in the case of the residue of combinations, the tendency appealed to is so general that it would explain all ritual whatever and therefore throws but little light on any. Why is the integrity of the individual endangered by contact with blood, and why is the malaise produced by this pollution got rid of just by this or that form of purificatory ritual? To say that these are just arbitrary combinations is surely to abandon the problem. There is, I think, a somewhat similar difficulty in Lévy-Bruhl's treatment of what he calls *transgressions,* with which

Pareto's discussion has some affinity. For example, it is not an explanation but only a restatement of the problem to say that the horror of incest is due to the fact that it is treated as a transgression.[2]

Somewhat unexpectedly, Pareto brings under the residue of the integrity of the individual the demand for equality by inferiors. He interprets this demand as really a hidden desire for another kind of inequality or selfish privilege. Perhaps this is not as pessimistic a view as that of Freud, who suggests that social justice means that we are ready to deny ourselves many things so that others may have to do without them as well.[3] But what direct evidence is there of the real motives which inspired the leaders of humanitarianism or the mass of their followers? In general, Pareto's attack on humanitarian ethics hardly calls for detailed analysis here. His arguments are very far from being presented with the detachment which he considers so necessary in a logico-experimental sociology and they abound in value judgments. Since such judgments are in Pareto's view nothing but the expression of "sentiments," his discussion has merely biographical interest insofar as it throws light on Pareto's own mentality.

In his treatment of the residue of sex Pareto brings out with great gusto the vagaries and inconsistencies of sexual morality and he stresses the well-known fact that behind the condemnation of sex there is often hidden an excessive preoccupation with it. He might have generalized this and shown how in the case of other impulses the repression of self takes revenge in the reprobation of others. In this discussion even more than elsewhere the fundamental weakness of his method is revealed. In his anxiety to stress the constant and invariable elements in sex he fails to come to grips with the medley of social forces affecting the morals of sex relationships and to deal with the variations that have been observed in them. One almost gets the impression that the rules regulating the relations between the sexes and the respect for chastity are based on nothing but disguised sexual greed and jealousy. There is no study of the need to canalize and control the sexual impulses in view of the manifold derangements of which they are susceptible, no examination of the relation of sex to tenderness and affection and the social impulses, or of the problems connected with precocious sexuality, or of the influence on sex relationships of the institutions of property and the family. In short, there is no treatment of the numerous factors, sociological and psychological, which must be taken into consideration in a just estimate of sex regarded as a constant and invariable drive.

[2] Cf. Lévy-Bruhl, *Le Surnaturel et la nature dans la mentalité primitive.*
[3] Cf. Sigmund Freud, *Group Psychology and the Analysis of the Ego.*

The theory of the derivations is intended to furnish a psychology rather than a logic of error—that is, to reveal the hidden forces which lead to error and make it acceptable rather than to disclose the logical structure of erroneous reasoning. Clearly the derivations must be rooted in the residues. There is, in fact, a double connection between them. First, men have a strange hankering after logic and they are not satisfied unless they can give reasons for their actions and beliefs. This Pareto regards as being one form of the residue of combinations which supplies the drive both for logical and nonlogical reasoning. But, second, particular derivations owe their strength and influence to other residues and the sentiments underlying them. That the ultimate driving power lies in the sentiments or their residual manifestations and not in the theories which are offered to account for behavior can be seen, Pareto argues, from the fact that the feelings or sentiments remain essentially unaltered despite changes in derivations and theories. He is fond of using, in this connection, examples derived from the history of morals: "A Chinese, a Moslem, a Calvinist, a Catholic, a Kantian, a Hegelian, a Materialist, all refrain from stealing; but each gives a different explanation for his conduct." Strangely enough, Pareto claims greater constancy for moral rules than is needed for a rationalist ethic, and he makes no attempt whatever to account for the variability of the moral judgment. The residue of the integrity of the individual will account for the laws of theft, but only if you are content to neglect the enormous variations that are found in the laws of property and consequently in what is regarded as theft, and so with other institutions. While both the varying and constant elements in morals contain both rational and nonrational elements, I do not think that Pareto provides any method for estimating their relative strength—for determining, for example, the role of reason in the history of law or indeed of any social or political movement—though nowadays no one would be concerned to deny the importance of the irrational or even unconscious factors in human life.

The interest of Pareto's treatment of the derivations lies largely in his acute and penetrating criticism of many famous social theories—for example, of Benthamism or of the General Will—for which it provides an occasion. It is not particularly successful as a systematic exposition of the sources of prejudice and modes of sophistication. The derivations are grouped under four headings: affirmation, authority, accord with sentiments, and verbal arguments. Under the first are included assertions claiming authority simply as assertions. The examples that he gives are maxims such as "Silence is an ornament to all women"; "Neither do nor learn aught that is shameful." These correspond, I think, to what

Mill calls fallacies a priori, mere assertions claiming to be self-evident. It is not easy to see where derivation comes in here, since, by definition, no reason is given for the assertion, unless what is meant is that if challenged the answer will be just their indisputability. Pareto does not discuss the psychological factors which produce the feeling of self-evidence, nor why assertions that are regarded as self-evident in one age are considered nonsensical or false in another. Occasionally the examples chosen beg important questions of theory, as when aesthetic judgments are interpreted as unconscious conversions of subjective likings into assertions of objective fact. I doubt whether the derivations of affirmation form a distinct class, and in most instances they pass readily into those resting on authority or verbal argument. The derivations of authority have long been familiar, and among the writers whom Pareto quotes in other connections, he might here have referred to Bentham, who has given an elaborate discussion of them.[4] The derivations of accord with feeling present a good opportunity for a consideration of the subjective factors of belief, and Pareto has much of interest to say on the influence of the self-assertive and the social tendencies upon belief. Here his analysis would have been greatly improved had he paid attention to the work of modern psychology, and especially the psychology of the unconscious. In his discussion of the derivations of verbal argument, the logical aspect is not kept very distinct from the psychological. Perhaps the most valuable part of his exposition is his insistence on the tendency of abstractions to persist and to become the nuclei of powerful emotional dispositions.

Pareto has no doubt that the residues remain constant or undergo only slight and slow change even over long periods. But though this may be true in a sense, the proof offered is not very convincing. The residues are so vaguely defined that it is easy to find what is alleged to be the same residue in what are apparently very different social movements. In this way it is argued, for example, that behind ancestor worship, polytheism, Catholicism, Protestantism, nationalism, socialism, [and] humanitarianism there is the same residue of group persistence. So again the residue of individual integrity is regarded as constant, because though it is not so strong in the modern plutocracy as it was, say, in the feudal nobility, the loss is made up by the growth of self-respect on the part of the lower classes and in the recognition that even criminals have a personality deserving of consideration. A humanitarian may be pardoned for thinking this "compensation" a matter of some importance. Even more surprising is the claim that the residues of combination have

---

[4] Cf. Bentham, *Works,* Vol. II: *The Book of Fallacies.*

not changed much if the class is considered as a whole, on the ground that territory formerly occupied by magic, theology, and metaphysics is now increasingly occupied by experimental science which is also a product of the residue of combinations. Units of comparison so pliable and interchangeable are hardly what one would expect to find in a logico-experimental sociology.

The most interesting and suggestive part of Pareto's treatise is that concerned with the dynamics of social change and the factors determining social equilibrium at any one time. The social system is conceived as made up of the elements which have hitherto been considered in abstraction but which in fact are in a relation of mutual dependence. The elements in question are the residues, the derivations, and the interests, and since these are differently distributed in the population, account has to be taken of individual differences and of the amount of circulation or movement from one group to another that occurs in given societies. The important influences, he thinks, are those exerted by the interests—that is, broadly—of economic factors on the residues and upon their distribution in the different social classes and the converse influence of the changing distribution of the residues on the interests. On the other hand, the influence of theories of derivations on the residues is slight, if not negligible. The interaction of these elements is such as to result in undulations or oscillations, movement in one direction usually setting up compensatory movements in the opposite direction, with the result that change is not in a straight line but is cyclical in character.

The individual differences that Pareto considers at length are those in the intensity or strength of the residues of combinations and persistent aggregates. He lays special stress on one particular classification. In both the ruling classes or elite and in the masses, though in different proportions, two types are to be found. There are, on the one hand, individuals of the speculator type, enterprising, eager for new experiences, imaginative, expansive, fertile in new ideas. Contrasted with them are people of the *rentier* type—timid, conservative, anxious to preserve what has been won, averse to anything new. The differing relative proportions in which these two types are combined in the governing class and the extent to which recruitment from below is permitted determine the different types of social structure and civilization. In the political sphere, for example, if the governing class consists of individuals in whom Class 2 residues predominate over Class 1 residues, we find types of government which rely chiefly on physical force and on religious and similar sentiments; on the other hand, if the ruling class is chiefly of the speculator type, we find types of government relying chiefly on intelligence and cunning, and appealing either to the sentiments of the multitude, as in the theocratic forms of government, or else playing upon the interests, as in the demagogic plutocracies of modern times. The changes that occur as a result of the predominance of one or other of these types are not, however, in a continuous direction. Compensatory movements occur, whether as a result of internal changes or of war, and oscillations of varying length are thus produced. It is to be noted that the distinction between the speculator and *rentier* types does not quite correspond to that between liberal and conservative in the political sense, since the speculators will ally themselves with or make use of liberal and conservatives alike—and even of anarchists if it suits their purpose. Revolutions occur mainly when the ruling class, relying too much on the combination residues, develops an enervating humanitarianism and is disinclined to use force, especially if it cultivates a policy of exclusiveness and does not find ways of assimilating the exceptional individuals who come to the front in the subject classes. On the other hand, a governing class may also encompass its own ruin by accepting, for their economic value, individuals who are well endowed with Class 1 residues, and this may end in the government passing from the lions to the foxes. History shows, Pareto thinks, that changes in the proportions between Class 1 and Class 2 residues in the élite do not continue indefinitely in one direction, but are sooner or later checked by movements in a counterdirection. In this way the modifications in the élite are shown to be among the major factors determining the undulatory form of social change. They are correlated, it is claimed, not only with political transformations but also with economic cycles and with oscillations in thought and culture. Thus in periods of rapidly increasing economic prosperity the governing class comes to contain greater numbers of individuals of the speculator type, rich in Class 1 residues, and fewer of the opposite type; while the converse is the case in periods of economic depression or retrogression. With these alternations are connected also the oscillations that Pareto traces in the history of thought, expressed roughly in the conflict between "reason" and "superstition," skepticism and faith.

It will be noted that in this theory Pareto is not merely replacing the Marxist conception of a struggle between bourgeoisie and proletariat by that of a struggle between speculators and *rentiers*. It is essential to his thesis that the residues are differently distributed in the ruling and ruled groups, and it is on the balance of the residues in both groups that social equilibrium depends. Further, it is in this part of his inquiry that Pareto

makes the transition from individual psychology to sociology proper—
that is to say, to a study of interactions between individuals. His view
does not imply that the course of events is determined by the schemes
of individual speculators who rule the world by deliberate and concerted
stratagem. Their policy is the resultant of a complex set of forces and an
infinite number of acts, each initiated by the particular circumstances of
the time, but leading collectively to results which individually they do
not foresee, despite the fact that they may have a clearer conception of
their own interests than the masses have of theirs. Here, as elsewhere in
the *Treatise,* Pareto insists on the great complexity of social interactions
and on the need for replacing the notion of one-sided causality by that
of mutual dependence of the factors involved.

How far the theory of the circulation of the élites is to be interpreted
in biological or genetic terms is not very clear. Pareto undoubtedly
thinks that the residues are determined by inherited constitution. Further, it would seem that in his view "aristocracies" tend to die out, in
the sense of leaving no descendants: "History is the graveyard of aristocracies." On the other hand, one gets the impression that, according to
him, the residues are remarkably constant in a given society taken as a
whole apart from infiltration of individuals from other societies. The
changes that occur are rather in the distribution of the residues in the
different portions of the population and the opportunities offered for
their manifestation. Such changes might well occur without involving
any genetic changes in the stock and be largely socially conditioned.
Pareto refers now and again to the work of the anthroposociologists—
e.g., Lapouge and Ammon—but he seems to have paid little attention to
modern studies of individual differences and the effects of differential
fertility, and one cannot be sure of his attitude to them. As the residues
clearly involve temperamental traits in addition to cognitive ones, and
as the evidence of individual differences in temperamental traits is very
slight, perhaps he would not have been able to get much help from these
studies.

Pareto supports his theory of social change by numerous examples
derived from the history of Greco-Roman civilization and of modern
Europe. Brilliant as the exposition is, it is hardly adequate to establish
the periodicity of social and political movements as a regular law, or
the correlations alleged between these movements and the history of
thought and culture. The proof of such a law would require a much
more exact social morphology than he provides and an extension of the
inquiry to non-European civilizations. It would also require independent

evidence of the mental makeup of the different social groups, especially of the individuals directly concerned in social movements, and a more exact determination of the nature and extent of what he calls *the circulation of élites*. It may be remarked that he makes very little use of the work of others. Occasionally he might have found support for some of his theories. It is worth mentioning that Pirenne's later study of European capitalism, and the explanation that he gives of the alternations traced by him between periods of innovation and periods of stabilization, appear to be in line with Pareto's views.

If the occurrence of undulatory movements in history be granted, there remains the important problem of their significance from the point of view of long-range trends. Pareto himself grants that in economic production and in the arts and sciences there has been on the whole a movement forward, or as he expresses it, Class 1 residues and the conclusion of logico-experimental science have forced a retreat on group persistences. But he insists that this growth in the power of reason has not affected political and social activities to any great extent, and that in any case there is no ground for the belief in continuous progress. The notion of progress is never mentioned by him without bitter derision. But it will be noticed that, though according to him there can be no reliable criteria of progress, he does not hesitate to speak of decadence, which requires criteria of the same kind. To me it is clear that Pareto has developed no adequate method for estimating the role of reason in law, morals, and politics, and that he vastly underestimates what has on the whole been achieved in these directions. The growing interconnection between economic and social and political movements which he himself stresses is an important phenomenon and one which may compel humanity to make increasing use of rational agencies. The fact also that the notion of conscious control of social change in its application to humanity as a whole is relatively new must be taken into consideration in estimating future trends. No one nowadays believes in automatic progress or in indefinite and unlimited perfectibility. What is asserted is that it is theoretically possible to formulate a coherent ideal of human endeavor, and that from a study of the failures as well as the successes of mankind in dealing with its problems, there is ground for the belief that such an ideal permits of realization if men are prepared to work for it. Pareto's denial of human progress rests upon (1) his disbelief in any rational ethics; (2) his view that history so far has disclosed no significant changes but only oscillations. As to (1), I do not find that he provides any reasoned justification for his disbelief. As to

(2), it seems to me that he greatly exaggerates the constant elements in human history, and that if there is no law of human progress neither is there any law of cyclical recurrence. From the point of view of policy, in any event, if a choice is to be made between persistent aggregates and combinations, I see no reason for not choosing combinations.

SIX

A MANIFESTO OF OUR TIME

FRANZ BORKENAU

ON ELITES

ONLY IN ONE SECONDARY respect is the theory of residues and derivations connected with the theory of elites. The latter stands out as an independent body of concepts, to be discussed separately. And certainly the group of ideas here concerned is the most interesting in Pareto's sociology, and probably the one containing the greatest amount of objective truth. . . .

The first of [his] axioms is the necessary existence of differentiation among men. This differentiation, Pareto very justly contends, takes place in every respect. As men are of different physical strength and different mathematical or poetical talent, so they differ in respect of economic ability, general intelligence, and fitness to rule (2025). This, we believe, is an undeniable fact. Certainly differentiation of surroundings is not sufficient to account for all differences between man and man. It is true that aptitude develops in a favorable and is retarded in an adverse milieu. But it is equally certain that differences of talent in different respects are found among people living in very similar conditions. This argument is decisive in confuting some naïve egalitarians who seriously believe in the abolition of all natural differences between men as a consequence of a possible abolition of all institutional differentiation. In addition, there seems to be evidence that no society, however it was organized, could give really the same share in government to all its citizens, though formal rights may be entirely equal. . . .

Following on this, Pareto takes a second step. He assumes that the economic, political, and social gradation of society corresponds to the natural differentiation in abilities. Partly, this argument is tautological,

From *Pareto*, by Franz Borkenau (New York: John Wiley & Sons, Inc., 1936), pp. 106-11, 114-17, 129-30, 157-58, 163, 164-68. Reprinted by permission of John Wiley & Sons, Inc.

for he insists that abilities—in his conception—are not the same as objective ability in any sense, but simply ability to do what is done in social life. Economic ability, for instance, is not meant to be utility for the procuring of the highest standard of wealth for the society, but the ability to secure individual economic success in a given society. If this society has unreliable business habits, then economic success will mainly depend on the ability to cheat, and the economic elite in such a society may consist of the best cheats. Undeniably, there is a great deal of truth in the argument. . . .

An even stronger argument could be made in favor of Pareto's view. There is no doubt that a leading group . . . need not only be highly gifted in some special direction, but must consist on the average of what are usually called *strong personalities*, possessing to a high degree some general aptitude. Intelligence tests in American schools have shown beyond question that the average intelligence of bourgeois children is higher than that of the children of the poor. . . . One may assume that the very best of the lower class climb into the upper class, so that the remainder of the former may be somewhat inferior to the average of the latter. But, on the other hand, the children of the higher classes must be supposed to grow up in a sheltered position, protecting them from falling quickly even if they lack talent, and this fact presumably alters the balance in favor of the poor. If the final outcome is definitely in favor of the upper class, some natural difference in talent is likely to have its part in it. This part must be diminishing where the circulation of elites—the climbing of the poor into the ranks of the rich—is seriously hampered. This result would completely agree with Pareto's assumption. . . .

There are, however, two other axioms hidden in Pareto's theory of elites, arguments conducive to further steps in this theory. The first takes domination as an immediate consequence of the differentiation of abilities, and the second assumes a direct quantitative correspondence between the distribution of abilities and the distribution of elites. . . .

As to the first argument, like so many other essential points of his doctrine, Pareto never explains it *expressis verbis*. He distinguishes between parts of the elite which do not rule (such as the scientific or artistic elite), and the ruling part of the elite (2032). He seems to assume that the mere fact of a group of men being able and willing to rule is sufficient to explain the existence of domination. Abhorring any research into the "origins" of institutions, it never occurs to him that possibly the existence of a group of men with qualities of domination may not be the actual reason but only one among different conditions for the coming about of domination.

. . . Marx believed domination to be simple "superstructure," or "reflex," or consequence of economic differentiation, but closer research has shown that political rule has an existence of its own, independent of economics. Pareto, on his side, takes domination as a simple "super-structure," or "reflex," or consequence of natural differentiation between men, and his view is exposed to the same doubt and criticism as Marxism in this respect.

Does he not, in reality, contradict himself? Communities, during a long war, need a leading group of warriors, he contends most justly. We may assume that the community will either prove able to produce such a group and to put it into political power, or will break down. But have the warriors (for instance the Roman "military emperors" in the third century B.C.), then, really come into power as a simple result of their military qualities? Far from it. . . . War was the condition of their coming into power and this war was not the result of their own rule (since it broke out when others ruled). This Pareto acknowledges in another connection, insisting strongly in his criticism of democracies upon their liability to drift into war in spite of their peaceful temper (2178). . . . Does this not imply that situations form elites at least as much as elites form situations?

. . . Domination must be explained as a social need and not as a desire or intention of the elite. If the necessity for domination is understood, then and then only the function of the dominating group can be made intelligible. . . .

. . . If elites are the very best and strongest, why then do they degenerate? Why do they decline in numbers? As a matter of fact, high-bred pedigree animals do not. But "the aristocracies do not last. For one reason or another, after a certain time they disappear (2053). . . . To us it seems to demonstrate that biological facts, though probably involved in the phenomenon of political differentiation, are not sufficient to account for it. . . . To us it seems evident that the continuance and disappearance of aristocracies are both due to a change in social milieu. In rising, elites change completely the atmosphere of life. When their status is low, they have been stimulated by their sufferings and by the possibility of success. At the top of society, they usually soon become more anxious to keep what they have than to conquer what they lack. Instead of stimulating conditions, enervating conditions supervene. . . . Military aristocracies, as long as they have been in conditions of continual warfare, generally do not show any decay in numbers or in their characteristic qualities, as can be shown throughout the last centuries by the Prussian aristocracy. Aristocracies living in a milieu of activity and enterprise do not decline either, as can be seen from the long-lasting strength of the aristocracy of Venice. But aristocracies which are spared hard struggle, decline. . . .

. . . Two types of elites are distinguished and identified by exhibiting quick and slow circulation, the one dominated by Residue 1, the other by Residue 2 (2178). And these two types of elites are again identified with two economic types: one being the speculator, following the lure of new combinations; the other being the *rentier,* who keeps anxiously to a fixed income (2233). Out of these two types of elites arise two types of social order. The one is conservative, military, religious, using force as the main method of government. The circulation of elites is slow; economic stimulus, weak. In the opposite case economic interests supercede military ones: the costs of government are high, but so is economic stimulus; the conservative virtues decline, and finally the leading class, degenerating into humanitarianism, proves unable to keep the political power. Revolution or defeat in war ensues and puts an end to this part of the cycle. For Pareto assumes that there is a continuous change between these two forms of government. . . .

Pareto is convinced that history proceeds by cycles or undulations. In this he agrees with Hegel—without, of course, being aware of it. There is only one essential difference between the two. Hegel insisted upon the recurrence of the same problems and of the same forms of social life in different civilizations, but he considered the differences as well, believing every civilization to be characterized by one specific dominating concern. . . . Now Pareto here as in other instances stresses exclusively sameness. And in the case of the cyclical movement, where experimental evidence is and must be lacking, this assumption takes the aspect of a metaphysical axiom overtly proclaimed. . . . Here Pareto is very near Nietzsche's idea of eternal recurrence, but Nietzsche's hope in the breaking of the eternal cycle through the appearance of superman is absent. . . . Pareto is a man whose political and social ideal has been broken, and who, opposed to the dominating ideal of his day (or rather to the declining ideal of his day), is unable to oppose another ideal to it and makes pessimism his program and his belief. For the characteristic fact is that pessimism in this context is not simply a contemplative attitude and an unfavorable judgment on life, but gives rise to a political ideology intended to act, an ideology of force, suppression, and conservatism. . . .

THE IMPORTANCE OF PARETO'S SOCIOLOGY

. . . Is this sociology worth careful study? Taking into account only the objective scientific value of his theories, one might be entitled to doubt it. . . . [Pareto's] sociology has been described as an attempt to apply behaviorism to social science. . . . But Pareto's sociology is not really behavioristic. . . . Though, of course not entirely devoid of empirical elements, . . . [it] is in reality a philosophy of society, a social creed, determined mainly by violent political and even purely personal passions. . . . In this respect, Pareto's sociology certainly does not rank very high.

But let us consider the objective value of the new elements introduced into social science by Pareto. The theory of cycles is not to be counted in this respect, as it is by no means Pareto's own. There remain the theories of residues, derivations, and elites as the essential elements of his system. . . . The theory of residues is apt to focus increased attention on the study of sentiments, before considering their transformation in the process of social adjustment. Pareto does not want to be a psychologist, and he certainly is not one. But the real merit of the theory of residues lies in the stressing of the axiom that there can be no satisfactory sociology without psychology. . . .

The theory of derivations is very valuable indeed in putting us on our guard against accepting "ideologies" at their face value. Here, Pareto has followed the indications of Marx and Nietzsche, two authors who deeply influenced him. . . .

[Pareto] is most original and most consistent and successful in his theory of the elites. He certainly does not stand alone with [it] . . . but he has given the theory a more systematic development than any of his predecessors. . . .

Generally speaking, his talent seems to be essentially a critical one. . . . The theory of residues and derivations gives a real knockout blow to dying rationalism, whereas the theory of the elites pierces the shades of egalitarianism. It was his violent hatred of humanitarianism and democracy which was at the root of these critical theories, and the creative power of the author seems to reach exactly as far as his hatreds, and to vanish as soon as they are exhausted. There would be hardly any reason, from the merits enumerated in this survey, to number Pareto under the important sociologists.

But, as a matter of fact, he is very important. . . . There are very few points in Pareto's teaching worth including in the common stock of our knowledge of society. But social philosophy is at least no less an expression of the aims and views of certain social groups and of certain new tendencies of thought and behavior which transform society, than a contribution to science. . . . In Pareto's work for the first time the powerful tendency towards a change of the political machinery and social organization since embodied in Bolshevism, Fascism, National Socialism and a score of similar movements has found clear expression; clearer here than in the work of Georges Sorel, who alone could be ranked with Pareto as a precursor of the political and social changes we behold in our days. . . .

SEVEN

PARETIAN POLITICS

RAYMOND ARON

THE CONCEPTUAL FORMALISM of Pareto's work does not prevent us from discerning both his prejudices and the concrete cases he is aiming at. He hates the plutocrats who, as he saw it, controlled France and Italy; he has contempt for them and their humanitarian ideologies. He looks upon the revolutionary syndicalists as the heirs of middle-class democracy (1857), but he also foresees fearfully a bureaucratization of the kind that marked the final stages of the Roman Empire. He believes the mixture of Residues 1 and 2 to be most favorable to society, but in the same breath he desires—perhaps not quite conscious of the likely consequences—a strong state which will allow full economic freedom to the speculators while at the same time keeping them under control (2549).

To be sure, Pareto does not openly endorse or suggest anything; however, his experimental uniformities virtually point at a distinctive theory of action. He who knows and understands the reciprocity of influences operating in the social system is in a position to foresee the consequences of the changes he intends to introduce. Ideal ends are to be disregarded simply because of the permanently given exploitation of the masses. In consequence, the nature of all governments remains unchanged. Likely objectives are determined by the social interest; effective means, by mass psychology. From this objectivist sociology one can distill a certain policy—a policy which is the most intriguing and exciting aspect of the whole *Trattato*. By way of a dialectical reversal, the pretense at total objectivity leads forthwith to an attitude of utter cynicism. The critic ought to pay attention, not so much to the conceptual details, as to the method by which this reversal—or should we call it *sleight of hand?*—is taking place.

"Paretian Politics" (original title: "La sociologie de Pareto"), by Raymond Aron. From *Zeitschrift für Sozialforschung*, VI (1937), 489-521, passim. Translated by the editor. Reprinted by permission of the author. (See above, Introduction, n. 166.)

Even if the uniformities established by Pareto would in their entirety be in agreement with experience, the *Trattato* still would not be, for that reason, "a masterwork of the human mind." [1] The formalistic character of this sociology, if the propositions are taken at face value, is such that it singularly weakens the import of the conclusions. If Pareto and his faithfuls differ with this, the reason is they take for granted that *the general is already the fundamental.* Just because elites and governments exist in all societies, it does not follow that all elites and forms of authority are one and the same. . . . Pareto accepts with the same confidence the most uncommensurable testimonials, the most doubtful sources, if they reconfirm his preconceptions and give satisfaction to his hatreds. . . . Let us admit that his account of the financial scandals which vitiated the French and Italian parliamentary regime is accurate. Still, to equate the history of the French Third Republic with that of the Paris plutocrats is to ignore the great solidity of the regime in the French provinces and the French countryside. . . . Corruption, a general phenomenon found everywhere, must be distinguished from political and economic combinations typical of a certain society at a certain time of its development. Anecdotes and generalities are not enough to help make such a distinction—which leads us to the main point.

Our major grievance against the *Trattato* is its ambiguity: the ease with which Pareto slides from logic to psychology, and from psychology to sociology. In brief, the first half of the work is marred by its reliance on a logic and metaphysic of science; the second half suffers from an opposite defect: what ought to be sociology turns into an equivocal psychology of class and the class struggle. On first sight, the combination of these two conflicting accusations would seem to be paradoxical. The paradox, however, disappears once we remind ourselves that, between the first and second half of the *Trattato,* the classification of the residues changes its significance, until only those of Classes 1 and 2 remain: the instinct of critique and innovation, as opposed to the conservative, religious sentiments. . . . A question comes to mind: Did it really take hundreds of pages to rediscover the maxims of bourgeois wisdom: that the people need religion while intelligence and skepticism are the property of the elites?

The very nature and, indeed, the weakness of the theory of residues and derivations is revealed in full when we compare it, on the one hand, to the Freudian psychology of complexes, and on the other, to the Marxist critique of ideologies. The analysis proceeding from the justification or rationalization to the complex penetrates much deeper into

---

[1] The expression has been used by [G. H.] Bousquet and [Louis Auguste] Rougier.

human consciousness than commonplace knowledge is capable of doing. The pseudological content of the justification is explained, together with its origin. The method gives us both the power and the right to confront appearance with reality, and the idea which the individual has of himself with his authentic being (all these terms to be taken in their psychological sense). Applied to a historic case, the method retains its advantages. It makes it possible to understand both the specific nature of the ideology and the reasons for its success. One reservation, to be sure, is necessary: if particular [historical] examples are subsumed under one concept—if, for instance, all rebellions are attributed to *ressentiment*—this would, at best, identify only one of the psychological conditions of historical phenomena; it would not help us to interpret sociologically, say, the proletarian movements of the nineteenth century.

Put differently, the analysis of ideologies, in order to avail itself of the advantages of individual psychology, must combine it with historic understanding. Not only will it not neglect the single instance, but it will insist on stressing its originality. The analyst will take care to relate it to the social constellation before settling on some general law of behavior. Such is, exactly, the character of the Marxist approach which refuses to dissolve all derivations in the name of some eternal logic and to relegate them to a catalog of stable sentiments. . . .

Pareto's method, then, is neither that of Freud nor that of Marx. Whether he deals with cult or rite, custom or creed, religion or medicine, he never tries to render the phenomena intelligible by an inquiry into their origins or the attendant circumstances. He does not concern himself with moral preferences, prehistoric modes of thought or feeling; he even disregards impulsions. The sentiments of which he speaks correspond exactly to the facts he states: the former are a literal translation of the latter. The cult of the dead is explained by the sentiment inspired by the body of the deceased; asceticism, as a propensity for suffering; persecutions are called forth by the desire for uniformity; magical practices bespeak the belief that words have cosmic force; the family proves the persistence of aggregates. Now we know! Pareto has no right to vent his ridicule on other people's interpretations, since he offers none himself. He claims to be a positivist; in fact, he is a throwback to scholasticism. . . .[2]

Although not a member of the Fascist Party, Pareto was nevertheless known to be a sympathizer. He saluted the advent of Fascism, which confirmed his prediction: the replacement of a cunning elite by a violent

[2] Cf. Borkenau, *Pareto* (London, 1936), p. 75.

one. In turn, he was acclaimed by the regime and made a royal senator. It is true that Pareto personally was for moderation; he believed in independence (for the few). The totalitarian character of Mussolini's state would have been doubly disappointing to Pareto, had he witnessed the suppression of the intellectual freedom of the ruling class and the sharp limitation of that economic freedom which he held to be most favorable to the growth of social wealth. . . .

But we do not propose to study here Pareto's personal relations with Italian Fascism. What matters to us is not the subjective psychological affinity but the implicit meaning of his work. . . . We shall try to establish the essential liaison between Pareto's thought and a typology of fascism.

The *Trattato* intimates a political type who will act logically and make use of the experimental uniformities in order to achieve his ends. That kind of politician would become the heir of the empiricists and realists, but he would be a lucid, conscious hypocrite. He would try to exploit the residues; he would promote such derivations as are likely to turn into residues. He always would appeal, not to reason, but to sentiments. He would endeavor to inculcate useful creeds, with no concern about their quality (one who wants to convince the crowd must never reason, but he must appear to reason).[3] On the other hand, he would appeal to the class interest of the elite. Himself emancipated from the residues to be upheld among the masses, he manipulates those myths which would enhance the energy of others—myths whose illusory character is clear to him. Propaganda and ideology would be the tools of governmental action, and the social balance resting on the skill of leadership and the fanaticism of the masses, with the grandeur of the nation as the supreme goal.

Without doubt what we have here is one type of fascist: the intellectual, or semi-intellectual, purged of all prejudices and despising intellectuals. All the theories of the *Trattato* become clear once they are understood as a design enabling such a man to organize and justify his conduct.

A certain number of equivocations . . . round out the portrait: the juxtaposition of a complete relativism and a naïve dogmatism. Nothing can, by definition, be said about ultimate values, so the national interest should be understood in terms of subjective evaluation only. But this relativism is immediately forgotten and the trite demands of the national interest (in a material sense) becomes the *summum bonum*. In the name of skepticism, the ancient creeds and rudimentary fanaticisms are revived.

---

[3] *Les Systèmes socialistes,* Vol. I, p. 126.

But it is not enough to train a man to be an able politician; he must also be endowed with a good conscience. Fascism is antiliberal, antihumanitarian, antidemocratic, and antirationalist. Because the antithesis moves on the same ground as the thesis, the dialectical negation must be shown to be impossible. In order to escape the Marxist conclusion, one changes the subject. The socioeconomic structure is demoted to secondary importance. The concept of the class struggle is kept; far from being rejected, it serves to justify the absolutist character of the regime.[4] But the class struggle is understood in terms of individual rather than collective psychology, so as to strengthen the conviction that class conflict is enduring, under all skies and in all societies.[5]

This substitution does not, by itself, prove the superior truth of any cause, but no proof is needed. Violence is now the passport to sucess—and success is the guarantee of being right. The fervor and creative will of the elites make programs and the study of priorities superfluous.

One understands now why Pareto pays little or no attention to historic situations, why he is unwilling to distinguish between forms of exploitation, why he has so great a need for generalities and none for the investigation of specific problems. . . . While Marxism insists on the originality of modern class conflict, Pareto denies it and dwells instead on the features common to all regimes. . . . The mechanism of his thinking, the political thrust of his scientific methodology, become transparent.

The whole *Trattato* stands revealed as one gigantic derivation, drawn from the two residues of hate and an exclusive interest in the relationship of governors and governed. . . . The historic promptings for this ideology are no less evident. The more bourgeois democracy declines, the less possible it becomes to speak for all classes: the liberal appeal has lost its magic.[6] This being so, and because behavior is nonlogical, belief in progress yields to the negation of all hope. The *grand bourgeois* turns fascist. This gentlest of all men adopts the course of intellectual ferocity. And yet, he cannot quite deny his own true nature: it desires a violent elite, but one intelligent enough not to begrudge the great ones of this world their claim to leisure and the pleasures of the mind.

By the same token, it is safe to say that, although quite useful as a key

---

[4] Pareto's exaggerations about bourgeois humanitarianism, about the concessions granted to the working class and the soft treatment meted out to strikers—all this reads today like an appeal to the bourgeoisie to get tough.

[5] With Pareto, the class struggle becomes an aspect of the existential struggle, in *Les Systèmes socialistes,* Vol. II, Chap. XIV.

[6] The disillusionment of the bourgeois and economic liberal, Pareto, is at the root of all his violence.

to Fascism, Pareto's doctrine will forever be confined to a small circle. For, once Fascism has attained power, the Paretian formula will have to be disguised behind an ideology of general appeal. A government which needs religion will consider cynicism a great danger; it can have no use for cold analysis. That which every page Pareto wrote attests to—the reality of class conflict—must be denied at any price and called *a fabrication of the intellectuals*. The more effective the prescription, the less needed the physician. Other sides of fascist thought—totalitarianism, racial metaphysics, the religion of the nation-state—will take first place. Even for the Fascist leaders other intellectual nourishment than his will have to be prepared, because the true believer is a better propagandist than the hypocrite. Pareto's insights will be put into practice and—disowned. . . .

EIGHT

MORPHOLOGY AND SOCIAL PSYCHOLOGY IN PARETO

JOSEPH A. SCHUMPETER

THERE IS NOTHING surprising in the habit of economists to invade the sociological field. A large part of their work—practically the whole of what they have to say on institutions and on the forces that shape economic behavior—inevitably overlaps the sociologist's preserves. In consequence, a no-man's land or everyman's land has developed that might conveniently be called *economic sociology*. More or less important elements that hail from that land are to be found in practically every economic treatise or textbook. But, beyond this, many economists—and especially those who define economics proper rather strictly—have done sociological work. A. Smith's *Moral Sentiments* and Wieser's *Gesetz der Macht,* are both outstanding instances of a large genus. But few, if any, men in the list of great economists have devoted so large a part of their energy as has Pareto to what at first sight seems to be an extracurricular activity, and few, if any, owe so much of their international reputation to what they have done in that field. But his achievement is not easy to characterize and to appraise. The enthusiastic applause of some and the hostility of others are both understandable, but neither can be taken quite seriously because the nonscientific sources of both are painfully obvious in most cases. Although several minor works and a large number of newspaper articles would have to be considered in order to give a satisfactory picture, we need not go beyond the *Systèmes socialistes,* the *Manuel* (especially Chapters 2 and 7) and the *Trattato di sociologia generale.*

"Morphology and Social Psychology in Pareto" (original title: "Vilfredo Pareto, section III: The Sociologist"). From *Ten Great Economists: From Marx to Keynes,* by Joseph A. Schumpeter (New York: Oxford University Press, Inc., 1951), pp. 134-42. Copyright 1951 by Elizabeth Boody Schumpeter. Reprinted by permission of Oxford University Press, Inc.

Let us begin with two aspects of Pareto's sociology that are perfectly obvious and the reverse of difficult to characterize. First, although Pareto the economist touched upon a large number of extremely concrete and practical problems throughout his long life, his purely scientific contribution is in the realm of the most abstract economic logic. It is, therefore, quite understandable that he should have experienced a wish and, in fact, a need to erect alongside his pure theory another building that would shelter facts and reasonings of a different kind—facts and reasonings that would do something toward answering the question how the elements taken care of by his economic theory might be expected to work out in practical life. Second, we have seen that in his earlier days, at least as long as he lived in Italy, he had taken a passionate interest in the debates on questions of economic and general policy. The born thinker that he was must have been struck by the impotence of the rational argument, and the question must have intruded upon him of what it really is that determines political action and the fate of states and civilizations. Again, it is quite understandable that, as soon as he had settled down to a life of thought, this question should have emerged from the sphere of easy and superficial answers that all of us are prone to give when immersed in our daily work, and that he should have attempted to raise it to the plane of scientific analysis. This amounts to saying that primarily and fundamentally his sociology was a sociology of the political process. Of course, everything that man does or thinks or feels and all his cultural creations and his attitudes toward cultural creations are bound to come in somehow or other when we think about the political process, which then becomes but a special case. But it was this special case which fascinated Pareto and for the sake of which he erected and adorned a much larger structure.

Next, still moving on ground that is relatively easy to survey, we shall consider his method. Pareto himself emphasized again and again that he simply applied the same logico-experimental methods that had served him for the purposes of economic theory to the task of analyzing the "experimentally" verifiable reality of other aspects of social life, allowing himself to be guided here as elsewhere by the example of the physical sciences. This was, of course, a complete delusion. It is easy to observe, for instance, that he made large and in part illegitimate use of psychological interpretations for which there is no analogy in the physical sciences and that his material, such as it was, was the product of observation and not of experiment—a difference which is fundamental from the standpoint of method. I am afraid that what he really meant to emphasize, when trying to formulate his rules of procedure, was simply the detachment of the philosopher who does not identify himself with any party, interest, or creed. The possibility of such detachment raises, of course, a very well-known fundamental difficulty and one that Pareto was the less qualified to overcome because he failed to see it. Actually he used two different analytic schemata: one that may be called a morphology of society and does invite the use of facts that are, potentially at least, amenable to observation in a similar sense as are the facts of anatomy or biology; and another that pertains to social psychology. Both schemata are indeed illustrated or even, to some extent, verified by historical and contemporaneous instances, but neither is *derived* from them by anything like a logico-experimental method: both are reflexes of a highly personal vision of the social process that owes much to Pareto's background, practical experience—and resentments. The affinity of the morphological schema with Darwinian selection and of the sociopsychological schema with parts of the teaching of Tarde, Durkheim, Lévy-Bruhl, and Ribot is obvious. Still more so is the relation of both with the current of thought . . . that issued in derogatory criticism of the doings of parliamentary democracy—the current that was anti-intellectualist, antiutilitarian, antiequalitarian and, *in the special sense defined by these terms*,[1] antiliberal. But the force of the man created from these materials something that was nevertheless specifically his own.[2]

The morphological schema centers in the proposition that all societies consist of heterogeneous masses of members—individuals or families— and are structured according to the aptitudes of these members for the relevant social function: in a society of thieves, the *ex hypothesi* widely varying ability to steal would determine social rank, and hence influence upon the government of the society. Pareto seems to assume that these abilities, while capable of improvement and of decay, are substantially innate, though he makes little effort to establish this. Moreover, though distributed continuously in the population, they lead to the formation of classes, the "higher" ones of which have and use the means of buttressing their position and of separating themselves from the lower strata. In consequence, there is in the lowest strata a tendency to accumulate

---

[1] This proviso is very necessary. There are other meanings of the word *liberal*, one of which would describe Pareto's position much better than could any other term. Similarly, there is a sense in which he might be justly called a great humanitarian. But it is not the one which he applied to *individus dégénérés, d'intelligence et de volonté faibles (Manuel,* p. 130.)

[2] It is highly instructive to observe how different the results are that different men arrive at not only from the same facts but also from the same intuitions. Graham Wallas was an orthodox English radical and a Fabian. But in *Human Nature in Politics* he drew a picture that was not in the least more flattering to the slogans of political democracy than was Pareto's.

superior ability that is prevented from rising, and in the topmost stratum, in the aristocracy or elite, a tendency to decumulate energy through disuse—with resulting tension and ultimate replacement of the ruling minority by another ruling minority that is drawn from the superior elements in the *couches inférieures*. This *circulation des élites* does not, however, affect the principle that it is always *some* minority which rules, and does not do anything to bring any given society nearer to the ideal of equality, though it does produce equalitarian philosophies or slogans in the course of the struggles that ensue. With a turn of phrase that recalls the first sentence of the *Communist Manifesto*, Pareto proclaimed that history is essentially a history *de la succession des aristocracies* (*Manuel*, p. 425). But his presentation of this part of his argument is so very sketchy and he leaves his readers with so much to interpolate that I am not at all sure that I have rendered justice to his thought. Nevertheless, I had to make the attempt. For some such argument is necessary in order to put his social psychology into its proper light.

The sociopsychological schema centers in the concept of the nonlogical (not necessarily illogical) action. This concept recognizes the well-known fact—well-known, in particular, to economists—that the great mass of our everyday actions is not the result of rational reasoning on rationally performed observations, but simply of habit, impulse, sense of duty, imitation, and so on, although many of them admit of satisfactory rationalization ex post either by the observer or the actor. So far there is nothing in Pareto's psychosociology that could be unfamiliar to anyone. What is unfamiliar, however, is his tremendous emphasis upon the additional facts that a great number of actions—and let us add at once, beliefs—are being rationalized, both by actors and by observers, in ways that will not stand up under scientific analysis and, more important, that some actions and beliefs are altogether incapable of being rationalized in any way that will. The importance of this second step for a sociology of the political process becomes obvious if we take a third one: Pareto maintained that the large majority of all the actions and beliefs that make up that process are of the type mentioned last. Take, as an instance on which we all agree, the idea of the Social Compact or, as an instance on which most of us agree, Rousseau's theory of the *volonté générale*. Only, according to Pareto, practically all the actions, principles, beliefs and so on prevailing in the collective mind of electorates belong in the same category. And a large part of the *Trattato* consists in illustrating this, often amusingly, sometimes instructively.

It will serve our purpose to put this point strongly, more strongly than

Pareto himself ever put it. The masses of thought and the conceptual structures that form the conscious surface of the social and, in particular, of the political process have no empirical validity whatever. They work with entities such as liberty, democracy, equality, that are as imaginary as were the gods and goddesses who fought for and against Greeks and Trojans in the *Iliad,* and are connected by reasonings that habitually violate the rules of logic. In other words, from a logical standpoint, they are nonsense unalloyed. This makes a political philosophy that is best described by its diametrical opposition to that of Jeremy Bentham. It should be observed, however, that this diagnosis of the political myths (Sorel) did not induce Pareto to overlook the function that this logical nonsense may fill in national life. After having gone through with an analysis that is severely positivist in nature, he refused to draw the conclusion that would seem the obvious one to the positivist. While political creeds and social religions—with Pareto there is very little difference between these two—contribute to dissolution in dissolving civilizations, they also contribute to effective organization and action in vital civilizations. This is a very curious attitude for a thoroughgoing positivist to take and will perhaps be cited at some future time as an outstanding example of the mentality of an epoch that destroyed one type of metaphysical beliefs while ushering in another. It reminds me of the advice which I have heard some psychoanalysts give to some of their patients— namely, the advice to cultivate, with a view to possible remedial effects, a sort of synthetic belief in God. There is, of course, no contradiction between maintaining that social and political creeds have no empirical significance and admitting that some of them may make for social cohesion and efficiency. But the social philosopher who should thereupon undertake to advise the adoption of the latter would run into the same difficulty as our psychoanalyst: so long as his analysis is being accepted his advice must be ineffective, for no synthetic God can be trusted to help; so soon as his advice is accepted his analysis will have to be rejected.

That tissue of creations of our imagination Pareto called *derivations.* The argument adumbrated in the preceding paragraph abundantly shows that they are not without importance as factors that help to shape the historical process. It was Pareto's opinion, however, that this importance is relatively small and that substantially these derivations do no more than verbalize something more fundamental that comes much nearer to determining actual political behavior and the sum total of nonlogical actions. Now if we defined this more fundamental something in terms of group interests, and if we then went on to define these group interests in terms of the social location of groups within a society's productive organization, we should be, to say the least, very near Karl Marx's view of the matter, and there is in this point actually a strong affinity which I think it important to emphasize. In fact, if we adopted this line of reasoning, there would be only two major points of difference left between Marxian and Paretian political sociology. On the one hand, Pareto introduced explicitly an element that is only implicitly present in the Marxist analysis: the importance for the explanation of an actual stretch of history, of the greater or smaller degree of social flexibility that a given society displays, or, in other words, the importance of the fact that there exists an optimum of vertical mobility and of resistance to it that will better than others guarantee what might be termed *stability of political change*. On the other hand, we need only recall our sketch of Pareto's social morphology in order to realize that with Pareto the historical process is not so much the result of the conflict of comprehensive social classes as it is the result of the conflict of their ruling minorities. It is submitted that, while both differences are to the credit of Paretian sociology, they do not amount to more than corrective improvements upon the Marxist schema. I might add the fact that property relations per se are much less in evidence with Pareto than they are with Marx, and that this also constitutes a claim to superiority of the Paretian analysis. But it will be readily seen that this point is really implied in the other two.

Actually, however, Pareto did not follow up this line of analysis. With him the link between the tissue of delusions which he called *derivations* and the objective determinants of actual behavior was supplied by what he called the *residues*. I am conscious of the danger of being unfair if, for the sake of brevity, I define these residues as impulses generally found to be present with human beings that revive, and not in a very inviting manner, the old psychology of "instincts." We need not discuss the list that Pareto drew up—and which contains such items as an instinct of combinations, the sexual impulse, and so on—especially as Pareto himself does not seem to have been very satisfied with it. It is sufficient to point out the obvious methodological objection to any such procedure; even if Pareto's residues and the "laws" of their association and persistence were much more satisfactorily analyzed than they are, they would still be labels rather than solutions of problems, and call for professional investigation of a kind for which Pareto lacked the equipment. It is therefore quite understandable that Pareto's work has exerted so little influence upon professional sociology and social psychology, and that professional sociologists and social psychologists have but rarely displayed a sense of the greatness of the structure as a whole.[3]

But those and other shortcomings are not decisive. Pareto's work is more than a research program. Also, it is more than mere analysis. The fundamental principle that what individuals, groups, and nations actually do must find its explanation in something much deeper than the creeds and slogans that are used in order to verbalize action, conveys a lesson of which modern men—and none more than we economists—stand much in need. We are in the habit, when discussing questions of policy, of accepting at face value the slogans of our own and, indeed, of a bygone time. We reason exactly as if the Benthamite creed of the eighteenth century had ever been valid. We refuse to realize that policies are politics and to admit to ourselves what politics are. We cultivate the subnormal and do our best to suppress whatever there is of strength and sparkle. In conditions such as these, Pareto's message, however one-sided, is a healthy antidote. It is not, like his economics, a technical achievement of the first order. It is something quite different. It is an attempt to preach a sermon.

[3] Professor Talcott Parsons' analysis of Paretian sociology stands almost alone in the Anglo-American sociological literature.

NINE

THE ITALIAN CONTEXT: PARETO AND MOSCA

FRANCO FERRAROTTI

PARETO AND POSITIVISM

THE ADHERENTS OF CROCE, together with all those learned men who from the early years of this century accepted his neo-Hegelian premises, in the final analysis had an easy time in attacking the theories of the most noted of the Italian sociologists, Vilfredo Pareto, from a philosophical and more specifically methodological point of view. The task of the critics was indubitably facilitated by Pareto's obstinate refusal to make any effort to assure the preciseness and autonomy of sociological research on the level of its philosophical base:

> Let's forget the names and look at the things . . . we have better things to do than to waste time trying to determine whether sociology is or is not an autonomous science—whether it is anything other than the philosophy of history under another name—or arguing at length concerning the methods to be followed in its study.[1]

Although he begins his work with this declaration, which might seem to be devoid of pragmatism, Pareto in reality tries—and it is an ambitious effort because of its breadth and vastness of plan—to found sociology as an exact science, particularly in the three large volumes of his treatise on general sociology (four volumes in English translation).

In contrast to the sociological studies inspired by the philosophy of Comte—studies which are inclined to fall into metaphysics in spite of

From "Sociology in Italy: Problems and Perspectives," by Franco Ferrarotti. Translated by W. G. Lanlois, in Becker and Boskoff, *Modern Sociological Theory in Continuity and Change* (New York: Holt, Rinehart & Winston, Inc., 1957), pp. 702-7. Copyright © 1957 by Holt, Rinehart & Winston, Inc. Reprinted by permission of the publisher.

[1] Vilfredo Pareto, *Trattato di sociologia generale*, Vol. I, p. 1.

all protestations of "positivism"—Pareto uses the logico-experimental method—that is to say, he declares that his research is based exclusively on experience and observation. The repugnance that dogmatic or a priori sociologies arouse in him finds vituperative expression:

> We have an abundance of "humanitarian" sociologies, for all those that are being published now are of that sort; we don't lack metaphysical sociologies, and among them are to be classed all those which are "positivist" and humanitarian; we have a small number of Christian sociologies, Catholic and other; let it be conceded, without wanting to slight all these sociologies, that we are here engaged in the exposition of a kind that is exclusively experimental, like chemistry, physics, and other similar sciences.[2]

Guided by this method and with these criteria, Pareto presents an analysis of a huge, heterogeneous collection of evidence, including among other things entire historical periods, the rise and fall of cultures and nations, and the classic description of the circulation of the elites. The fundamental aim of this long, ponderous work of research, and its ultimate justification, probably consists in the attempt to verify inductively the law of social equilibrium, which Pareto conceives in accordance with his own methodological premises in mechanistic terms and which he can therefore express in mathematical language through a system of equations.

Aside from the intrinsic limitations of his "social equilibrium," concerning which serious doubts have been raised even recently,[3] and the traditional series of objections that can be leveled against a purely mathematical method when it is applied to the descriptive analysis of the world of human beings and its manifold, multidimensional relationships, the weakness of the monumental sociological work of Pareto seems to lie, from the point of view of recent developments in the social sciences, in its macrosociological character. This is particularly true in a period in which sociology is renouncing in ever more decisive manner those ambitions typical of the "imperialism" or encyclopedism of Comte, in favor of the study of well-defined social phenomena, such as the primary group and the community. It appears to be constantly more cognizant of the necessity of going beyond the essentially mechanistic organization from which Spencer's teaching is not immune. We are in fact going from a macrosociology, or a general, encyclopedic sociology characteristic of the last century, toward a sociology that is both extremely careful in

[2] *Ibid.*, p. 4.
[3] See David Easton, "Limits of the Equilibrium Model in Social Research," *Profits and Problems of Homeostatic Models in the Behavioral Sciences* (Chicago, 1953), pp. 26-40.

circumscribing the field of its own specific inquiry and philosophically more sophisticated and defensible. To express it with the suggestive phrase of Gurvitch, we are evolving a sociology *en profondeur*[4] that recognizes its obligation—at a certain stage of its development—to take into account both psychology and history.

All this is certainly not sufficient to justify the critical demolition of Pareto by the neo-idealist followers of Croce and Gentile, particularly Guido de Ruggiero, who writes in so many words:

> Without bothering with the Pleiad of minor authors, I shall restrict myself to calling attention to a very conspicuous and recent example of a man who is generally considered a great master in Italy—I mean Vilfredo Pareto. I have read his treatise on general sociology with a great sense of sadness. The author, a writer of great historical erudition, of acute political sense and of admirable scientific restraint, has succeeded in wasting his outstanding qualities in a work organized abstractly and mechanistically.[5]

The judgment of de Ruggiero, effectively summing up the position of a more mature Crocean philosophy vis-à-vis sociology, accused of burying "the laws (of thought) beneath the chaotic mass of facts," [6] has found followers and has often been amplified in recent works.[7] Pareto is reproached above all for the schematic character of his theoretical analysis, which results in the famous dichotomy of the residues (or part that is constant, instinctive, nonlogical) on the one hand, and the derivations (or part that is variable and deductive, tending to explain and justify the residues) on the other. Another point of reproach and criticism is found in the unwarranted, confused, and undoubtedly complex subdivisions to which this dichotomy gives rise. Pareto divides the residues into six classes: (1) residues of the instinct of combination; (2) residues of the persistence of aggregates; (3) residues (or needs) of the manifestation of sentiments though overt acts; (4) residues of sociability; (5) residues of the integrity of the individual; (6) sexual residues. Moreover he distinguishes the four classes of derivations, masks by means of which facts are rationalized: (1) simple affirmations; (2) affirmations supported by an authority; (3) affirmations in accordance with sentiments or principles; (4) affirmations dependent on exclusively verbal proofs. Each class of residues is formed by many elements and the four classes of derivations include seventeen different forms. The fifty-two residues (Pareto actually

---

[4] Georges Gurvitch, *La Vocation actuelle de la sociologie* (Paris, 1950), p. 49.
[5] Guido de Ruggiero, *La Filosofia contemporanea* (Bari, 1941), Vol. II, pp. 230-31.
[6] *Ibid.*, p. 231.
[7] This is the case with Giuseppe La Ferla, *Vilfredo Pareto: filosofo volteriano* (Florence, 1954).

enumerated this many) can enter into various combinations among themselves and with the seventeen forms of the derivations. Thus one can easily see that certain reproaches were not completely unjustified and that, in the heat of argument, all sorts of criticisms were leveled against him.

Whatever may be our over-all opinion of the scientific validity of the sociological work of Pareto, there is no doubt that the contributions of this man, who time and time again has been compared with Voltaire and even with Abbot Galiani, and by North American scholars with Thorstein Veblen,[8] have been numerous and of great importance. Among these it is sufficient to note the definition of the logico-experimental method applied to the social sciences, the distinction between the logical and the nonrational elements in human conduct, the recognition that beliefs, myths, and dreams are very real "facts" for the social scientists, the theory of residues and derivations (however artificial and complicated it may appear), the concept of the elite, and, finally, the conception of social causation as a process in which many variables may be functionally interactive.

MOSCA AND METHODOLOGICAL BALANCE

In general, the criticism of the Croceans has been less sharp toward Gaetano Mosca, one of the most noted and astute promotors of the Italian social sciences.[9] It is probable that this results from the fact that Gaetano Mosca, in contrast to other eminent Italian social scientists (such as Roberto Michels, Vilfredo Pareto, and Achille Loria), accepts fully and with all its implications the historical method, rejecting the single-factor fallacy, which he characterizes as consisting in "simplist formulas that claim to explain a very complex phenomenon by means of a single cause." [10] The same Benedetto Croce, reviewing Mosca's work on the elements of political science, wrote:

> The dominating concept of the book is by this time well-known because it is linked to the name of Mosca: it is the idea of the political or ruling class in which the political life of the state is really focused: a class which

---

[8] W. Rex Crawford, "Representative Italian Contributions to Sociology," in H. E. Barnes (ed.), *An Introduction to the History of Sociology* (Chicago, 1948), p. 555.

[9] Among Gaetano Mosca's works, those particularly worthy of mention are: *Teoria dei governi e governo parlamentare,* 2nd ed. (Milan, 1925); *Elementi di scienza politica,* 2nd ed. (Turin, 1923), 2 vols.; *Il principio aristocratico e il democratico nel passato e nell'avvenire* (Turin, 1903); *Cenni storici e critici sulle dottrine razziste* (Rome, 1933); *Storia delle dottrine politiche* (Rome, 1933; Bari, 1951).

[10] See Gaetano Mosca, *Elementi di scienza politica,* 5th ed. (Bari, 1953), Vol. I, p. 19.

is quantitatively a minority but qualitatively a majority because it possesses awareness and possibilities for action. This concept is of the greatest import-ance for the interpretation of political history, an interpretation that is sought in vain in such external causes as climate, ethnic situation, etc., or in any other kind of externals, i.e., political forms considered as values in themselves, that is to say abstract and empty, such as monarchy, republic, and the like.[11]

In spite of this clear recognition of the validity of the methodological base of his research, the historical method to which Mosca claims he conforms is evidently strictly inductive and hence comparable to the em-pirical method of the natural sciences. As such, Croce cannot accept it. However, in order not to be accused of pedantry, Croce abstains from a criticism that might appear purely formalistic. He writes: "While Mosca enunciates and demonstrates truth, it is evident that he is philosophizing and philosophizing well," even if it would be easy to demonstrate that Mosca "reaches those truths by means of a method different from the inductive, naturalistic one." [12]

Besides the exact formulation of the concept of the "ruling class," Mosca is particularly apt and effective in those passages where he attacks the banalities and false problems that in his time were still taken as accepted truths. Thus, for example, in pointing out the various biases and prejudices against which Spencer warned scholars of social phe-nomena to guard themselves (national, religious or political prejudices, etc.), Mosca is able to point out that "the true safeguard against this sort of error is in knowing how to elevate criticism itself above the beliefs and opinions that are general in our epoch or in the particular social or national environment of which we are a part." [13] Further along in his treatment of the question, he takes the opportunity to explode the myth of a presumed antagonism or opposition between the state and society, about which so much has been written.

Starting in fact from his fundamental proposition that "in all socie-ties . . . there exist two classes of people, the governing and the gov-erned," [14] Mosca affirms that

> . . . antagonism between state and society cannot exist since it is possible to consider the state as that part of the society that fulfills its political function. Thus all questions regarding the interference of the state come to be viewed in a new light. Rather than study what should be the limits of the action of the state, one should seek to ascertain what is the best type of political

---

[11] See Benedetto Croce, in *Critica*, XXI (November 1923), pp. 374-78, reprinted as *Premessa* to Mosca's *Elementi di scienza politica*, 5th ed. (Bari, 1953), p. viii.

[12] Croce, *op. cit.*, p. ix.   [13] Mosca, *op. cit.*, p. 73.   [14] *Ibid.*, p. 78.

organization—that is to say, the one that permits all the elements having a given political value in a given society to be best utilized and developed, best subjected to reciprocal control and to the principle of individual responsibility for the acts which they carry out in their respective functions.[15]

The position of Gaetano Mosca appears particularly convincing when he criticizes the concept of social law as elaborated by Auguste Comte as being simplist and schematic. Rather judiciously, he notes how the famous Comtean "law of the three stages" cannot logically provide the base for "making a clear and precise chronological distinction between the various human societies by assigning them to one of the three periods Comte names, i.e., theological, metaphysical, and positive." [16] He concludes that "in this, as in so many other cases, simplification does not adapt itself well to the sciences that have to do with the mentality of man, a very complex animal, full of contradictions, who is not always concerned with being logical and coherent." [17]

Equally incisive and appropriate is the criticism advanced by Mosca against the Spencerian distinction between military states, founded on the coercion which the governing class exerts on the governed, and industrial states, based, on the contrary, on a contract—that is, on the free consent of those who make up the state. In opposition to the thesis of Spencer, Mosca demonstrates how "any political organization whatsoever . . . is concurrently spontaneous and coercive; spontaneous since it derives from the nature of man, as has been observed ever since Aristotle, and at the same time coercive because it is a *necessary* condition, man not being able to live otherwise." [18]

Moreover, the ideas of Mosca, like those of Pareto and of Michels, for that matter, were able—in the field of politics—to lend themselves to a justification of Fascism (or at least to a justification of the principle of the "charismatic leader" which was reminiscent of Weber's principle and which at the time was personified by Mussolini) independently of the personal political positions of these writers. Ironically, on the other hand, with the advent of Fascism to power the possibility of conducting free research in the social sciences ended, and in the universities the chairs of sociology and of political science became chairs of "Fascist doctrine."

[15] *Ibid.,* p. 212.   [16] *Ibid.,* p. 218.   [17] *Ibid.,* p. 221.   [18] *Ibid.,* p. 230.

TEN

THE FETISHISM OF POWER
SIDNEY HOOK

Not so many years ago the conquest of power was the central theme of all left-wing social theory oriented to political activity. Today, in the light of the consequences of totalitarian rule, concern with power is primarily with its abuses, its destruction of life and corruption of the spirit. The naïveté of the messianic reformer has given way to weary skepticism. The young Davids of radicalism seem to have laid aside their slings for the Book of Ecclesiastes—or for a safe berth with the New Deal. For most of the disillusioned, the main political task is conceived as preventing fascism from coming to power, not by winning power for socialism, but by strengthening liberal capitalism. Suspicion of the excesses of all power makes easier the acceptance of the customary abuses of existing power.

This new attitude toward power is revealed more in moods than in explicit argument, though theoretical formulations have not been lacking. But it is to books of an earlier day that we must turn to find the weightiest critiques of political power. Mosca, Pareto, Michels, writing in an age when optimism was as general as pessimism is today, raised all the crucial problems which have now come to the fore. They fortified their conclusions on the nature of political power with a mass of historical material and a nicety of analysis which commands respect even when it does not elicit agreement.

The translation into English of Gaetano Mosca's *The Ruling Class* offers an opportunity to evaluate both the strength and the weakness of this recurrent philosophy of political power. Like most doctrines that catch hold easily, the basic thesis is simple and recommends itself with a high initial plausibility to anyone who has had some political experience. It asserts that political power never rests upon the consent of the major-

"The Fetishism of Power," by Sidney Hook. From *The Nation*, CXLVIII: 20 (May 13, 1939), 562-63. Reprinted by permission of the author and *The Nation*.

ity, that irrespective of ideologies or leading personalities all political rule is a process—now peaceful, now coercive—by which a minority gratifies its own interests in a situation where not all interests can receive equal consideration. As Mosca himself puts it: "Political power always has been, and always will be, exercised by organized minorities, which have had, and will have, the means, varying as the times vary, to impose their supremacy on the multitudes." In peaceful times, the means are public myths and secret frauds; in crisis, force. Whichever side wins, the masses who have fought, bled, and starved are made the goat. Their saviors become their rulers under the prestige of new myths. The forms change, but the essential content remains. This is put forth as a "law" of all social life which can be demonstrated to the satisfaction of everyone except the dull, the pious, and candidates for political leadership. It is a law accepted by every political partisan as obviously true for other organizations but as a slander when applied to his own.

The reactions to this position in recent discussions have been astonishing. They tend to confirm some corollaries Mosca has drawn from his thesis about the distribution of political intelligence. One group does not argue the truth of the theory on the evidence but asserts that, since its acceptance makes for defeatism, it must be wrong. Another group applauds Mosca's theory or some variant of it and deduces therefrom the comforting view that revolutions are never justified; this, despite Mosca's contention that revolutions do not depend upon any theory of political power. Some contest the truth of his findings on the nature of political power because on some other unrelated points he is clearly mistaken. The most sophisticated opponents of the thesis first state it in such a way as to suggest that according to it all power is necessarily evil and should never be employed. They then have little difficulty in showing that this leads to a *reductio ad absurdum,* for men must act, and this involves a choice between alternatives all of which demand implementation by some power.

In the interests of clear analysis we must distinguish between Mosca's descriptive generalizations of the actual uses and abuses of political power in the past and present, and the theoretical explanation he offers of them. As descriptive generalizations, Mosca's conclusions are valid, once differences in the form of political rule have been properly noted. It is true that every political organization is, in effect, run by a minority. It is true that vital illusions, chicanery, and naked force have been three important props of all political rule. It is true that every successful mass movement—even with a democratic ideology—has compromised some of its basic principles, on occasions all of them. The history of

Christianity, of German Social Democracy, of the Russian Communist Party indicates in a dramatic and focal way all this and more. But in explaining these phenomena and in predicting that the future must always be like the past Mosca falls back upon a psychological theory of human nature considered independently of its social context. Almost every one of his explanations and predictions involves an appeal to an original nature conceived as essentially unalterable despite its varying expressions. Mosca's antiquated terminology can be brought up to date by translation into the language of dynamic psychology or psychoanalysis. But the controlling assumptions are the same no matter what the terms. The laws of political power are frankly characterized as psychological. They flow from fixed and unchangeable elements in the nature of men. Mosca has no hesitation in sometimes referring to them as "wicked instincts." It is from this conception of original sin that Mosca's dire prophecies flow.

The fact that the argument from human nature must be invoked to support the thesis is prima facie evidence that the entire position is unhistorical. Everything Mosca says may be granted except when he speaks in the future tense; for the genuine problems of power are always specific, are always rooted in the concrete needs of a particular people at a determinate time. Any conclusion based on his findings about the futility of social change and struggle is therefore a non sequitur; it betrays political animus, and if grounded at all, is derived from other considerations. The belief that there is an invariant core of properties which constitutes the "essential" character of human nature rests on gross data drawn from history and on a faulty technique of definition. Habits, traditions, and institutions play a much more important role in political behavior, and are more reliable in predicting the future, than any set of native impulses. By isolating the latter from their objective cultural setting, selecting from among them an alleged impulse to dominate, fight, love, or flee, the pattern of human nature can be cut to suit any current political myth.

Despite the fact that Mosca's "laws," when presented in psychological dress, have no empirical warrant, they can be reformulated so as to bear relevantly on particular situations in which intelligent choice between different modes of power is possible. They then function as "cautions" or "guides" to possible dangers that attend transference of power from one group to another. The task then becomes one of devising safeguards —an occasion for experiment, not for lamentation. And most safeguards do not make accidents impossible; they make them less frequent. Sufficient evidence has been assembled which indicates the probable sources of future corruption and oppression. It would require a treatise to explore this theme, but in a preliminary way we can indicate the spheres of social life in which conflicts will arise, necessitating safeguards against oppression.

The first sphere of conflict and possible oppression is obviously economic. Most socialists grant this readily enough for the past but deny that it holds for collectivist society. Yet it is apparent that under no system operated by finite creatures in a finite world can all men be equally served in everything and, what is just as important, equally served at once. That there will probably be some differences in standards of living, no matter what the level of productive forces, none but a utopian will deny. But there are differences and differences. Conflicts there will be, but their kind, generality, and intensity will depend upon the specific mechanisms adopted to reflect and negotiate the interests of different groups of producers and consumers. Socialists have always asserted that there is no genuine political democracy without economic democracy. In a collectivist economy the converse is even more emphatically the case.

The second sphere of possible abuse of authority is administrative. Every administrator intrusted with responsibility for making decisions that may affect the jobs, pleasures, and life careers of other human beings may function as a tyrant. The greater the area of administration, the greater the danger. Especially when efficiency is the goal is it easy to palm off injustice as a necessary evil. Here, too, the situation is one that must be met, for better or for worse, by contriving checks and reviews with a maximum of publicity.

Finally, there is the undeniable fact that many people love the exercise of power. For some it is a compensation for frustration; for others it is a way of acquiring prestige, glory, a sense of vitality or importance; for almost everybody it is a temptation to prefer those we like and to overlook those we despise. Everyone has his own list of people whose absence he thinks would be a boon to the world. But what follows from all this? Nothing that need dismay anyone who is not a saint or a fool. Here, as everywhere else, once we surrender the dogmas of an unalterable human nature or inevitable laws of organizational progress or corruption, we can do something to mitigate and counteract, and to establish moral equivalents.

Whether we are talking of pain or injustice or power, there is no such thing as *the* problem of evil except to a supernaturalist. There are only evils. The more we know about the pathological lust for power, the conditions under which it thrives, the instruments it uses, the myths behind

which it hides—and the more public we make that knowledge—the
better can we cope with the problem of taming it. Skepticism is always
in order; but no more than in science need it lead to paralysis of activity.
More knowledge is always desirable, but we know enough to make at
least a beginning. And if we are interested in democratic socialism, by
keeping our eyes on both Germany and Russia we certainly know what
to avoid. Despite the swelling chorus of disillusion there still remain
alternatives to the insanity of uncontrolled myth and the inhumanity of
uncontrolled power.

ELEVEN

GAETANO MOSCA AND
THE POLITICAL LESSONS
OF HISTORY

H. STUART HUGHES

AMONG AMERICAN STUDENTS of political science and history, Gaetano Mosca is usually considered as a kind of second-class Pareto. The leading ideas ascribed to the two thinkers are similar—the theory of elites, of the role of force and deception in history, in short, of a neo-Machiavellianism derived from a common Italian heritage. As sharp critics of parliamentary democracy and socialism, Pareto and Mosca appear to occupy similar places among the precursors of Fascism—half-unconscious, perhaps, of what they were doing, but still in some ultimate sense responsible for the collapse of Italian democracy and the advent of Mussolini. From this standpoint, Pareto looms as the larger figure. His range is wider, his books are longer, his "scientific" apparatus is more impressive, and his criticism cuts deeper. Moreover, the Fascist chief himself honored Pareto and was happy to number him among his intellectual inspirers; apparently he never mentioned Mosca. Conversely, the latter's eventual opposition to Mussolini's regime was too quiet to attract much attention: the sweet notes of reasoned dissent reached the outside world through Croce alone, and other voices sounded muffled and ineffective. On all counts, then, Mosca has seemed a lesser figure; he wrote more gracefully than Pareto and his views were more moderate—but those were the only respects in which his work ranked higher.

The accidental circumstance that Pareto's *Trattato di sociologia generale* appeared in English translation five years earlier than Mosca's

"Gaetano Mosca and the Political Lessons of History," by H. Stuart Hughes. From *Teachers of History: Essays in Honor of Laurence Bradford Packard,* edited by H. Stuart Hughes with the collaboration of Myron P. Gilmore and Edwin C. Rozwenc (Ithaca, N.Y.: Cornell University Press, 1954), pp. 146-67. Copyright 1954 by Cornell University Press. Reprinted by permission of the publisher and the author.

Elementi di scienza politica partly explains the greater prestige the former work enjoys.[1] But even in Italy, where the two books were equally available to the reading public, Mosca's took second place. Although his theory of the political class quite obviously antedated Pareto's formulation of the "elite" concept, Mosca experienced the greatest difficulty in maintaining his claim to priority. The result was a polemic that went on for two decades, to the eventual weariness of both the contestants and the other learned figures who were drawn in. There was no doubt that Mosca was the injured party. Pareto affected a lofty disdain for the whole controversy and simply "erased Mosca's name even from his footnotes." [2] But at the same time there must have been something profoundly irritating to the sage of Lausanne about the pertinacity with which a less-well-known scholar ten years his junior kept insisting on his title to an idea that was by no means totally original and that could plausibly be regarded as no more than the product of the general intellectual atmosphere in western Europe just before the turn of the century.

It is not the purpose of the present essay to argue against the prevailing impression and to give Mosca his due. It is rather my intention to point out once again the obvious—if frequently overlooked—difference between the practical conclusions in which the two theories terminate, and in so doing to suggest that this contrast is due in great part to a different attitude toward history—an attitude that in Mosca's case was the product of a longer personal experience. Mosca's sense of history as an experienced reality, even against his expressed intention, worked gradual and subtle changes not only in his political ideas but even in the presuppositions behind them.

I

The difference between Pareto's and Mosca's practical conclusions is too well-known to require elaboration. Pareto died, as he had lived, the sworn foe of parliamentary democracy. He had experienced only the

---

[1] Introduction by Arthur Livingston to Gaetano Mosca, *The Ruling Class (Elementi di scienza politica)*, translated by Hannah D. Kahn (New York, 1939), p. xxxvi. Mr. Livingston, who was responsible for the American editions of both Pareto's and Mosca's work, explains that the latter was originally intended to appear first. In the succeeding footnotes I shall refer to the fourth (and final) Italian edition rather than to the translation, since Mr. Livingston has somewhat rearranged the original order of Mosca's presentation.

[2] Renzo Sereno, "The Anti-Aristotelianism of Gaetano Mosca and Its Fate," *Ethics*, XLVIII (July 1938), 512. For an exhaustive summary of the question of priority, see Alfonso de Pietri-Tonelli, "Mosca e Pareto," *Rivista internazionale di scienze sociali*, VI (July 1935), 468-93.

first year of Mussolini's new government; he had expressed his reservations about it—but these were on matters of emphasis rather than principle. Mosca lived nearly two decades longer, virtually through the whole of the Fascist dictatorship. He had ample time to see what was happening, and he early came to a negative judgment, although once the regime was consolidated, he prudently kept his opinions to himself. This difference in age, however, was not decisive. Mosca had reached his new conclusions even before Pareto's death; the second edition of his *Elementi,* published a few weeks after Mussolini came to power, already shows his transformation from a critic of parliamentary democracy into its defender—a skeptical defender, indeed, but an extremely effective one. The difference lies, rather, in the divergent experience of the two writers during the quarter-century preceding the March on Rome; while Pareto was living in scholarly seclusion and enjoying his self-imposed exile in Switzerland, Mosca was actively participating in Italian political life. The day-to-day contact with political reality was insensibly modifying his theoretical judgments and even the concept of history on which they were based.[3]

Mosca's original idea of history closely resembled Pareto's. It was a simple, straightforward view, reflecting both the heritage of the Enlightenment and the more recent teachings of French positivism. In its didactic emphasis, it recalled the Enlightenment. Like Voltaire or Gibbon, Mosca set out to ransack the records of past ages for instructive examples that would yield general truths on the political behavior of mankind. He had read widely and thoroughly both in the classics and in the published literature of European history. And he seemed able to remember nearly everything he read; as a young man of twenty-five, in the introduction to his first political work, he somewhat naïvely congratulated himself on the advantages he owed to his unusually retentive memory.[4]

Mosca was not only looking for examples. He was also seeking "laws." Here his debt to Taine was manifest and amply recognized. Like his French master, Mosca was radically dissatisfied with the methods and categories ordinarily employed by political writers. He found them imprecise, emotionally grounded, and generally unrelated to the recorded facts of political behavior. And the result had been that the study of politics and sociology had lagged far behind the other scholarly dis-

[3] The only detailed biographical and critical study of Mosca that has appeared to date is by Mario Delle Piane, *Gaetano Mosca: Classe politica e liberalismo* (Naples, 1952).

[4] Gaetano Mosca, *Teorica dei governi e governo parlamentare,* 2nd ed. (Milan, 1925), pp. 5-7.

ciplines. It had not yet become a "science."[5] Mosca implied, although he refrained from making too flat-footed a claim, that his own works would rank as the founding documents of this new science.

This was positivist thinking with a vengeance. Mosca's scientific self-confidence, his cold disdain for sentimental ideologies, and his emphasis on force as the basis of human society were strictly in consonance with the prevailing temper of the post-Darwinian age. From this standpoint, he was by no means the innovator that he claimed to be—he was simply the typical bright scholar of his time. Yet he was too open-minded to allow himself to become imprisoned in his own formulas. He did not rest content with the materialist, mechanical explanations that to contemporary readers make the work of Taine so repellent. And he was careful to avoid the trap of historical determinism. The "political classes" whose role in history he was charting he subjected to no inexorable law of degeneration and fall from power. Their fate lay in their own hands. As Mosca's American editor has pointed out, it was simply "wrong political decisions that headed them toward decline instead of toward higher levels of civilization."[6] Hence Mosca's theory of society, as opposed to that of his leading predecessors and contemporaries, was "open" rather than "closed." It would have satisfied the rigorous requirements of the great living theorist of the "open society." Like Karl Popper, Mosca in effect argues that "we must learn to do things as well as we can, and to look out for our mistakes," and further, that "progress rests with us, with our watchfulness, with our efforts, with the clarity of our conception of our ends, and with the realism of their choice."[7]

Moreover, proud as Mosca was of his theory of the political class, and stoutly as he defended it from all competitors and detractors during more than half a century of catastrophic political changes, he never seems to have taken it with the deadly seriousness characteristic of most discoverers of new ideas. Mosca's mature work, despite the dogmatism of its major premise, is far from dogmatic in tone. It flows along pleasantly and easily in a style that combines the old-fashioned, piled-up periodic sentence with great simplicity and clarity of expression. It is full of sly asides, tantalizing hints of ideas that will never be developed, quiet jests —in short, of an ebullient Mediterranean good humor. The dominant tone is one of urbane skepticism. His own theory, Mosca implies, while

---

[5] Mosca, *Teorica* . . . , *op. cit.,* pp. 11-18; Gaetano Mosca, *Elementi di scienza politica,* 4th ed. (Bari, 1947), Vol. I, Chap. 1.

[6] Livingston, Introduction to *The Ruling Class, op. cit.,* p. xxi.

[7] Karl R. Popper, *The Open Society and Its Enemies,* revised ed. (Princeton, N.J., 1950), p. 463.

it is doubtless the best produced to date, is, after all, only a theory. And all theories should be taken rather lightly. It is probable that Mosca never expected his ideas to have much effect—as indeed they did not—or to be taken . . . too literally by his contemporaries. It would be enough if he had planted in their minds the suspicion that the contrasting political ideologies they so vociferously supported were essentially fantasies—pious frauds of widely varying social usefulness. Subsequently, when Mosca entered politics himself, his conduct was far from doctrinaire. Untroubled by apparent contradictions, he serenely permitted himself to be guided by his naturally pragmatic temper. Thus, although unconvinced of any practical advantage accruing to Italy from the Tripolitan War, he declared himself a colonialist and even consented to serve as undersecretary of state for colonies during World War I. "It is frequently better," he is reported to have remarked, "to make a bad deal than to cut a poor figure." [8]

The same good-humored disclaimer of infallibility cannot be found in Pareto. About many aspects of human behavior, Pareto was deeply skeptical—witness the conventional charge of cynicism brought against him. But about his own mental processes, his own conclusions, he permitted himself little doubt; in this respect he remained closer than Mosca to the original positivist faith. Pareto was content to respect the ultimate mystery of human motivation—but he was convinced that he had at least discovered enough about the laws of social mechanics to provide an adequate guide to mass manipulation.[9] Hence his writing has a rigidity of categorization and an asperity of tone that are found only in Mosca's earliest work. Moreover, Pareto's sociological writings are all of one piece. Only seventeen years elapsed between the publication of the first volume of the *Systèmes socialistes* and that of the final volume of the great *Trattato*. And during this period the author's ideas underwent no significant alteration. He simply reworked them to give them a more "scientific" terminology and presentation. Once Pareto had retired to the shores of Lake Geneva, his attitude was fixed for all time; distinguished visitors came and conversed with the master, but the reverberation of the earth-shaking storms beyond the borders of Switzerland did not alter Pareto's fixed ideas any more than they upset the ordered, if rather eccentric, routine of his daily living.[10] Even the advent of

---

[8] Robert Michels, *Italien von Heute: 1860-1930* (Leipzig and Zürich, 1930), p. 181.

[9] This is essentially the view of Karl Mannheim in *Ideology and Utopia* (New York and London, 1949), p. 123.

[10] For Pareto's domestic arrangements, see Manon Michels Einaudi, "Pareto as I Knew Him," *The Atlantic Monthly*, CLVI (September 1935), 336-46.

Mussolini and the award of a seat in the Italian Senate could not induce him to return to Italy.

In Mosca's case the gap between the youthful moment of discovery and the ultimate retouches applied to his theory for the last edition of the *Elementi* published during his lifetime was a matter of fifty-seven years. In the interval the political configuration of Europe had changed utterly. For Mosca this was no particular source of dismay, either theoretical or practical. Serene in his conviction that most political leaders were garrulous fools, he was not surprised by what had happened. On balance, he concluded, his theory had stood up well. There was little he wished to retract or alter. Even where he confessed that youthful intrepidity had led him to overstate his case, he noted "with a certain satisfaction" that the "fundamental principles" did not "need many corrections." [11] And "several of the most important predictions" that he had made had been "confirmed by events" either "in whole or in part." [12] Nevertheless the passage of time had left its mark. Under the stress of enlarged experience, the "open" element in Mosca's thinking began to predominate over what was merely positivist and doctrinaire.

To many of us today, Mosca's basic notion of history may seem profoundly unhistorical. The problem of historical knowledge never troubled him; he never questioned the credentials of his data. They were simply given "facts," transferable blocks for the political theorist to build with. To the end of his days the concept of history as a drama taking place in the mind of the historian never seems to have occurred to him —despite the fact that he was the contemporary, the countryman, and presumably (as a fellow senator) the acquaintance of Benedetto Croce. On the surface, Mosca retained his positivist allegiance. But somewhat deeper down, a more refined feeling for historical change gradually asserted itself. Despite his own professions, despite his denials of subjectivity, his essential historical-mindedness broke through. This is part of what Croce had in mind when he found a great deal of good sense in a book like the *Elementi* that rested on "philosophical presuppositions" so radically different from his own.[13]

II

This paradox is already apparent in Mosca's first published work. In a little treatise entitled *Teorica dei governi* (1884) that was intended

---

[11] Preface to second edition (1925) of Mosca, *Teorica* . . . , *op. cit.*, p. iv.

[12] Preface to third edition (1938) of Mosca *Elementi* . . . , *op. cit.*, pp. 5-6.

[13] Benedetto Croce, review of the second edition of Mosca's *Elementi* . . . , *La Critica*, XXI (November 20, 1923), 374-78; see also Delle Piane, *op. cit.*, p. 52.

to define the permanent truths of political behavior—derived from historical observation, it is true, but themselves timeless and unchanging —Mosca revealed how deeply his thought was anchored in his own historical situation. With a lordly scorn for his predecessors, Mosca dismissed their theories as based on faulty "historical preconceptions." He alone had discovered the "key to the great secrets of history."

> All the political history of mankind in all times, in all nations, and in all civilizations can ultimately be summarized under two major points of view: on the one hand, the degree of coordination of the various political classes, the number of resources that they are able to gather in their own hands, and the force of their collective action; on the other hand, the various elements that make up these classes, their different methods of imposing their rule, their rivalries, their struggles, their compromises and "combinations." [14]

And so he went on to elaborate in their first and most dogmatic form the basic theories associated with his name—the doctrine of the necessary predominance of an active minority in all times and under all forms of government, even those that call themselves the rule of one man or of all the citizens, and the parallel concept of the "political formula," the convenient myth that conceals the harsh realities of class rule under the respectable cloak of religious or ideological legitimacy.

This emphasis on class considerations in politics already begins to locate Mosca in a specific historical situation. As Karl Mannheim has pointed out:

> It is almost possible to establish a sociological correlation between the type of thinking that appeals to organic or organized groups and a consistently systematic interpretation of history. . . . A class or similar organic group never sees history as made up of transitory disconnected incidents. [15]

Thus it appears to be no accident that during the past century the great integrated views of history have been associated with the aspirations and fortunes of fairly well-defined social classes. They have expressed the struggle of the urban working classes for economic improvement and social equality, as in the case of Marxism. Or, as with the theories of Pareto and Spengler, they have been phrased as last-ditch appeals to a tottering oligarchy to "shore up its fragments" of prestige and authority by infusing new life into the traditional aristocratic values. Finally—as in the case of Toynbee, or, in our own country, F. S. C. Northrop—they have been efforts to restore self-confidence to a great middle class, structurally unintegrated and unsure of its own political allegiance, by lifting

---

[14] Mosca, *Teorica* . . . , *op. cit.*, pp. v, 17, 35.
[15] Mannheim, *op. cit.*, p. 126.

to a higher plane of spiritual contemplation and extra-European validity, the somewhat shop-worn credo of liberalism inherited from the Enlightenment. In this schematic arrangement, Mosca's theories fall somewhere between the second and third categories. They began by more closely resembling the former and ended as a vigorous reaffirmation of liberal principles.

Thus Mosca, as a discerning and clear-headed anti-Marxist, confronts Marx with his own terminology. Unlike the conventional American refutation of Marxism, which denies the whole class interpretation of history, Mosca's theory accepts it but redefines it in such a way as to reverse its implications.

> The existence of a political class does not conflict with the essential content of Marxism, considered not as an economic dogma but as a philosophy of history. . . . There is no essential contradiction between the doctrine that history is the record of a continued series of class struggles and the doctrine that class struggles invariably culminate in the creation of new oligarchies which undergo fusion with the old.[16]

But in Mosca's hands, the classes cease to be historical actors in their own right. They become simply a series of passive audiences, disciplined claques pathetically anxious to applaud the posturings of narrower groups drawn from their own ranks. History, Mosca assures us, cannot be the story of the political vicissitudes of classes conceived as entities— a moment's reflection shows this to be a technical impossibility. It can only be the record of the rise and fall of oligarchies. And if this is the case, then the whole apocalyptic vision of the new world of classless harmony simply vanishes into thin air. The new world will be very much like the old one. Mosca does not deny the possibility of human progress: the word occurs frequently in his writings, and the great ethical purpose behind his work is to confirm the progress that has already been made and to preserve the conditions essential to further advances. His own era—the last quarter of the nineteenth century—Mosca feels to be superior in nearly all respects to its predecessors. But this superior level of civilization is precarious and desperately threatened. A new political class is striving by methods of fraud and violence to displace the old oligarchy whose leadership has brought the European world to its current position of eminence. Under these circumstances, a revolution—the displacement of one oligarchy by another—far from opening up glittering vistas of further progress, would imperil and perhaps destroy the progress that has already been made.

[16] Robert Michels, *Political Parties*, new ed. (Glencoe, Ill., 1949), pp. 390-91.

Redefined in this fashion, the class interpretation of history is transformed from a revolutionary into a conservative doctrine. It becomes a vehicle for restoring the self-confidence of the European ruling classes, whose will to govern has been sapped by the Rousseauist dogmas of democracy and social equality. In effect, Mosca's teaching gives back to them a good conscience about their privileges. If history is simply a succession of oligarchies, it tells them, and political equality a mirage, then it is foolish to worry about one's own position as an oligarch. The democratic gestures inspired by such scruples will be worse than futile; they will pave the way to power for a new oligarchy—far inferior in talent, in ethical standards, and in respect for individual rights to the political class that is currently governing the European parliamentary states. Rather than pursuing the will-o'-the-wisp of democracy, it would be better to take thought for the strengthening and improvement of the existing class regime.

Such was the final lesson of Mosca's neoconservative theory. In the 1880's, after a century of ideological debate, it brought a refreshing breath of realism and practical sense into a political atmosphere stale from the passionate repetition of conflicting slogans and credos. It is only in this context that Mosca's thought can properly be understood. As with the work of so many other political writers, it must be read as an answer to something that has been said earlier. It is neoconservatism —or, to use a contemporary term, sophisticated conservatism—in the sense that it is both postdemocratic and postsocialist. Like the majority of nineteenth-century conservatives, like Tocqueville or Burckhardt or Metternich himself, Mosca considered democracy no more than a brief halt on the way to socialism; the latter was already implicit in the Rousseauist "political formula." But unlike De Maistre and the original theorists of the counterrevolution, in repudiating democracy Mosca did not simultaneously reject the whole liberal tradition of the Enlightenment. On the contrary, he accepted the Enlightenment in its broadest emphasis on rationalized procedures, personal freedom, and limited government. At the same time, he sought to free this tradition from the democratic accretions that had drastically altered its original outlines and that threatened eventually to destroy it. In the light of the experience of two generations of parliamentary government, he argued, one could at last locate precisely where liberalism had gone astray.

It was as a young but already self-conscious member of the liberal upper middle class, then, that Mosca composed his first treatise on politics. This class, which had figured in recent history both as the bearer and as the beneficiary of the liberal tradition, was in the 1880's the dominant group in the economic and political life of the three great parliamentary states of western Europe. In all of them, it was true, the upper-middle-class oligarchy shared power with the old aristocracy—but with each year that passed the balance seemed to incline more heavily in favor of the former. When Mosca wrote his *Teorica,* this happy state of affairs was still of recent origin. In England it had existed at the most for half a century; in France and Italy, for perhaps a decade. And yet it was already threatened with disruption. It was threatened not merely by the assaults of democracy and socialism. It was also being undermined by the malfunctioning of the very parliamentary institutions that had served as the vehicles of upper-middle-class supremacy.

In this historical situation, it was not surprising that Mosca should have devoted the whole second half of his little book to a critique of parliamentarism. After defining the eternal laws of political behavior, the intrepid young theorist quite logically turned his attention to the specific institutions through which these laws manifested themselves in his own time. One might study them, he noted, in England or in France, in the United States, in Austria, in Germany, in Spain, or in Italy. The reasons he gave for using his own country as his test case were not particularly convincing.[17] Presumably he chose it simply because he knew it best.

This choice of Italy, however, and the fact that Mosca was an Italian, were not merely incidental to what he had to say. They profoundly affected the character of his judgments on parliamentary institutions. For Italy in the 1880's was by no means the typical parliamentary country that Mosca claimed. On the contrary, it was an extreme and somewhat eccentric example of the general phenomenon. Still more, Mosca was a southerner, a Sicilian, and it was from southern Italian experience that he drew his most damaging instances of parliamentary malfunctioning. It was already enough that Mosca was writing from an Italian vantage point; the fact that he was a Sicilian compounded the distortion.

In fact, if one were deliberately to choose a time and a place that would display parliamentary institutions to their maximum discredit, it would be hard to find a more telling example than southern Italy in the 1880's. Ever since the fall of the "old Right" in 1876—an event which liberal conservatives of Mosca's type regarded as an unmitigated calamity —Italy had been ruled by a "Left" that was leftist only in name and that in practice represented little more than the replacement of the oligarchy of birth and talent that had founded the new Italian kingdom

[17] Mosca, *Teorica* . . . , *op. cit.,* p. 148.

with a less respectable "political class" of professional parliamentarians and officeholders. The franchise has just been extended to include a million and a half new voters—but still only about one out of every three adult male Italians was even theoretically entitled to participate in elections. And as a practical matter merely a fraction of those enfranchised actually exercised their privilege. Devout Catholics scrupulously refrained from participation in public life; thousands of other citizens shunned the polls through political apathy or distaste for the upstart regime that had overthrown their traditional allegiance. In Rome the parliamentary chambers had become the scene of an unabashed trading of votes against local favors. Under the supple manipulation of Agostino Depretis—prime minister for nearly a decade—party lines had dissolved and old oppositionists had been lured into the governmental majority. The word *trasformismo* had been added to the Italian language to epitomize all that was wrong with the country's parliamentary life.

It was quite obvious, then—and it took no great discernment on the young Mosca's part to detect it—that Italy was being ruled by a fairly narrow governing class. This was particularly the case in the south and Sicily, where quasi-feudal class relations persisted, where the bulk of the population was still illiterate, and where one or two "great electors"— a large landholder or other local potentate—could sometimes swing the vote of an entire constituency. Tightly knit cliques controlled the nomination of candidates and not infrequently called on the local *mafia* or *camorra* to enforce their will. What wonder that Mosca concluded—to cite his most celebrated thrust at the parliamentary system—that "it is not the electors who elect the deputy, but ordinarily it is the deputy who has himself elected by the electors." [18]

Presumably this was necessarily the case; under what Mosca's admirer, Robert Michels, has called "the iron law of oligarchy" no elective system could function otherwise. But in Mosca's early work the distinction between what is merely the normal condition of any political activity and what an abuse is not always made clear. The spirited polemical tone of the young author's writing frequently carries him beyond his expressed intention. At times he keeps rigorously to his professed position of detachment. As opposed to most other political commentators of the period, he is not shocked by the interference of the prefects in elections; indeed, he argues that in a majority of cases this may actually be a good thing, since it produces better candidates than those ordinarily chosen by the local political cliques.[19] At other times, however, Mosca gives way to his

---

[18] *Ibid.*, p. 250.   [19] *Ibid.*, pp. 196-97.

natural polemical bent and makes statements that sound like an unqualified condemnation of the whole parliamentary system. At such times
he betrays what is obviously a deep personal annoyance.

One source of this annoyance is theoretical. Mosca is exasperated by
what he regards as the hypocrisy of political rhetoric, and he is out to
expose how shamelessly the "democratic" politicians violate the principles they profess. At all costs, he wishes to set the record straight.
Beyond this, however, the careful reader can detect a class grievance.
As a member of the educated upper middle class, Mosca understandably
regards himself as belonging to the natural elite of the new Italian
kingdom. Properly, this class should be managing the affairs of the
state. And to a large extent such is still the case. But through a cynical
manipulation of the parliamentary system, the natural elite of the country is being displaced by a new and unsavory class of politicians and
profiteers. Mosca protests against this state of affairs and looks around
for a way to change it. An Italian Henry Adams, he resents being de-
frauded of his birthright.

It comes as no surprise, then, when at the end of his *Teorica* he pre-
dicts the end of the parliamentary system. Even the apparent stability
of Britain, he notes, rests less on its parliamentary institutions than on
the continuity of its governing class.[20] But here Mosca's theoretical difficulties begin: it is one thing to expose the deficiencies of parliamentary
government; it is something far more difficult to devise a new system to
replace it. Mosca is too acute a political observer to imagine that a
return to a frankly aristocratic regime is possible. The idea of representative government—however fallacious the reasoning behind it—is far too
deeply rooted to permit that. And so when he comes to outline his
remedies, he appears somewhat at a loss. After all the vigor of his condemnation, he has few concrete changes to offer. A return to the letter
of the Italian constitution, with executive authority again in the hands
of the King, and a new method of appointing senators so as to make
them truly independent of political considerations—this is virtually all
he proposes. And he advances it somewhat lamely and diffidently, as
though conscious that it is actually a reactionary proposal, unrealistic
and impossible of attainment. He seems already to suspect that this is
not a practicable way to attain his highest goal—"a true renewal of the
whole political class . . . on the basis of personal merit and technical
capacity."

Such is the direction in which Mosca's theory is actually heading.
And his second great desideratum is even more revealing—a "reciprocal

[20] *Ibid.*, pp. 266-67, 299.

control among all the members [of the political class] so as to avoid, so far as is humanly possible, the arbitrary and irresponsible action of a single individual or group of individuals." [21] In this statement Mosca leaves open the way for his eventual reconciliation with the parliamentary regime itself.

III

In its original form the *Elementi*—published in 1896, twelve years after the *Teorica*—did not depart very far from the main principles embodied in the earlier work. It was longer, more detailed, more systematic in organization, and more moderate in tone. The theories of the political class and the political formula, however, were still its central features. And the windy abstractions of democracy and socialism remained the chief targets of Mosca's quiet scorn.

Nevertheless the emphasis had changed. Partly this change reflected the author's altered circumstances of life. In 1885, after the publication of the *Teorica*, Mosca became an unpaid lecturer on constitutional law at the University of Palermo. He was still at the bottom of the academic ladder and still confined to a Sicilian horizon. In the following decade he virtually severed his connections with Sicily. Although remaining a junior lecturer, he transferred to the University of Rome, where he could study national political life at the center rather than on its eccentric periphery. And, in addition to his university work, he had found a paying position that gave unequaled opportunities for observing politics at close hand. As editor of the journal of the Chamber of Deputies, Mosca occupied a unique vantage point for acquiring an education in the realities of parliamentarism.

The day-to-day view of a parliament in action, as opposed to merely observing electoral abuses in the local constituencies, seems to have mollified the uncompromising critic of representative institutions. In 1896 Mosca was not prepared to retract anything that he had said earlier; he still regarded the conventional justifications of parliamentary rule as largely fictitious. But from the practical standpoint he was more prepared to see the advantages of representative government and less eager to point out its failings. Parliamentarism—in the sense of a regime that concentrates in the parliament "all prestige and all power"—he still considered "one of the worst types of political organization"; it was simply the "irresponsible and anonymous tyranny of the elements that prevail in the elections and speak in the name of the people." But properly controlled and limited in their powers, representative bodies

[21] *Ibid.,* pp. 263-64, 300.

offered at least two great advantages. They permitted public opinion—
or, as Mosca more skeptically phrased it, "certain sentiments and certain
passions of the crowd"—to find an echo "in the highest spheres of government." And they guaranteed the "participation of a certain number
of socially valuable elements in the rule of the state." In this fashion,
representative institutions could help in attaining what Mosca still
regarded as the prime desiderata of good government—a system that
would permit "all the elements that have political value in a given
society to be used and specialized to the best advantage, and to be subjected to reciprocal control and the principle of individual responsibility
for what they do in their respective spheres of action."

All this was familiar to readers of the *Teorica*. At the same time the
original version of the *Elementi* shows Mosca already beginning to shift
his emphasis from the first to the second of his requirements for good
government. He still speaks of the importance of recruiting and maintaining the best possible political class. He is still the technician striving
to lay the theoretical foundations for a more competent oligarchy. But
now he emphasizes more frequently than he did before the necessity of
checking the oligarchs in the exercise of their functions. The danger
of "arbitrary and irresponsible action" looms larger in his thought. "The
true moral guarantee of representative governments," he finds, "is the
public discussion that takes place in the assemblies." [22]

Necessarily, then, Mosca is led to re-examine his theory of the political
formula. He reiterates his contention that all such formulas are equally
mythical, but he is now more ready to distinguish between those of them
that are socially useful and those that are dangerous. Specifically, he sep-
arates the two main "intellectual currents" that have produced the parliamentary formula. The democratic doctrine of Rousseau he finds almost
wholly noxious. But the theory of limited government associated with the
name of Montesquieu he considers "not fundamentally mistaken." [23]
Actually Mosca might have gone much farther. Had he been less anxious
to assert his own originality as a political writer, he might have been
more generous in recognizing his debt to the great French theorist. He
might have granted that on all essential points he and Montesquieu are
in agreement. For, like Montesquieu, the Mosca of the *Elementi* draws
"a sharp dividing line between despotism and all other forms of government." And, though an uncompromising foe of despotism in all its
guises, he is too skeptical to "elaborate any radical solution" as a substitute for it. He lacks faith "in the capacity of men to effect and maintain a radically new society. . . . His awareness of the ambiguous char-

[22] Mosca, *Elementi . . . , op. cit.*, Vol. I, pp. 207, 209, 212.   [23] *Ibid.*, Vol. I, pp. 272-73.

acter of progress, his insistence on slowness and caution in legislative changes—all this makes for a conservative but not necessarily reactionary attitude toward life." [24] These conclusions of a contemporary writer on Montesquieu describe with amazing accuracy the position that Mosca had reached midway in his career as a political theorist.

IV

The two decades following the publication of the first edition of the *Elementi* completely altered Mosca's circumstances of life. In 1896, just after the *Elementi* appeared, he had been made a professor at the University of Turin. This event established him as a man who had arrived in life—just as it shifted his orientation from Sicily to the northern part of the country. By 1908 he had attained a position of sufficient eminence so that he could "have himself elected" a deputy. And from that point on the highest public honors followed in regular succession. From 1914 to 1916 he served as an undersecretary in the government, and in 1919 he was appointed a senator of the realm. Mosca's ambition evidently reached no higher. His elevation to the Senate automatically made him an elder statesman, and it was in that capacity that in 1923, the year following Mussolini's accession to power, he accepted a chair at the University of Rome.

Such substantial success in the realm of public life is almost unique in the biographies of political thinkers. In itself it may have had something to do with the increasing mellowness of Mosca's writing and the more favorable attitude he came to adopt toward the parliamentary system. But his experience as a deputy and senator also entered in; he was participating in the activity of the chambers during a period when talent and devotion to the public service were perhaps more conspicuous in those quarters than they had been during the last decades of the previous century. He was experiencing as a historical reality the advent of universal suffrage and the shaky beginnings of Italian electoral democracy. And he did not condemn the new developments in the unrestrained terms that he might have used in the past. This was the more noteworthy since the period immediately following his appointment to the Senate witnessed a further historical change that might well have destroyed his whole new-found tolerance toward the parliamentary system: the virtual breakdown of that system during the three years preceding the March on Rome.

It would have shown a superhuman restraint on Mosca's part if he

---

[24] Franz Neumann, Introduction to Baron de Montesquieu, *The Spirit of the Laws* (New York, 1949), pp. xix, xliii.

had refrained from reminding his fellow countrymen that they were
now experiencing what he had predicted nearly forty years earlier. This
is doubtless what he had in mind when in 1924 he congratulated
himself on the accuracy of his foresight. In an essay on the "crisis in
parliamentarism" published four years later, he stressed the gravity of
the current breakdown in representative institutions. It had come about,
he argued, largely through the "mistake" of conceding universal suffrage
—a mistake, however, "which had become more or less necessary through
the mentality of the times in which it was conceded." Once again he had
little to offer in the way of a remedy. He simply gave his implied endorsement to a system of weighted suffrage "in which the vote of the
poor and ignorant" would not count "exactly the same . . . as that of
the educated person and of the person who has had the ability to acquire
honestly a certain well-being." [25]

Yet at the same time he remained faithful to the basic principles of
limited, representative government. He surprised a number of his intellectual disciples by refusing to rally to the new Fascist regime.[26] More
than that, the very advent of the dictatorship reinforced his tendency to
take a more charitable view of parliamentary institutions. In the first
edition of the *Elementi,* he had stated that "the only practical criterion
for judging . . . political regimes is . . . by comparing them . . . with
those that have preceded them and, when possible, with those that have
followed them." [27] The coming to power of Mussolini gave him a chance
to apply this criterion—to judge the parliamentary system in the light
of what had succeeded to it. Mosca's verdict was unqualified. In December 1925, during the debate on the bill that in effect ended the
responsibility of the prime minister to the Parliament, Mosca rose from
his seat in the Senate to make the following declaration:

> I who have always sharply criticized parliamentary government must now
> almost lament over its downfall. . . . Certainly representative parliamentary
> government must not and cannot be immutable. As the conditions of society
> change political organizations are changed. But should the change have been
> rapid and radical, or should it have been slow and wary? This is the very
> grave question which vexes my soul. As an old adversary of the parliamentary
> regime, I believe that this problem must be solved in the most moderate and
> prudent manner.[28]

[25] Gaetano Mosca, "The Crisis in Parliamentarism and How It May Be Overcome,"
in *The Development of the Representative System in Our Times,* five answers to an
inquiry instituted by the Inter-Parliamentary Union (Lausanne, 1928), p. 84.

[26] Michels, *Italien von Heute, op. cit.,* p. 219.

[27] Mosca, *Elementi . . . , op. cit.,* Vol. I, p. 375.

[28] Quoted in Gaetano Salvemini's introductory essay to A. William Salomone, *Italian
Democracy in the Making* (Philadelphia, 1945), pp. xv-xvi.

Beneath the cautious phraseology, the implication was unmistakable. Mosca rejected Mussolini's brutal solution of the parliamentary crisis. In the showdown, his loyalty to personal freedom and limited government took precedence over his elitist yearnings, which the Fascists had actually gone far to satisfy. Moreover, the tone of his retrospective judgment on the parliamentary system indicated a revised attitude toward history. The elderly senator, now in his late sixties, was far less confident than he had been as an intrepid young theoretician of twenty-five. He was now less sure that his "key" to history had unlocked all its secrets. Nearly half a century before, he had discovered the theoretical formulas that seemed to explain both the political systems of past ages and the course that would be followed by the representative institutions of his own day. And the formulas had worked. They had indicated the crisis in the parliamentary system that in fact had come to pass. But still something had been lacking. The positivist-minded syllogisms in which Mosca had tried to imprison the variety of human political experience had failed to embrace all contingencies. The elusive stuff of history itself had slipped through the theoretician's deftly shaping fingers.

In four decades of lived history, all the elements of his problem had altered. The institutions had changed, but the change had not merely been one of degeneration, as Mosca had earlier predicted. Electoral democracy had come to Italy, but its coming had not been quite the unmitigated catastrophe that he had expected. The virtual universal suffrage extended to the Italian people in 1912 had not destroyed the country's representative institutions. In some ways it had actually strengthened them, by bringing a number of "socially valuable elements" into the Parliament and by adding to it new deputies of unquestioned talent. After all, Mosca himself had been re-elected to the Chamber under the new extended suffrage. It was true that the postwar years had seen the collapse of Italian parliamentary government. But its overthrow had come not from the forces of socialism and syndicalism, as Mosca had long predicted, but from a new and unexpected radicalism of the Right. As late as 1925 it was difficult to determine the precise nature of the Fascist regime. But the old political theorist understood it well enough to know that it was even less to his taste than the system of government that had preceded it. An elitist reaction against democracy had come— but not in the form he had hoped for. Or was it perhaps that his theories themselves had changed? Was it perhaps the shift from emphasizing the mythical character of all "political formulas" to an insistence on their qualitative differences that caused him to render a negative judgment on the new Fascist regime? If something similar had come in the 1880's,

might he have been willing to accept it? Or was it the theoretician himself who had gradually accommodated himself in practice to the characteristic institutions of his time? It was impossible to say—there were too
many variables. In place of the old clear-cut lessons of history, the flux
of human experience itself had taken over.

This new feeling for historical change is apparent in the second edition
of his *Elementi,* published early in 1923. For this revision of a work that
had already become a political classic, Mosca adopted an unusual and
extremely honest approach. Aside from adding a few explanatory notes,
he simply left the original text exactly as it stood. His later ideas and
reflections he appended to it as a somewhat shorter second volume.
While this arrangement makes for rather curious reading, it has the
advantage of displaying the young and the old Mosca side by side. The
leading ideas are the same—again it is simply the emphasis that has
altered.

Although this second volume must have been written almost in its
entirety before the March on Rome—since its publication followed so
soon thereafter—it already reveals Mosca's new attitude toward parliamentary institutions that we have seen embodied in his statements of
1925 and 1928. And in some respects this new version of the *Elementi*
goes even farther. It praises representaive government as the form of rule
that "has succeeded in coordinating a maximum sum of energies and
of individual activities for the benefit of the collective interest." And it
includes a qualified endorsement of "the democratic tendency" as "in a
certain way indispensable to . . . the progress of human societies."
Mosca adds a characteristic justification for this rather surprising change
of front:

> The democratic tendency, so long as its action does not tend to become ex-
> cessive and exclusive, represents what in vulgar language would be called a
> conservative force. For it permits a continual addition of new blood to the
> governing classes through the admission of new elements that have innately
> and spontaneously within them the attitude of command and the will to
> command, and so prevents that exhaustion of the aristocracies of birth that
> is wont to bring on the great social cataclysms.[29]

This, then, is the message of the *Elementi* in their final form—a tentative recourse to "the democratic tendency" to revive the European elites
that have so signally failed in their task of holding off the forces of
despotism. And it is the youth that must accomplish the fusion of the
old and the new elements in the political class. Mosca's second volume

[29] Mosca, *Elementi* . . . , *op. cit.,* Vol. II, pp. 126-127.

closes on a note of warm supplication—an appeal for political "vision"
to the "noblest part of the youth" of his country, in the hope that they
will rise to the responsibilities that the new age imposes upon them.[30]

V

The second volume of the *Elementi* represents the completion of
Mosca's work as a political thinker. In the last two decades of his life,
he felt himself too old to do much further writing. The period between
1923 and his death in 1941 saw the publication of two relatively minor
studies and of the few notes he added to his *Elementi* for the third edition, which appeared in 1938. It is on the final version of this work that
Mosca's reputation rests and that the contemporary relevance of his ideas
may best be judged.

To a skeptical age that has seen the destruction of so many hopes and
the blasting of so many illusions, Mosca's theory of society may well have
a peculiar appeal: . . . it seeks in one formulation both to explain the
revival of despotism that has characterized the past half-century of Western history and to establish on a more solid basis the permanent validity
of free government. The theory of the political class and the political
formula cuts both ways: it exposes what is abstract and unrealistic in the
doctrine of popular sovereignty at the same time as it insists on the
supreme importance of preserving a liberal, constitutional regime. In
drawing a sharp distinction between the liberal and the democratic traditions, it clarifies much that is imprecise and sentimental in contemporary
historical writing and the contemporary discussion of political issues.
And in establishing the priority of the former, both in time and in
importance, it seeks a way out of a dilemma as old as Aristotle—the
dilemma of a democracy that freely chooses to abdicate to tyranny. This
ancient problem has reappeared with renewed force in our own time.
The collapse of Italian, German, and French democracy in the period
from 1922 to 1940 and the present precarious situation of the restored
parliamentary regimes in those countries, have brought home to men's
minds once again the age-old danger that democracy may degenerate into
despotism.

Mosca's answer to this question was aristocratic, conservative, and
largely ineffective. To check the excesses of democracy, he had nothing
more promising to offer than a weighting of the suffrage in favor of
education and property and a strengthening of the powers of non-elective
officials. The very hesitation with which he advanced these remedies
suggests that he half suspected how unrealistic they were; democracy, he

[30] *Ibid.*, II, 242.

admitted, "had become more or less necessary through the mentality of the times." Hence his specific proposals have little relevance for the contemporary world. It is, rather, his insight into the functioning of representative government that is useful to us—that and his insistence that the talent and ethical level of the political class can alone guarantee the preservation and progress of a free society. This teaching is only superficially inapplicable to a modern democracy. It is "undemocratic" only under a definition of democracy that seeks to add to an equality of rights an equality of attainments and ideas. The latter definition is widely held today, particularly in the United States. But it is coming under increasingly heavy attack from those who see the dangers to a free society that such a leveling of talents implies. For them Mosca's warnings carry a note of particular urgency. In a democracy—subject as it is to gusts of popular prejudice and passion—the systematic cultivation of talent, the persistent fostering of the higher-than-average individual, are indispensable to the proper functioning of free institutions.

We have seen how under the influence of a long experience of history itself, Mosca's concept of the political lessons of history gradually altered. We have seen how as an old man he was willing to grant what in his youth he would never have admitted, that under proper circumstances "the democratic principle" could actually function as a stabilizing force in society. Had Mosca lived a decade longer, he might have seen that a new turn of history had necessitated still a further revision in his theories. He might have recognized that in a country like the United States, with a standard of living unparalleled in history and the majority of its population assimilated in habits and attitudes to a vast middle class, his theory of a "political class" is no longer strictly applicable. It is too rigid to embrace the realities of our current society. In a situation in which the locus of political influence is almost impossible to establish, in which authority is diffused among a wide variety of mutually interacting pressure and "veto" groups, it is idle to speak of a clearly defined political class. In practice the rule of minorities still obtains; but their influence is exerted in so shifting and amorphous a fashion that it cannot be described any longer in terms of a specific ruling group.[31] Once more a loosening and reinterpretation of Mosca's categories is in order.

Nevertheless, even in such a society, the problem of the recruitment of political and administrative talent remains. It is perhaps the crucial problem that faces the United States today. Here the historical lessons taught by Mosca—for all their quaint conservatism—can still be studied with profit.

[31] David Riesman, *The Lonely Crowd* (New Haven, 1950), p. 252.

TWELVE

NOTES ON MOSCA
C. WRIGHT MILLS

In *The Sociological Imagination,* C. Wright Mills remarks: "In the book on the elite [*The Power Elite* (New York, 1956)] I had to take into account the work of such men as Mosca, Schumpeter, Veblen, Marx, Lasswell, Michel [*sic*], Weber, and Pareto." He then offers "two excerpts from preliminary notes on Mosca, which may illustrate what I have been trying to describe" (p. 202).

IN ADDITION TO his historical anecdotes, Mosca backs up his thesis with this assertion: It's the power of organization that enables the minority always to rule. There are organized minorities and they run things and men. There are unorganized majorities and they are run. (There are also statements in Mosca about psychological laws supposed to support his view. Watch his use of the word *natural.* But this isn't central, and in addition, it's not worth considering.) But why not also consider (1) the organized minority, (2) the organized majority, (3) the unorganized minority, (4) the unorganized majority? This is worth full-scale exploration? The first thing that has to be straightened out: Just what is the meaning of 'organized'? I think Mosca means: capable of more or less continuous and coordinated policies and actions. If so, his thesis is right, by definition. He would also say, I believe, that an "organized majority" is impossible because all it would amount to is that new leaders, new elites, would be on top of these majority organizations, and he is quite ready to pick up these leaders in his *The Ruling Class.* He calls them *directing minorities,* all of which is pretty flimsy stuff alongside his big statement.

One thing that occurs to me (I think it is the core of the problems of definition that Mosca presents to us) is this: from the nineteenth to the twentieth century, we have witnessed a shift from a society organized as 1 and 4 to a society established *more* in terms of 3 and 2. We have moved from an elite state to an organization state, in which the elite is no longer so organized nor so unilaterally powerful, and the mass is more organized and more powerful. Some power has been made in the streets, and around it the whole social structures and their 'elites' have pivoted. And what section of the ruling class is more organized than the farm bloc? That's not a rhetorical question: I can answer it either way at this time; it's a matter of degree. All I want now is to get it out in the open.

Mosca makes one point that seems to me excellent and worth elaborating further. There is often in "the ruling class," according to him, a top clique and there is this second and larger stratum, with which (a) the top is in continuous and immediate contact, and with which (b) it shares ideas and sentiments, and hence, he believes, policies (page 430). Check and see if anywhere else in the book he makes other points of connection. Is the clique recruited largely from the second level? Is the top, in some way, responsible for—or at least sensitive to—this second stratum?

Now forget Mosca. In another vocabulary, we have, (a) the elite, by which we here mean that top clique, (b) those who count, and (c) all the others. Membership in the second and third, in this scheme, is defined by the first, and the second may be quite varied in its size and composition and relations with the first and the third. What, by the way, is the range of variations of the relations of (b) to (a) and to (c)? Examine Mosca for hints and further extend this by considering it systematically.

This scheme may enable me more neatly to take into account the different elites, which are elites according to the several dimensions of stratification. Also, of course, to pick up in a neat and meaningful way the Paretian distinction of governing and nongoverning elites, in a way less formal than Pareto. Certainly many top-status people would at least be in the second. So would be the big rich. *The clique* or *the elite* would refer to power, or to authority, as the case may be. *The elite* in this vocabulary would always mean *the power elite*. The other top people would be *the upper classes* or *the upper circles*.

So, in a way, maybe, we can use this in connection with two major problems: the structure of the elite; and the conceptual—later, perhaps, the substantive—relations of stratification and elite theories. (Work this out.)

From the standpoint of power, it is easier to pick out those who count than those who rule. When we try to do the first we select the top levels as a sort of loose aggregate and we are guided by position. But when we attempt the second, we must indicate in clear detail how they wield power and just how they are related to the social instrumentalities through which power is exercised. Also we deal more with persons than positions, or at least have to take persons into account.

Now power in the United States involves more than one elite. How can we judge the relative positions of these several elites? Depends upon the issue and decisions being made. One elite sees another as among those who count. There is this mutual recognition among the elite, that other elites count; in one way or another they are important people to one another. Project: select three or four key decisions of last decade—to drop the atom, to cut or raise steel production, the G[eneral] M[otors] strike of [19]45—and trace in detail the personnel involved in each of them. Might use 'decisions' and decision-making as interview pegs when you go out for intensives.

THIRTEEN

POWER SOURCE AND POWER FLOW

J. H. MEISEL

THE THIRTY-FIVE PAGES which make up the fourth chapter of the second *Elementi* (Chapter XV of *The Ruling Class*) are very likely the best Mosca ever wrote. Entitled "Various Principles and Tendencies Affecting the Formation and Organization of the Ruling Class," this section . . . represents the author's answer to his own stern summons: if the doctrine of the ruling class is to be meaningful at all, "the comprehensive and generic demonstration" must be supplemented "with an analytic study." [1] Here is the proof of the pudding; the full potentialities of the new method are established beyond any reasonable doubt.

Plato—the Plato of *The Laws*—has the first as well as the last word of the chapter. His twofold scheme, deriving all existent variants of government from the two archetypes, democracy and monarchy, serves Mosca as a starting point. . . . The author uses the term "principle" when he refers to the direction of the power flow in a political community. There are, of course, only two ways in which that flow could move: "authority is either transmitted from above downward . . . or from below upward." In the first case, Mosca says, the autocratic principle is at work. He might have called it "the monarchic principle," but the autocratic won out, being more inclusive, since it could be applied to nonmonarchic types of government as well.

Conversely, when authority is assumed to reside with all, or a part, of the people, Mosca chooses to speak of "the liberal principle," preferring the term *liberal* to Plato's "democratic," since democratic denotes the sovereignty of all the people, whereas "liberal" would also include all

"Power Source and Power Flow." From *The Myth of the Ruling Class: Gaetano Mosca and the Elite,* by James H. Meisel (Ann Arbor: The University of Michigan Press, 1958 and 1962), pp. 198-201, 217-18, 220-21. Reprinted by permission of The University of Michigan Press.

[1] Gaetano Mosca, *The Ruling Class*, p. 336.

those systems which restrict the ballot, as in Rome and Athens, to a more or less large fraction of the total populace.

"Tendency," as distinct from "principle," is Mosca's label to identify the source from which the ruling classes are recruited. Here Plato's terminology is readopted by the author: the term "democratic" seems more suitable to indicate that an existing ruling class is open to the lower classes, or else that the ruling class ought to be open to the lower ranks.[2] This tendency "is constantly at work with greater or lesser intensity in all human societies." [3]

The same is true of "the aristocratic tendency" which is at cross purposes with democratic methods of selection. It is the label for the human urge "to stabilize social control and political power in the descendants" of the ruling group.

Now all this is at first a bit confusing. Was it necessary to inflict upon the reader, at this advanced stage of the discussion, four new, complex, easily confounded terminologies all in one heap? From this objection one might easily proceed and try to simplify the matter. Could the four terms be reduced to two? Why not pair off "the autocratic principle" with "the aristocratic tendency" and "the democratic tendency" with "the liberal principle"?

But Mosca has been waiting for just that attempt, and he is quick to point out to us our mistake: "At first glance it might seem that the predominance of what we call the 'autocratic' principle should go with what we call the 'aristocratic' tendency; and that the opposite principle which we call 'liberal' should go with the tendency that we call 'democratic' . . . . That, however, would be a rule that is subject to a great many exceptions." [4] Not a few autocracies recruited their officials from the lower classes, and elective systems could be mentioned in which the electors were identical with the political class in control. So intermixed are the two principles and the two tendencies that it is difficult to isolate them properly. But nothing less will do if we intend to understand which way society is moving.

Accordingly, the four components of the system are now taken up in sequence and the pluses and the minuses in each case toted up.

Much can be said in favor of the autocratic principle. "A political system that has been so widely recurring and so long enduring among peoples of the most widely various civilizations . . . must somehow correspond to the political nature of man. The artificial or exceptional thing never shows such great tenacity." The political formulas of autoc-

[2] *Ibid.,* pp. 394, 395.   [3] *Ibid.,* p. 413.   [4] *Ibid.,* p. 395.

racy, based on a theocratic, charismatic, or dynastic principle of authority, are "simple, clear, and readily comprehensible to everybody."

Against autocracy speaks the fact that "it does not allow the peoples
that have adopted it, and especially their ruling classes, to attain all of
the moral and intellectual development of which civilized mankind is capable." In some way, size and cultural accomplishment of a community
seem to be correlated: thus, autocracy appears to be the system most
congenial to large communities.[5] The glory that was Greece, or Florence,
issued from parochial ground. Another correlation can be found between
duration and intensity of cultural achievement: the actual flowering of
Athens lasted only 150 years (479-323 B.C.), and Rome's greatness did not
last much longer (203-31 B.C.). The United States and England are the
modern nations which proclaim the triumph of the liberal principle. But
English institutions deserve to be called *free* only after the Glorious Revolution (1688), when "the great North-American Republic" was not even
born. The real greatness of both countries did not come until much
later, Mosca says. In other words, it is too early to say whether Anglo-
Saxon liberty is going to outlast the Greco-Roman span of a hundred and
fifty years. That is, in any case, what Mosca seems to think when he says
that apparently the liberal principle tends "to prevail at those exceptional periods in the lives of the peoples when some of the noblest
faculties of man are able to show themselves in all their intensity and
energy." However, those enormous outbursts of creative force seem
almost always to be followed by a kind of collective fatigue. It is then
that "human societies feel, as it were, an overpowering need for a long
sleep." That is the time when Rome submitted to the autocratic rule of
the Augustus Caesar.[6]

This periodization, linking periods of historic creativity or barrenness
with certain types of government, has a definite Spenglerian note, but
possibly it was the secret, unacknowledged influence of Giambattista
Vico's *Corso* and *Ricorso* that inspired our author at this point. . . .

Commenting on the wide application the aristocratic principle has
found in the past, Mosca wisely leaves room for the human factor. His
four tendencies and principles are not to be considered iron laws. One
instance will suffice to demonstrate their flexibility: "In countries where
the autocratic principle and the aristocratic tendency jointly prevail, the
[ruling] group is usually made up of members of the highest nobility."
That will be so in all instances where the incumbent of the highest
office is a man of only average ability. But when the monarch happens

<hr />

[5] *Ibid.*, p. 397.   [6] *Ibid.*, p. 398.

to be a great ruler, "he sometimes succeeds in breaking the ring of aristocratic cliques that serve him—or more often rule him—and he snaps
it by elevating to the highest positions persons . . . of ordinary birth.
. . . ." In doing so, he brings about a change from the aristocratic to
the democratic tendency, thereby not only not abandoning the autocratic
principle but, in most cases, reinforcing it against the cabals of his
court. . . .[7]

Close intellectual and moral ties, we are informed, connect the first
and second strata of the ruling class, the top group being "more or less
imbued with the ideas, sentiments, passions, and, therefore, policies" of
the secondary level. . . . Unless the top rulers have come from an alien
race of conquerors, the upper stratum would quite naturally rise from
the larger body (which unites in itself one or several of the indigenous
social forces). They would rise the way a medieval king had to be first a
primus inter pares, first among his peers, before he could become the
absolute prince, *legibus solutus.*

What is true of the small inner circle applies equally to the secondary
elite. Again, unless it came into existence through an act of conquest, it
has to—and does—come from the ruled majority. To restate once more
Mosca's general idea of the way civilizations grow: they crystallize out of
a multitude of little power centers until some kind of unity has been
achieved. (The unifying agent need not be a central government, but
could be—as was the case with feudalism—a cultural, religious bond and
institution.)

That is integration in its horizontal aspect: centripetal. The same
process takes place also in a vertical direction: power flows toward the
apex of an ever-higher-rising social pyramid. It is permissible to say that
Mosca's law of social and political organization is identical with his
law of the "democratic tendency." Nor is that an accident. Whether he
likes it or not, his whole theory of the political class has a cryptodemo-
cratic character. It is one not concerned with conquerors, and only at
the very outset with the men of military valor. The political class is not
even any more exclusively the wealthy class. Professional skills, knowledge, training have become the indispensable tools of political control,
and these tools are in the hands of the educated class—Mosca's class. This
class is still, essentially, the middle class, but with education having
become general, the flow of intellectual energies is no longer confined
to it. The new elite comes from the masses.

[7] *Ibid.,* pp. 403-4.

Mosca is aware of it, and he calls the connection between masses and the second layer of the ruling class even "more certain and less varying than the other" (the connection between the two strata of the ruling class itself).[8]

. . . The greatness of a statesman may be measured, Mosca says, by his "success in transforming ruling classes by improving the methods by which they are recruited and by perfecting their organization." In that sense, Augustus was a man of greatness, for "he revived the old Roman ruling class, which had been decimated by almost a century of civil warfare, by introducing new elements into it." Vespasian, too, comes in for praise because he "raised representatives from many of the more illustrious families of Italy to senatorial rank." [9] [Here] the author almost but not quite succeeds in reaping the full benefits of his own method. What Vespasian did was to broaden but also to lower the basis of the ruling class, by drawing the provincial notables into the second stratum, to which he had himself just barely belonged.[10]

In this connection Mosca . . . makes it very clear that even the most consummate practitioner of statecraft may be helpless if the situation is beyond repair. This time, he exploits the advantages of his own method to the full in using the example of Byzantium. As long as "its ruling classes still retained . . . considerable resources in intellectual power and patriotism, and the subject peoples were still able to supply large revenues to the public treasury and numerous soldiers to the army," the Empire could hold out. But when those classes were "run down," the end was only a matter of time.[11]

In other words, to spell out what the author fails to say, but clearly wishes to convey: the upper stratum of the ruling class depends on the lower; both, in turn, depend upon the common people: if these are vigorous, the ruling class can perform wonders; if they are abused, *finis imperii*.

By implication Mosca says . . . : The doctrine of the ruling class is a myth, in the sense that it directs attention to a single aspect of the social process which is slated to epitomize and symbolize the working of the whole. It is, however, not the whole but a mere part, although perhaps the most intelligible and enticing part. But taken by itself, the ruling elite is not an "intelligible field of study." . . .

[8] *Ibid.*, p. 433. [9] *Ibid.*, pp. 431, 432. [10] Cf. *The Myth of the Ruling Class*, p. 85.
[11] Mosca, *The Ruling Class*, p. 433.

FOURTEEN

THE POLITICAL ELITE
AND BUREAUCRACY

CARL J. FRIEDRICH

POLITICAL THOUGHT HAS persistently been inclined to presume that government is a task calling for specially qualified men of exceptional capacity, virtue, and intelligence. This inclination is only a specialized version of the view that most human achievements are the creations of great men. Such theories, extolling the deeds of the select few, have exercised a profound influence, and not without reason. . . . It can certainly be said that men differ in power, influence, authority, representative quality, as well as the capacity for freedom in its three dimensions. But the problem of political theory is to determine to what extent such differences can be said to "constitute" an elite, which is more than a category in a system of classifying men. It is one of the basic errors in much of the writing on political elites that it argues from the existential judgment that people can be classified according to standards of excellence in performance to the existential judgment that an elite exists. But unless such an assortment of persons (a class in the mathematical or statistical sense) also possesses the characteristics of a group with internal cohesion and a consequent capacity for acting jointly, it is hardly justified to speak of them as a political elite. Therefore, a tentative description of the political phenomenon which may properly be called a *political, ruling,* or *governing elite* may be as follows: it is a group of persons who are distinguished by exceptional performance in politics, who effectively unite (monopolize) the rule of a particular community in their hands, and who possess a sense of group cohesion and a corresponding *esprit de corps,* usually expressed in cooptation; a political elite excels in the ability to secure power and rule.

"The Political Elite and Bureaucracy." From *Man and His Government,* by Carl J. Friedrich (New York: McGraw-Hill Book Company, 1963), pp. 315-21, 332-34. Copyright © 1963 by McGraw-Hill Book Company. Reprinted by permission of the publisher.

It may, however, be argued that it would be useful to distinguish a political elite in the statistical sense of those who are "good at politics" from the "ruling" or "governing" elite we have just characterized.[1] We hesitate to accept this suggestion because of the potential confusion as well as the doubtfulness of so designating those who are "good at politics"; for is anyone who is "good at politics" likely to be unrelated to the ruling and governing, if the term "good at politics" is given a specific governmental connotation? It is, of course, true, that in situations of breakdown and revolutionary crisis, a revolutionary leader may be very good at politics, and yet quite unrelated to a "ruling" or "governing" elite of the political order he and his movement seek to overthrow. But he is likely to be the ruler, indeed usually the autocratic governor, of his organization.[2] Our concept of the elite is not restricted to a particular group or level of community formation; it applies to any group whatever. The political elite, seen as ruling and governing, may of course be differentiated according to political community formation: official elites, revolutionary elites, ecclesiastical elites, and so forth.[3]

Perhaps the most striking instance of an elite theory failing to consider the group aspect of political elites (though implying it repeatedly) is that of Vilfredo Pareto and of Gaetano Mosca.[4] Pareto, who systematized and developed Mosca's ideas on this score, sought to give the theory a broader sociological basis. The relationship of the two writers is somewhat controversial.[5] Pareto's elite theory, being of broader scope, rests upon this

[1] This point was first made by Robert Dahl in a discussion of the main thesis of this chapter, on April 13, 1961; cf. for the issue, his study of 1962.

[2] The specific issues of party rule, as seen by Lenin, are discussed below, Chap. 28. [I.e., in *Man and His Government*—ED.]

[3] A very interesting general discussion of political elites was organized by the International Sociological Association at their Fourth World Congress in 1959, under the chairmanship of A. P. d'Entrèves; the proceedings were edited and published by Renato Treves, 1961. The main papers were presented by E. Pennati, N. Bobbio, G. E. G. Catlin, W. L. Guttsman, J. La Palombara, G. Lavau, J. H. Meisel, G. Sartori, and A. Touraine. Only a partial, general agreement emerged. Bobbio, in concluding remarks (pp. 207-209), identified two main areas of discussion and possible agreement, one that political elites are minorities (agreed), and the other that they must be organized. On the latter point there was disagreement. As we show in the text, it is not a matter of organization but the more general question of group cohesion and self-identification.

[4] Gaetano Mosca, *Elementi di scienza politica* (1896), *The Ruling Class* (1939); Vilfredo Pareto, *Trattato di sociologia generale*, 2nd ed. (Florence, 1923), *The Mind and Society* (New York, 1935), esp. Secs. 2031-59; J. H. Meisel, *The Myth of the Ruling Class* (Ann Arbor, 1958); Robert Michels, *First Lectures in Political Sociology*, translated by A. de Grazia (1949).

[5] Pareto, *The Mind and Society, op. cit.*, contains an able discussion of the problem by Arthur Livingston on pp. xxxvi ff. However, because of his partiality toward Pareto, this author somewhat exaggerates when he claims: "There is no dialectical or historical

author's criticism of the rationalist concept of man, as found in nine
teenth-century economic and sociological thought. . . . Such criticism
overshot the mark. . . . Pareto argues from the hardly disputable premise that in any branch of activity, such as a trade, those participating in
it can be arranged according to their performance. Pareto does not hesitate to suggest that there exists an "elite" of thieves composed of those
who are best in that activity. It is clear that such a concept is purely
statistical and refers to persons with particular characteristics—namely,
those which make them best in what they are doing. One could also call
it functional, in that excellence is for purposes of classification defined in
terms of the function the particular individual performs. No attempt is
made by Pareto to show that such an "elite" operates as a group. This
might not be a fatal objection in the case of such persons as doctors,
engineers, and scientists, though even here organizations such as acade-
mies suggest that for certain purposes effective cooperation among the
best may be desirable.

Having defined the elite in a purely statistical way, Pareto proceeds by
simply dividing this elite into two classes, a *"governing elite,* comprising
individuals who directly or indirectly play some considerable part in
government, and a *non*governing elite, comprising the rest." [6] This distinction is not stated satisfactorily as it stands. It should distinguish
political from nonpolitical elites. Pareto's own interest in the circulation
of elites should have served to restrict the elite concept to those who
play a part in the government, even when that term is not taken too
formally. There is, however, a further difficulty in that nonpolitical elites
need actually to be further subdivided for purposes of political analysis.
These several nonpolitical elites, economic, social, technical, and cultural,
vary greatly in their relevance for politics among themselves, and in different situations. Thus, to give just one illustration of great moment at
the present time, the technical elite which constitutes the core of the
military establishment is much more relevant to American politics in the
second half of the twentieth century than it was in the first.[7] Along with
this ascendancy of the military, cultural elites, especially scientific elites,

---

connection between Pareto's theory of the elite and Mosca's theory of the ruling class."
For Pareto's "governing elite" seems largely identical with Mosca's "political class" or
"ruling class." Cf. also the stimulating, and in the main convincing, discussion in
Meisel, *op. cit.,* Chap. 8 and pp. 356-60.

  [6] Pareto, *op. cit.,* Sec. 2032.

  [7] This is the sound kernel in Mills, *The Power Elite* (1956), Chaps. 8 and 9; he over-
stated his position when including the top military in an American "power elite." The
notion of such a power elite is largely statistical. Yet, Mills rightly emphasized the
ascendancy of the military.

have assumed decidedly more important roles in American politics in the course of the twentieth century.

The main difficulty with distinguishing between a political and a non-political elite stems, however, from another crucial fact. The problem of elite formation is complicated in two directions in the field of government. To begin with, only a *cooperating* group of the "best" could be said to be "governing"; for government is a complex whole. All that we have shown in earlier parts of this work and will elaborate later as characteristic of the governmental process implies that. Furthermore, arguments involving the importance of an elite, from Plato to contemporary writings,[8] have always tacitly assumed it. Surely, if Plato's guardians were found here and there, indiscriminately dispersed among the rest of the community, they could not accomplish their task. Plato, accordingly, is especially concerned with their forming a close-knit group by the sharing of property, of meals and, as the saying goes, of wives (though presumably wives share the husbands as well). Similarly, the communist elite of Marx's doctrine is a firmly organized party, and Lenin perfected the master's notions in this respect.[9] Indeed Pareto himself in writing of the "governing elite" seems to envisage them as a cohesive group when he says, for example, "Every people is governed by an elite, by a chosen element in the population."[10] The close-knit character of such elite groups does not exclude the possibility of a gradual transformation, of course; every governing elite is subject to such changes. This common observation led Pareto to the formulation of his celebrated "law," based upon his conception of the circulation of classes. "In virtue of class circulation, the governing elite is always in a state of slow and continuous transformation," he wrote.[11] That is to say, new persons join or are admitted to this group, which possesses, evidently, a life of its own. But as so often, this brilliantly speculative author alleges more than the facts which he adduces warrant. Change and transformation there are, certainly. But these changes do not seem to exhibit regularly or even casually a *circular* motion. Rather, they resemble the kind of transformation by which a piece of forest is slowly altered by the gradual substitution of other species; there may be built-in circular regularities, such as the succession of hardwood and softwood trees, but no data are offered by Pareto to suggest it. He merely offers some vague generalities, such as that "velocity in circulation has to be considered not only absolutely, but

[8] Mills, *op. cit.*, and Meisel, *op. cit.*, give extensive references; cf. also Dahl, "Critique of the Ruling Elite Model," *APSR*, LII:2 (1958), 463-69.

[9] Lenin, *What Is to Be Done?* (1902), especially Chap. 4, Secs. C-E.   [10] Pareto, Sec. 248.

[11] *Ibid.*, Sec. 2056.

also in relation to the supply of and the demand for certain social elements," [12] or that "the upper stratum of society, the elite, nominally contains certain groups of peoples, not always very sharply defined, that are called aristocracies." [13] There follow then some random observations on aristocracies, culminating in the dictum that "history is a graveyard of aristocracies," discussed further below. The reason for Pareto's failure to develop significant insights is due to his not recognizing the cohesive group character of political or governing elites. As such, governing elites are the result of specific constellations of political factors conditioning their development.

If this is true, then obviously the formation of such groups may be subject to specific conditions, and they may be found in some societies but not in others. Both Pareto and Mosca adduce evidence in support of their contention that they are found in all societies, but this evidence is inconclusive in two respects. In the first place, it is drawn from history and therefore would prove only that past societies have always contained elites; a different argument, philosophical and general, in terms of human nature for example, would have to be adduced if their disappearance were to be excluded. No such argument is offered by these authors, though writers like Plato and the theorists in his tradition abound with contentions of this sort. But there is the further difficulty that the historical evidence is quite incomplete and merely serves to show that such elites have existed and actually governed in some societies. That this is true, no one will want to question. In these instances, as Pareto's own evidence tends to suggest, the governing elite is apt to be self-appointed and self-renewing, with a great many variations in the methods of cooptation. The crucial fact is, however, that the elite itself sets the standard of excellence by which particular men are to be evaluated. Plato's royal lie is the most famous instance of the hypocrisy involved in all such self-evaluations. Most of the historic elites have not aspired to such spiritual heights as Plato did. More usual standards have been distinguished: blood descent, riches, and military valor, to mention only the most usual measuring rods.[14] More recently, Marx and his followers have made "class consciousness" the mark of a governing elite, and in the Communist

---

[12] *Ibid.*, Sec. 2044.

[13] *Ibid.*, Secs. 2051 ff. Pareto recognizes, of course, that these reflections are of long standing.

[14] Mannheim, *Ideology and Utopia* (1936), speaks of blood, riches, and accomplishment (*Leistung*), including of course military exploits. This inclusion of accomplishment in general obscures, however, the analysis of the governing or ruling aspect of an elite, but Mannheim, not being especially concerned with governing elites, is justified in putting it that way.

states of our time the ideological commitment of the ruling party has been the "visible" sign of such election.

The difficulty with all such standards for determining who "belongs" to an elite is that there is no readily available yardstick for assessing the performance in the field of government. As we said, it is quite possible to classify persons engaged in technical functions, such as lawyers, doctors, engineers, farmers, cooks, and so forth. There may be considerable difference of opinion, but because of the technical standards involved, a measure of rational agreement can be considered achievable. These purely technical standards can be used because agreement on the value to be achieved can be presupposed. When a doctor is called, health is to be served, when a lawyer, legal rights, and so forth. But can the same be said for "governing" or "ruling"? Plato asserted it in his well-known comparisons of rulers with shepherds, ship captains, doctors, and the like.[15] But he was wrong. The multiplicity of values involved in community living and the consequent difficulty in assessing performance exclude the possibility of treating excellence in government in analogy to excellence in these other activities. Pareto's own evidence in support of the contention that a "governing elite" is the projection of a class which happens to be dominant in society—in close parallel to Marxist views, incidentally—suggests the conclusion that only a fairly cohesive group with common value judgments and interests is likely to agree on the quality of performance of any person engaged in government.

Recently, an attempt has been made to substitute "power" for other kinds of performance criteria in constructing a statistical concept of the elite.[16] To do so was thought "important in the light of the common supposition that to put the concept of elite to the fore in political science is to deny from the outset the possibility of democratic institutions." An elite is then defined as "those with most power in the group." There would be added a "mid-elite" with "less power" and the "mass" with least power. Apart from the objections arising from limiting the term *elite,* even when meant politically, to power-wielders, it is evident from the previous analysis that this elite concept is strictly statistical—that is to say, [it] simply classifies persons according to the amount of power they possess. Whether such a statistical classification seems interesting in view of the difficulty of constructing an adequate index of power in

---

[15] Plato, *The Republic,* Sec. 345; *Statesman,* Sec. 302 A; and *The Laws,* Sec. 758 A for key references; there are some interesting variations on the theme in the *Statesman, The Laws,* and elsewhere, but they do not affect the basic issue.

[16] Lasswell and Kaplan, *Power and Society,* 1950, pp. 62, 201 ff. It should be borne in mind, however, that these authors do not use the terms *power* and *influence* in the same sense as is done here; for them power is *the participating in making decisions,* while *influence* is *value position potential* (pp. 75, 58).

quantitative terms will not be discussed here. These authors rightly remark that no more than such a statistical class is "contained in such assertions as Pareto's that 'every people is governed by an elite, by a chosen element in the population'; what is said, in effect, is that every people is ruled by—rulers." It seems highly questionable, however, whether in light of this discussion the decision of these authors to retain a statistical concept of the (governing) elite is justified; the paucity of generalizations derived by them from their analysis would suggest abandoning it. It deserves notice that their elite concept is different and distinct from their concept of the ruling class; it is not the class that rules, as in Mosca, but the class "from which the rulers are recruited and in whose interest they exercise power." In other words, their ruling class concept is identical with Marx's concept of the oppressing, exploiting class as expressed in the justly famous phrase of the *Communist Manifesto:* "The modern state power is only a committee which administers (executes) the common business of the bourgeois class," which shows that the exploiting class is also the ruling class. Clearly, such a ruling class, seen as a reservoir from which the rulers or governors, the governing elite, are drawn, is seen as a collective led by those who are conscious of its role and its identity. Indeed, "class consciousness" is, for Marx,.the key characteristic of true elite, and hence the communists are the elite of the proletariat, whereas the "elite" which is merely characterized by being a statistical classification of those who have the most power is quite different from a class-conscious leadership which could be, though it need not be, a mere collection of power-wielders. Only such an elite exhibiting group cohesion and a capacity for monopolizing rule possesses the self-identity necessary for political functioning. . . .

[In the section omitted here, the author reviews the history of the theory of elites, from Saint-Simon, Carlyle, and Nietzsche to Mosca, Michels, Pareto, and Mannheim. He discusses governing and "value" or "culture-shaping" elites in nondemocratic societies and questions the applicability of elitist concepts to democratic systems. He pays particular attention to elitist tendencies in party organizations and—here our text resumes—bureaucracies.]

Current discussions about a governing or ruling elite usually include all or part of the bureaucracy. Sometimes a government bureaucracy is distinguished from the rest; at other times, not. One recent author contrasts the normative notion of a "genuine" bureaucracy, described as "an organized hierarchy of skills and authorities, within which each office and rank is restricted to its specialized tasks," with a "pseudobureaucracy" outside government. To such a view, the bureaucrat "or civil servant" is "above all an expert whose knowledge and skill have been attested to by qualifying examination, and later in his career by qualifying experience." Such "normative" use should be avoided.[17] The various ways of describing the governing or ruling elite would invariably include the upper reaches of the bureaucracy, if by bureaucracy is meant the class of persons in a community who perform specific functions of an administrative kind as members of an organization in which such functions are differentiated as well as centrally controlled and supervised (thus forming a hierarchy), being specially qualified for the performance of these functions. Characteristically, such persons exhibit certain specific behavioral traits, more especially objectivity, consistency, and discretion.[18]

Bureaucracy thus employed as a term for designating a particular class of persons forming an organized group may be either diversified and pluralistic or unified and centralistic. If it is united and centralistic, it constitutes part of the governing or ruling elite, indeed often constitutes the central core of such an elite, as in ancient China and in the absolute monarchies of modern Europe. In the totalitarian autocracies two rival bureaucracies are operative, those of the party and of the government. Since virtually all members of the upper echelons of the government bureaucracy are also party members, the two bureaucracies together constitute the governing elite.[19] In constitutional democracies, a number of bureaucracies are in competition with each other, notably those of the several parties of the government, including the military (in federal systems these are multiplied), of business organizations and of the trade unions. Churches, universities and other sectors of social life also exhibit an increasing trend toward bureaucratization.[20] The conflicts among these several bureaucracies and the consequent disorder have raised, especially in periods of emergency, the cry for "coordination," if not of "integration." During the two world wars, such coordination was in a measure accomplished in all the major democracies. In normal times the vig-

[17] Mills, *op. cit.*, pp. 235 ff. Mills' definition is based upon Max Weber's as modified by later discussions; cf. Robert K. Merton, *et al.*, *Reader in Bureaucracy* (1952), especially the critical evaluation, pp. 27 ff. Also S. N. Eisenstadt, "Bureaucracy and Bureaucratization," *Current Sociology*, VII:2 (1958), 99 ff., and "Internal Contradictions in Bureaucratic Politics," *Comparative Studies in Society and History*, I:1(1958), 58 ff.

[18] Carl J. Friedrich, *The New Image of the Modern Man* (1950), Chap. II; Max Weber, *Wirtschaft und Gesellschaft* (1922, 1925), Part I, Chaps. 3-5, Part III, Chap. 6; Lasswell and Kaplan, *op. cit.* (1950), p. 205, stress the hierarchical aspect, which they define as "a structure of power relationships of varying amounts of power"—a definition which, while not incorrect, is insufficient, just as is their definition of an elite. Merely the amount of power, even if it were determinable, does not suffice to characterize a hierarchy.

[19] Friedrich and Brzezinski, *Totalitarian Dictatorship and Autocracy*, 1956, Chap. 16.

[20] This trend has been ridiculed by Parkinson, *Parkinson's Law* (1957); it is the subject of many serious studies, for example, the section on the "growth" of bureaucracy in Merton, *et al.*, *op. cit.*, pp. 60-113, and on the "bureaucrat," pp. 353-96.

orous competition and rivalry among the several bureaucratic *corpora* is not only accepted, but surrounded with a halo of approval; doctrines such as that of free enterprise embody that viewpoint. The diversification and rivalry between the bureaucratic elements is further evidence for the conclusion that no inclusive governing elite exists in the constitutional democracies, though such an elite may well exist in certain organizations which constitute parts of the system as a whole. Indeed, in many of the highly bureaucratized units, such as large-scale business enterprises and certain churches, the bureaucracy is in fact the governing elite. The need for excelling in performance in order to maintain their position within the community at large tends, however, to make these governing elites wide open to new elements, and hence to foster rapid transformation even in these constituent elements.

In conclusion, it might be desirable to repeat the tentative description given at the outset as it has been elucidated in the preceding pages. We said that a ruling or governing elite, in short, a political elite, is a group of persons who are distinguished by exceptional performance in politics, who effectively unite the rule in their hands, and who possess a sense of group cohesion and a corresponding *esprit de corps*. Such political elites are an important and widespread phenomenon, and they characterize the operation of many forms of rule, more especially totalitarian dictatorship. Evidently the persons composing them are not necessarily linked by blood ties, but may enter the elite on the basis of excelling in a considerable variety of performances. The above discussed "circulation of elites" is a cumbrous way of referring to this phenomenon, which is intrinsic to the very nature of any elite, but more particularly of a governing elite. The notion that a hereditary nobility is a particularly significant and efficacious kind of political elite, entitled to and worthy of special admiration, was found to be a mirage, although the cultural and political contribution of a hereditary nobility may be considerable under favorable circumstances. Other elites than a governing one are, in any case, probably as much or more worthy of admiration, including the scientific elite of our time. Democracy has every reason to foster the development of such nongovernmental elites, and even in the realm of government it has developed, in the administrative bureaucracy, a kind of technical elite in terms of performance. At the same time, a democratic political order is antielitist at its core; instead of relying upon the virtue and other standards of a self-appointed governing elite for securing responsible conduct, it depends upon the willingness of a sufficient part of the citizenship to participate freely in supervising and controlling the temporary rulers and to bring them to account.

SELECTIVE BIBLIOGRAPHY

WORKS BY VILFREDO PARETO

Cours d'économie politique. 2 vols., Lausanne, 1896-97.

Les systèmes socialistes. 2 vols., Paris, 1902.

Manuale di economia politica. Milan, 1906. French edition: *Manuel d'économie politique.* Paris, 1909.

Trattato di sociologia generale. Florence, 1916-23. English translation: *The Mind and Society.* 4 vols., New York, 1935.

Transformazione della democrazia. Milan, 1921.

Corrispondenza di Vilfredo Pareto, ed. by Guido Sensini. Padua, 1948.

The Ruling Class in Italy before 1900 (four essays). New York, 1950.

Lettere a Maffeo Pantaleoni, ed. by G. de Rosa. 3 vols., Rome, 1960.

WORKS BY GAETANO MOSCA

Sulla teorica dei governi e sul governo parlamentare. Turin, 1884.
Second edition: *Teorica dei governi e governo parlamentare.* Turin, 1925.

Elementi di scienza politica. Turin, 1896. Second edition (with a second, previously unpublished part), 2 vols., Turin, 1923. Fourth edition (with a Preface by Benedetto Croce), Bari, 1947. English translation: *The Ruling Class (Elementi di scienza politica),* translated by Hannah D. Kahn; ed. and revised, with an Introduction, by Arthur Livingston. New York and London, 1939. German translation: *Die Herrschende Klasse: Grundlagen der politischen Wissenschaft,* translated from the fourth Italian edition by Franz Borkenau (with a Preface by Benedetto Croce). Bern, 1950.

Lezioni di storia delle instituzioni e delle dottrine politiche. Rome, 1932 (Preface dated 1933). Second, revised edition: *Storia delle dottrine politiche.* Bari, 1937. French translation: *Histoire des doctrines politiques depuis l'antiquité jusqu'à nos jours,* translated, with an Introduction, by Gaston Bouthoul. Paris, 1936.

Partiti e sindacati nella crisi del regime parlamentare (collected essays). Bari, 1949.

BOOKS ABOUT PARETO

Franz Borkenau, *Pareto.* New York, 1936.

G. H. Bousquet, *Précis de sociologie d'après Vilfredo Pareto.* Lausanne, 1925.

——————, *Vilfredo Pareto, sa vie et son oeuvre.* Lausanne, 1928.

——————, *The Work of Vilfredo Pareto.* Hannover, Minn., 1928.

——————, *Pareto, le savant et l'homme.* Lausanne, 1960.

G. Eisermann, *Vilfredo Paretos System der allgemeinen Soziologie.* Stuttgart, 1962.

Tommaso Giacalone-Monaco, *Pareto e Sorel, reflessioni e ricerche.* Padua, 1960.

——————, *Pareto-Walras. Da un carteggio inedito 1891-1901.* Padua, 1960.

L. J. Henderson, *Pareto's General Sociology.* Cambridge, Mass., 1935.

Wolfgang Hirsch, *Vilfredo Pareto. Ein Versuch über sein soziologisches Werk.* Zurich-Brussels, 1948.

George Homans, *An Introduction to Pareto.* New York, 1934.

Giuseppe La Ferla, *Vilfredo Pareto, filosofo volteriano.* Florence, 1954.

Stanislao Scalfati, *Studi Paretiani.* Rome, 1932.

BOOKS ABOUT MOSCA

James H. Meisel, *The Myth of the Ruling Class. Gaetano Mosca and the "Elite."* Ann Arbor, 1958. Second edition, 1962. German translation: *Der Mythus der herrschenden Klasse.* Düsseldorf, 1962.

Ferrucio Pergolesi, *Appunti sulla "Scienza politica" di Gaetano Mosca.* Milan, 1957.

Mario delle Piane, *Bibliographia di Gaetano Mosca.* Florence, 1949.
——————, *Gaetano Mosca, Classe politica e liberalismo.* Naples, 1952.

Le élites politiche. Bari, 1961 (Symposium on political elites, Fourth International Congress of Sociology, Stresa, 1959).

CONTRIBUTORS

JAMES H. MEISEL, the editor of this volume, is a distinguished scholar in the fields of political theory and political sociology. He holds a doctorate from the University of Heidelberg, and is currently Professor of Political Science at the University of Michigan. His published works include *The Genesis of Georges Sorel* (1951), *The Myth of the Ruling Class: Gaetano Mosca and the "Elite"* (1962), and *The Fall of the Republic: Military Revolt in France* (1962).

WERNER STARK (born 1909). Lecturer in Sociology, Cambridge University, 1941-42; Edinburgh University, 1945-51; reader at Manchester University, 1951-63; Guest Professor, Purdue University, 1960-61; Professor of Sociology, Fordham University, 1963. Works: *Jeremy Bentham's Economic Writings* (3 vols.); *The Sociology of Knowledge; Montesquieu: Pioneer of the Sociology of Knowledge; The Fundamental Forms of Social Thought.*

SIDNEY HOOK (born 1902). Professor of Philosophy, New York University (Washington Square), 1939; Chairman, Philosophy Department, New York University Graduate School, 1948; President, American Philosophical Association, 1959. Works: *Toward an Understanding of Karl Marx; From Hegel to Marx; Heresy Yes—Conspiracy No; The Quest for Being; The Ambiguous Legacy: Marx and the Marxists.*

NICHOLAS S. TIMASHEFF (born 1886). Lecturer in Sociology, Harvard University, 1936-40; Professor of Sociology, Fordham University, 1940-57. Works: *Introduction to the Sociology of Law; The Great Retreat; Sociological Theory, Its Nature and Growth.*

TALCOTT PARSONS (born 1902). Professor, Department of Social Relations, Harvard University, 1944; Chairman, 1946-56; President, American Sociological Association, 1949. Works: *The Structure of Social Action; Essays in Sociological Theory Pure and Applied; The Social System; Toward a General Theory of Action* (with Edward A. Shils and others); *Family, Socialization and Interaction Process* (with others).

MORRIS GINSBERG (born 1889). Professor of Sociology, London School of Economics, 1929. Works: *The Psychology of Society; Essays in Sociology and Social Philosophy* (Vol. I: *On the Diversity of Morals*; Vol. II: *Reason and Unreason in Society*; Vol. III: *Evolution and Progress*).

FRANZ BORKENAU (1900-1957). Functionary of the Comintern until 1929; went to England after his break with communism, then to Spain; Professor of Modern History, Marburg University, 1945; Editor-in-chief of *Ostprobleme,* a review dealing with problems of communism. Works: *Pareto; The Spanish Cockpit; World Communism; European Communism.*

RAYMOND ARON (born 1905). Professor of Sociology in the Faculty of Arts, University of Paris; Member of the American Academy of Arts and Sciences. Works: *German Sociology; Introduction to the Philosophy of History; The Century of Total War; The Opium of the Intellectuals; France, Steadfast and Changing; The Fourth Republic,* and numerous others.

JOSEPH A. SCHUMPETER (1883-1950). Lectured in economics at the Universities of Vienna and Graz, Austria; Professor of Economics, University of Bonn, 1925-32; sometime Austrian Minister of Finance; Professor of Economics, Harvard University, 1932-1950. Works: *The Theory of Economic Development; Business Cycles; Capitalism, Socialism and Democracy; Imperialism and Social Classes; Ten Great Economists: From Marx to Keynes.*

FRANCO FERRAROTTI (born 1926). Fellow in Sociology, Universities of Florence and Rome; founder and managing editor of "Quaderni di Sociologia," 1950. Works: *Il Dilemma dei Sindacati Americani; Socologia: saggie e ricerche; Sindacalismo Autonomo.*

H. STUART HUGHES (born 1916). Professor of History, Harvard University, 1957; Chief, Division of Research for Europe, U.S. Department of State, 1946-48; Departmental Director, Russian Research Center, Harvard University, 1948. Works: *Oswald Spengler, a Critical Estimate; An Essay for Our Times: The United States and Italy; Consciousness and Society; An Approach to Peace, and Other Essays; History as Art and as Science: Twin Vistas on the Past.*

C. WRIGHT MILLS (1916-1962). Associate Professor of Sociology, Columbia University, 1948; Professor, 1956; visiting lecturer at Brandeis University, the University of Copenhagen, the United States Air War College. Works: *White Collar: The American Middle Classes; Character and Social Structure* (with H. H. Gerth); *The Power Elite; The Causes of World War Three; The Sociological Imagination; Listen Yankee: The Revolution in Cuba; The Marxists.*

CARL J. FRIEDRICH (born 1901). Professor of Government, Harvard and Heidelberg Universities; President, American Political Science Association, 1961. Works: *Responsible Bureaucracy* (with Taylor Cole); *Foreign Policy in the Making; Constitutional Government and Democracy; Inevitable Peace; The New Image of the Common Man; Man and His Government.*

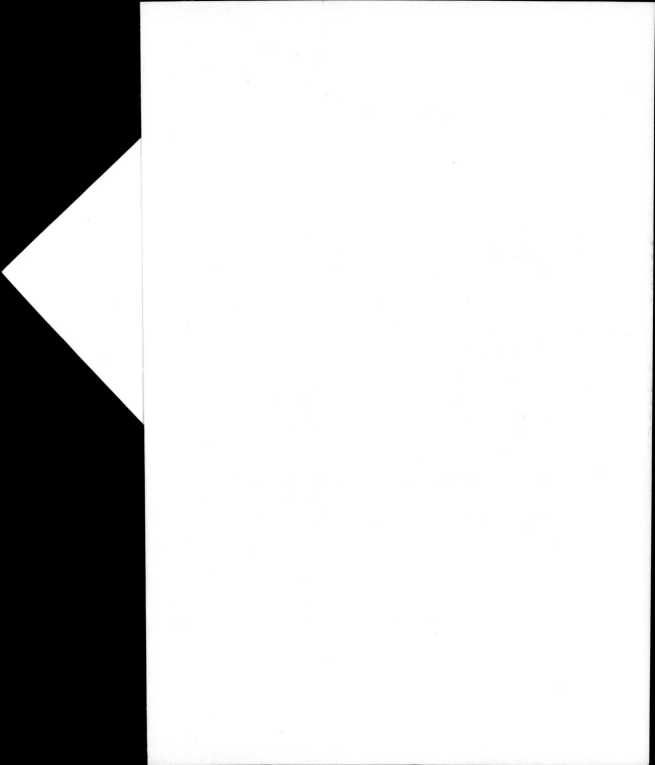

DATE

GAYLORD

PRINTED IN U.S.A.